Aztec Ceremonial Landscapes

Aztec Ceremonial Landscapes

Edited by
Davíd Carrasco

Foreword by
William L. Fash

University Press of Colorado

Paperback Edition 1999
International Standard Book Number 0-87081-509-1

Published by the University Press of Colorado
P.O. Box 849
Niwot, Colorado 80544

Printed in the United States of America.

The University Press of Colorado is a cooperative publishing enterprise supported, in part, by Adams State College, Colorado State University, Fort Lewis College, Mesa State College, Metropolitan State College of Denver, University of Colorado, University of Northern Colorado, University of Southern Colorado, and Western State College of Colorado.

The paper used in this publication meets the minimum requirements of the American National Standard for Information Sciences—Permanence of Paper for Printed Library Materials. ANSI Z39.48-1984

Library of Congress Cataloging-in-Publication Data

To change place.
Aztec ceremonial landscapes / edited by Davíd Carrasco.
p. cm.
Includes bibliographical references and index.
ISBN 0-87081-509-1 (pbk. : alk. paper)
1. Aztecs—Rites and ceremonies. 2. Nahuas—Rites and ceremonies.
3. Sacred space—Mexico. I. Carrasco, Davíd. II. Title
[F1219.76.R45T6 1999]
972'.5018—dc21 99-18834
CIP

To Paul and Margo Wheatley
in appreciation of their friendship and guidance.

Contents

About the Contributors

Philip P. Arnold is a historian of religions at the University of Missouri-Columbia.

Salvador Guil'liem Arroyo is an archaeologist active in the excavations at El Templo Mayor and Tlatelolco in Mexico City.

Anthony F. Aveni, Russell B. Colgate Professor of astronomy and anthropology at Colgate University, is one of the pioneers of archaeoastronomical studies and has published numerous works, including *Skywatchers of Ancient Mexico* and *Empires of Time.*

Elizabeth Hill Boone is director of pre-Columbian studies at Dumbarton Oaks, Washington, D.C., editor of *The Aztec Templo Mayor,* and author of *The Codex Magliabechiano and the Lost Prototype of the Magliabechiano Group.*

Johanna Broda is an anthropologist and ethnohistorian with the Instituto de Investigaciones Históricas, professor at the Universidad Nacional Autónoma de México, and author and co-editor of numerous works on ancient Mexican society and religions, including "Templo Mayor as Ritual Space."

Davíd Carrasco is a historian of religions and director of the Mesoamerican Archive, University of Colorado, Boulder, and author of *Religions of Mesoamerica: Cosmovision and Ceremonial Centers.*

Jane Stevenson Day is director of the Department of Anthropology, Denver Museum of Natural History, Denver, Colorado, with a special interest in the pre-Columbian arts of Costa Rica.

Doris Heyden is an archaeologist and ethnohistorian at I.N.A.H. and (with Fernando Horcasitas) is translator and editor of Diego Durán's *Book of the Gods and Rites and the Ancient Calendar.*

J. Jorge Klor de Alva is a professor of anthropology at Princeton University and author of many works on Nahuatl culture and language. He is coeditor with H. B. Nicholson and E. Quiñones Keber of *The Work of Bernardino de Sahagún.*

Peter L. van der Loo is a historian of religions at Northern Arizona University. He is the author of *Códices Costumbres Continuidad.*

Alfredo López Austin, author of *The Human Body and Ideology,* is a historian and professor with the Instituto de Investigaciones Antropológicas at the Universidad Nacional Autónoma de México, Mexico City.

Eduardo Matos Moctezuma is director of El Templo Mayor, Mexico City, and author of many works, including *Vida y Muerte en el Templo Mayor.*

Henry B. Nicholson, who wrote "Religion in Pre-Hispanic Central Mexico" for the *Handbook of Middle American Indians,* is a professor of anthropology at the University of California, Los Angeles.

Juan Alberto Román Berrelleza is a physical anthropologist active in the excavations at El Templo Mayor and Tlatelolco, Mexico City.

Lawrence E. Sullivan is director of the Center for the Study of World Religions and professor of history of religions at Harvard University. He is the author of *Icanchu's Drum: An Orientation to Meaning in South American Religions.*

Richard F. Townsend is curator of the Department of Africa, Oceania and the Americas at the Art Institute of Chicago, and author of *State and Cosmos in the Art of Tenochtitlan.*

Foreword

Changing Times and Changing Places in Aztec and Maya Studies

It is a rare event when a collection of conference essays presents both a comprehensive treatment of the intricacies and complexities of an important research problem, and a new vision of how those particulars can best be understood from a broad-based theoretical perspective. The present book represents just such an exceptional offering.

As pointed out by the volume editor Davíd Carrasco, studies of sacred landscapes and urban planning have generally tended to follow either of two perspectives. In the first, everything pivots around a central place that serves as an axis mundi for the integration of all people, domains, and meanings ascribed to a community by its members. For the kingdom of the ancient Culhua Mexica or Aztecs, this central pivot was the Templo Mayor or Great Temple, which was also the focus of a series of conferences in which the research reported upon in this volume were first presented. In the second perspective, the landscapes and the communities that shaped them are the basis for the creation of the center, and for the forms and meanings which that center assumes. From this vantage, the Aztec Great Temple was merely a reflection of all that had come before it, in the complex and long-lived evolution of a distinguished civilization in the Basin of Mexico over the course of three millennia. Under the leadership of its editor, the contributors to this book critically reviewed both these theoretical approaches, and a number of seminal works by historians of religion, anthropologists, and art historians. Their discussions then led them chart a new and extraordinarily productive course for the interpretations of their respective pieces of the larger picture.

This volume ushers in "a vision of place in which the terrain of the sacred is not concentrated, limited, or restricted to one or several locations," in Carrasco's words, where "change and transformation are the sustained pattern." Through this lens, Aztec ceremonies like the mountain-top child sacrifices of Atl Caualo are demonstrated to symbolize the ceremonial landscape of the entire Basin of Mexico during the first month of the year. Similarly, Carrasco's own path-breaking analysis of the human god-image or teotl ixiptla of the all-powerful creator deity Tezcatlipoca, reveals him to be a compelling figure precisely because of his transience and transformations across the ritual landscape, between social strata, and through time.

For the Aztecs, the richness of both the archaeological record and the ethnohistoric sources make such examinations doubly rewarding, allowing a multi-disciplinary effort at elucidating Aztec world-view and sacred geography. The volume has a nice balance between the fresh findings of recent archaeological investigations (in the chapters by Matos Moctezuma, Berrelleza, Arroyo, and Townsend), reflections on the meaning of visual imagery within the larger social and cosmological context (Boone, Arroyo, Matos Moctezuma, and Nicholson), astronomically and astrologically sited features (Aveni and Broda), examinations of the social and political implications of religion as distilled from a critical examination of historical tracts (Boone, López Austin, Arnold, and Klor de Alva), and expositions on vital religious precepts (Carrasco, López Austin, Nicholson, Heyden, Sullivan, van der Loo, and Day) within the perspective of all of the things that not only took place, but changed place, in rituals conducted at critical junctures in the ceremonial landscapes of ancient Mexico.

Such cross-fields approaches are now being pursued in many other parts of Mesoamerica. But rarely do they benefit from the richness of data, depth of experience and understanding, and strength of commitment to a conjoined scholarly effort as that which has been achieved by Carrasco and Eduardo Matos in their conferences and publications of the (Moses) Mesoamerican Archive. For my part, I have been moved by this volume to re-examine my own perspectives on the sacred geography of ancient Maya kingdoms such as Copan, Tikal, Palenque, and Chichén Itzá. The work of scholars such as Victor Turner and Evon Vogt can now be seen as demonstrating the importance that changing place, and time, through pilgrimages and their place-specific rituals, held for the ancient Maya. Likewise, we are now challenged to interpret the reasons why Classic Maya rulers selected the particular places they chose, to dedicate carved monoliths and sumptuous edifices in conjunction with calendrically timed rituals and anniversaries. The recent decipherments of place-names in the Classic Maya texts by scholars such as David Stuart and Stephen Houston now oblige us to expand and refine our interpretations of behavioral and physical remains at the shrines, buildings, courtyards, and communities we investigate, just as scholars have done in the Valley of Oaxaca since Alfonso Caso's path-breaking work on the toponyms there.

When viewed from the broad perspective afforded by the contributors to this book, ancient Maya ceremonial landscapes were teeming with sacred places, each resonating through the rituals that maintained traditions and pacified the ancestors and the gods who, like Tezcatlipoca for the 16th century Central Mexicans, were deeply respected, but also feared for their capricious, merciless, and omniscient aspects. This volume also serves as a timely antidote to the idea that each Maya kingdom was focused solely on the locus where the ruler or his apical ancestor resided. Rather than perceiving the ruler primarily as a political actor upon whose actions the short-term history of his kingdom revolved, we can interpret their acts through the window of their cyclical movements and integrative actions, along the lines of the teotl ixiptlas. In addition to focusing upon the rules of succession and the central temples and palaces, we can broaden our vision to the incorporate the nature of pilgrimages, rituals, and place-centered actions in the larger arena.

Now our understanding of a central temple or courtyard in a Maya kingdom as the pivot of the four quarters can be dynamically enhanced by a concerted look at each shrine and temple complex as marking a particular, vital part of the overall picture. Each such locus can profitably be seen by archaeologists, epigraphers, and ethnologists, as a place where other Mesoamerican peoples, like their later Mexica counterparts, "accomplished a domestication of space through the creation of ideal, reciprocal relationships linking ethnic groups to gods to landscape to ritual to tradition to ancestors." In places like Copan and Palenque, where shrines and elite residential areas are embellished with sculpted pictorial imagery and hieroglyphic texts, we can try to weave the mat of the ancient community by connecting all of the sacred spaces in terms of both movement and transformation through the landscape and through time.

In my view this book is a "must" for all who would seek to understand place-making, cosmogony, and world-view in ancient Mesoamerica. Those who embark on the journey of reading it will find themselves and their perceptions transformed—conceptually changing place—as a reward for their efforts.

William L. Fash
Cambridge, MA

Preface

This book is one of the fruits of a ten-year cooperative research project of the University of Colorado, through the Mesoamerican Archive directed by Davíd Carrasco, and the Great Temple Project of Mexico's Instituto Nacional de Antropología e Historia. The conference, "Aztec Ceremonial Landscapes," which took place June 19–23, 1989, at the Museo del Templo Mayor, demonstrated the close collaboration that has been established between both institutions, which have now deepened their commitment to carry out archaeological work in the ceremonial center of Tlatelolco, a site of historic importance.

We appreciate the participation of the colleagues who throughout the years have cooperated to gain a deeper knowledge of the pre-Hispanic Mesoamerican world and in particular the social and symbolic world of the Mexica. The meetings held at the University of Colorado's Mesoamerican Archive and in Mexico have permitted a more dynamic and productive interrelation among the participants; thus, archaeologists, anthropologists, historians, art historians, historians of religions, and archaeoastronomers have utilized their disciplines to broaden our knowledge.

This book is a sample of our collaboration, a collection of some of the research presented during the 1989 summer symposium. We hope that it proves of use to other researchers interested in the pre-Hispanic world. Different disciplines are represented here, a diversity reflecting the character we have tried to give to our meetings.

We would like to thank the generous support of the teams from the Mesoamerican Archive and the Templo Mayor. Without their work to organize the meeting, the event would have been impossible. Lois Middleton, Linda Cohen, and Georgina Alonzo were the hearts and minds of the organization of our discussions. We are deeply grateful to them. We also want to thank Raphael and Fletcher Lee Moses for their support and friendship.

EDUARDO MATOS MOCTEZUMA
TEMPLO MAYOR

Acknowledgments

I want to thank Lois Middleton for her extraordinary gifts of time, labor, patience, and guidance, which helped make this publication possible. Also, Scott Sessions served as overtime research assistant for the book, and he helped with the primary sources and the photographs. Linda Cohen helped us put things in order during the initial stages of the work.

William B. Taylor helped me think through the problems of "changing places" in Aztec ceremonies, as did Johanna Broda, Anthony Aveni, and Charles H. Long. Special thanks goes to Michio Araki, who enhanced our seminiar by his journey from Japan and his crucial comments.

As in all things done in the Mesoamerican Archive, I am indebted to Eduardo Matos Moctezuma, who has served as colleague, advisor, and firm friend through the years. His staff at the Museo del Templo Mayor enlarge our learning experience. Also, none of what I describe in the Introduction would take place at the University of Colorado without the generous friendship of Raphael and Fletcher Lee Moses and the administrative support of Chancellor James Corbridge, Vice Chancellor Bruce Ekstrand, and Dean Charles Middleton.

Finally, I am grateful to Luther Wilson, Jody Berman, and the entire staff at the University Press of Colorado for transforming our work into such a handsome result.

DAVÍD CARRASCO

Introduction: Aztec Ceremonial Landscapes

This book, generated by the scholars' conference "Aztec Ceremonial Landscapes" held at the Museo del Templo Mayor in Mexico City, is both a culminating point and a moment of transition in the study of Mesoamerican religions. It marks the completion of a cycle begun ten years earlier when the first international conference of scholars met at the University of Colorado in Boulder to reflect on the astonishing discoveries of the Coyolxauhqui stone and other ritual objects at the Templo Mayor in Mexico City. This volume also reflects a transition in theoretical discussions about the character of sacred spaces in the core area of the Aztec Empire. Since that first meeting and during collaborative discussions at numerous seminars, we have altered our point of view from focusing on a "centered mass"–that is, the Templo Mayor — to surveying a "sensitive grid" — that is, numerous interrelated ceremonial centers in the Basin of Mexico; thus the title of this volume: *To Change Place: Aztec Ceremonial Landscapes*. This emphasis on a change of place refers not only to how Aztec priests, warriors, rulers, and commoners changed social and symbolic place through movement and ritual action, but also how a working group of scholars, benefiting by the interaction of numerous disciplinary approaches, have developed elements of a new interpretive framework for the study of the dynamics of Aztec centers and peripheries. In this introductory essay, I want to describe the intellectual context for, and action of, the 1989 conference in Mexico City as well as the contents of this book.

The Setting

In that most remarkable of first novels by a young genius, Carlos Fuentes wrote about Mexico City in *Where the Air Is Clear*, that it was a

> city witness to all we forget, city of carnivorous walls, . . . city of motionless pain, city of immense brevities, city of fixed sun, city up to its neck in water, city of merry lethargy, city of twisted stinks, city rigid between air and worms, city ancient in light, old city cradled among birds of omen, . . . city of the violated outrage, city of resigned market plazas, city tempested by domes, city woven by amnesias, bitch city, hungry city, sumptuous villa, . . . city of the true image of gigantic heaven.[1]

It was in the heart of this prodigious, exploding city where the air is seldom clear, this city with endless cities and ceremonial centers pulsating within it, that our conference was held June 18–24, 1989. Hosted by Eduardo Matos Moctezuma, director of the Museo del Templo Mayor, and supported by García Moll, director of the Instituto Nacional de Antropología, our participants benefited by being together in the landscapes of museums, libraries, mountaintop centers, and the archaeological wonders of this "city of the true image of gigantic heaven." It was a significant development in the history of our collaboration to return together to the actual site of the excavation of the Great Temple of Tenochtitlan. Working together in Mexico enhanced the development of our ideas during the conference. Ten years earlier, in October 1979, many of the same scholars participated in the first conference, "Center and Periphery: The Great Temple and the Aztec Empire," at the University of Colorado in Boulder to discuss the exemplary role of the Templo Mayor in the organization and expansion of Aztec urbanism. Those discussions focused on the temple and economic tribute, human sacrifice and ideology, spatial symbolism in Teotihuacan and Tenochtitlan, magical flight and Mesoamerican cosmology. Our work, inspired by Proyecto Templo Mayor under the superb guidance of Eduardo Matos, uncovered some answers but more questions about the history and character of Aztec religion, social organization, and art.[2] Now, ten years later, our seminar group had the luxury of reflecting on those discoveries, questions, and problems within the jewel of a museum that housed so many of the objects, symbols, masterpieces, and fragments that were, in the words of Fuentes, "witness to all we forget." Within this setting, which served as our home base during the seminar, we were joined by new colleagues from Mexico, the United States, and Japan. Alfredo López Austin, who had participated in our original seminar in Boulder, rejoined the group and contributed greatly to our discussions. We were also pleased to include Professor Javier

Noguez from the Colegio de México, whose work on the formation of the cult of the Virgin of Guadalupe in Tepeyac assisted us in our field trip to the site. From the Museo del Templo Mayor, we benefited by the reports of new discoveries at Tlatelolco given by Juan Román Berrelleza and Salvador Guil'liem Arroyo. Lawrence Sullivan, a historian of religions whose work on South American religions provided a rich comparative relief, joined us for the first time. We were especially honored to welcome the historian of religions Professor Michio Araki and three graduate students from the University of Tsukuba in Ibaraki Prefecture, Japan. Their participation was a symbol of the process of deprovincialization in methodology and in comparisons with Asian cultures that is part of our seminar experience.

This enriched geographical, urban, and collegial setting was accompanied by new programmatic aspects to our 1989 conference. Previously, in 1987, a group of fifteen Aztec specialists and historians of religions gathered to discuss a selected group of seminal articles representing present views on Aztec ceremonial center/state organization in order to consider new avenues of research into the dynamics of center and periphery in the central Mesoamerican urban tradition. That conference, "Consultation on the Future of Aztec Studies: Center and Periphery in the Mexica World," strove to nurture a working group of scholars who would interact for a decade by focusing on a set of research problems of common interest within the field of Aztec studies. Up to this point, our work had been directed by the compaction of Aztec art, religious symbols, political authority, and military power within the centered mass of the Templo Mayor. Now, our goal was to shift the perspective in Aztec studies and look at Tenochtitlan, the Templo Mayor, and the consolidation of the Mexica worldview from the perspective of the periphery, from the points of view of such places as Texcoco, Tlatelolco, Mt. Tlaloc, Tlaxcala, and the ceremonial centers in between. As a means of laying out new lines of inquiry we focused an intensive discourse and debate on six articles considered both innovative and problematic in the study of Aztec social history and religious expression. These included Anthony Aveni's model of center and periphery dynamics in Aztec, Mayan, and Incan cultures; Johanna Broda's analysis of the puzzling manifestations of the Tlaloc cult at the Templo Mayor; Richard Townsend's seminal study of coronation ceremonies; Cecelia Klein's analogy of sin, social control, and human entrails; Jerome Offner's picture of the Texcocan empire; and Davíd

Carrasco's model of Aztec symmetry in astronomical, imperial, and ceremonial traditions. This method of interpretation — that is, the use of seminal works to stimulate discussion and criticism — resulted in an abundant set of correspondences about center and periphery including:

Center = Centroid or "the city that can be said to epitomize the pattern of society at large"
= The human body conceived as the nexus of cosmic forces on the terrestrial level
= The Templo Mayor as the pivot of the Mexica ceremonial and political/economic world
= The life and paraphernalia of the ruler as the quintessential expression of sanctified authority
= Tlatelolco as the focus of new research and comparisons with Tenochtitlan
= Texcoco as the heart of aesthetic and legal innovations
= Markets that combine redistribution and ceremonial exchange (between humans, and between humans and gods) in order to regulate internal and external relationships

These correspondences on the symbolism of the center were accompanied by correspondences to the geography and concept of the periphery:

Periphery = Distant societies and geographical areas (including seas) that served as resources for political and ritual symbolism in the capital
= Battlefields, specifically chosen spaces of combat and ritual where explosive political relationships were transformed and negotiated
= Plants and soils from outlying regions utilized in market exchange and religious/medical practices; these materials reflect the diverse ecological niches of Mesoamerican landscapes
= Frontiers — that is, the social and symbolic limits to political order and within cosmovision; these frontiers occasionally functioned as buffer areas for exchange and conflict
= Astronomical markers on the edges or within sight of the ceremonial centers, which functioned as sight lines or symbols of celestial events on the horizon
= Oceans; as the excellent display at the Museo del Templo Mayor shows, the oceans and marine animals were valued objects and symbols integrated into the floor of the *axis mundi.*

The 1987 seminar identified three types of dynamics between these centers and peripheries that animated the Mexica world, including the energy and action of the marketplace, the symbolism and action of warfare, and the ritual performances that mapped out the ceremonial world. It was posited that the ceremonial performances of the Aztec calendar presented a moving image of the entire society, centroid and center-periphery dynamics.

The 1988 conference, "Performance as Place: Aztec Centers, Aztec Action," began to combine research and theoretical materials in new ways. First, following our decision to shift our attention beyond the Templo Mayor, we benefited by the new discoveries of Proyecto Tlatelolco, cosponsored by the Instituto Nacional de Antropología in Mexico and the Mesoamerican Archive at the University of Colorado. The excavation yielded remarkable ritual burials of humans, pottery, obsidian, animals, musical instruments, and clay figurines. Eduardo Matos Moctezuma presented the results of two seasons of excavations at the start of the 1988 conference. "Excavaciones Recientes en Tlatelolco" was exhibited to over 1 million people in 1988 at the Museo del Templo Mayor in Mexico City. It was also exhibited October 1989 to January 1990 at the Museum of Natural History in Denver under the title "Lord of the Wind: Aztec Offerings at Tlatelolco, Mexico." The seminar also combined a critical analysis of a series of seminal works on ritual and cultural performance with original research from the Valley of Mexico.[3]

At the end of this conference, it was decided to form several subgroups (Tlatelolco, Atl Caualo, Toxcatl, Pulque and Pulque Gods) to gather reliable descriptions of specific ceremonial activities and their relations to sacred places. Eduardo Matos invited the working group to meet at the Museo del Templo Mayor for the 1989 conference. Six months before the conference and after consultation with members of the group I outlined our upcoming task in Mexico:

> Our assignment is to focus on a group of ceremonies described, pictured, and carved in the primary sources as a basis for interdisciplinary reflection and development of our model of center-periphery dynamics. I suggest that we organize our discussions under the notion of "ceremonial landscape," a landscape marked, mapped, and rejuvenated by complex sets of performances that communicated knowledge about the social and symbolic order of the Aztec world and its sacred foundation. This entire landscape, consisting of geographical, social, and architec-

> tural terrains, was subjected to a conscious design, systemic pattern, or cosmovision. I approach these terrains and performances with the notion of a metamorphic vision of place signifying the physical exuberance and symbolic transformations within ceremonies that cover large and diverse territories. From a continued study of sources it seems evident that not just ritual but most of Mexica social life can be viewed as sets of performances communicating an urbanized, hierarchical way of life. These public performances gave life to the ceremonial landscape and helped the world breathe with meaning.

This approach to Aztec society and ritual through the conception of a ceremonial landscape animated by a metamorphic vision of place draws upon the works of Paul Wheatley, Clifford Geertz, Victor Turner, and Richard Schechner. It combines the earlier emphasis on "place" with the new fashion to be attentive to "performance." As we approached the Mexico City meeting it became evident that our working group was "changing place" in the sense that we saw the Aztec city and ceremonial centers not only as a symbol but also as a series of performances. The emphasis had switched from the "center" to the "ceremonial" in the phrase *ceremonial center.* Further, unlike our previous emphasis on either the Templo Mayor or on viewing the Templo Mayor from the perspective of the periphery, we were now interested in ceremonial centers of various kinds and various places. It is to the scholarly action, part ceremonial and part spontaneous, that took place in the center of the "city ancient in light" that I now turn.

The Action and This Book

Our Mexico City meetings began with three presentations by the Tlatelolco working group led by Eduardo Matos Moctezuma. Together with Juan Román Berrelleza and Salvador Guil'liem Arroyo, the team presented several probing interpretations concerning the "chueco" *chacmool* discovered at Templo Mayor in 1989, and the skeletal materials recently discovered in Tlatelolco. We were also presented with a description of the mythic dimensions of the newly discovered mural of Tlatelolco, a rare moment in Aztec archaeology. The excitement accompanying these presentations was reminiscent, although on a smaller scale, of the electricity surrounding the earlier reports of treasures found during the excavation at the Templo Mayor.

Our sharing of these discoveries was followed by Davíd Carrasco's keynote address, "To Change Place: Tezcatlipoca, the Lord of Everywhere." Carrasco showed how his exploration into the ceremonial patterns of the festival of Toxcatl revealed a conception of spatial order and transformation that challenged both the conceptions of center and periphery developed in previous work.

This was followed by a well-integrated series of presentations by the Atl Caualo group consisting of Anthony Aveni, Edward Calnek, Phil Arnold, and Michio Araki, who opened up the spatial and symbolic character of the first month of the year when children, or "human paper streamers," were sacrificed on a number of mountaintops around the Valley of Mexico. These presentations showed that a remarkable sense of coordination of research and discussion had developed during the year. The presentations were enhanced by the remarks of Michio Araki, who made several tantalizing comparisons with the "land of the dead" symbolism in Japanese religions. One of the interesting possibilities that emerged was that Atl Caualo, with its prodigious displays and disguises and its long-distance pilgrimages to ceremonial precincts on mountaintops, symbolically cosmicized the *entire ceremonial landscape* of the Mexica during the first month of the year.

Following the first day of reflection on the discoveries at Tlatelolco and the research on Atl Caualo, we visited the shrine of Guadalupe on Tepeyac and traveled to the base of the nearby preconquest site of Yoaltepec to gain a sense of continuity and change in mountain ceremonial centers. We continued on to the unique ceremonial landscape of Teotihuacan where, under the guidance of Anthony Aveni, Doris Heyden, and John Hoag, we had the experience of not just traveling to, but feeling enveloped within, this unique imperial city.

On Wednesday, our conference began with Charles Long's response to Victor Turner's article, "Pilgrimages as Social Processes." Utilizing Loren Eiseley's idea that originality comes, in part, from reading the works of others, we revived the archive's practice of reflecting critically on a seminal article on ritual performance and landscape. In his article, originally published in the *History of Religions Journal* as "The Center Out There: Pilgrim's Goal," Turner saw pilgrimage as a rite of passage whose goals included both the experience of "communitas" and the liminal encounter with the sacred at the pilgrimage center. Significantly, Turner included a section on the pilgrimage and cult of Guadalupe at Tepeyac.

In my view, his article set the stage for new understandings of a ceremonial landscape. In Aztec religion, something akin to a liminal encounter with the sacred takes place at *many locations* on the way to the pilgrimage center as well as at the final destination. Through comparative examples, Long emphasized that while we are studying the Aztec case, it is valuable to reflect on the general human meaning of ceremonial movements through space. It was also valuable to hear Long reflect eloquently about the Aztec merchant class, the *pochteca*. In his view, the Aztec practice of economic exchange is a complex example not only of social dramas but also of symbolic metamorphosis.

Peter van der Loo provided a rich response and critique of Turner's model in his description of the Tlapanec pilgrimage, dedicated to rain deities, in which he participated several years earlier in northeastern Guerrero.

The reflection on social dramas gave way to Johanna Broda's gestalt of the Valley of Mexico. Her presentation was a remarkable synthesis of many years of work and collaboration and revealed the different ways that the Mexica took possession of the landscape. The Mexica accomplished a domestication of space through the creation of ideal, reciprocal relationships linking ethnic groups to gods to landscape to ritual to tradition to ancestors. Broda surveyed, with unusual depth, a number of mountaintop sites and suggested an enriched methodology for future studies.

Lawrence Sullivan's response was a poetic meditation on the "spectral" cultures of the Valley of Mexico. He helped us imagine what could be seen during ritual movements through the ceremonial landscape in the Valley when the air was clear!

This exchange was followed by Alfredo López Austin's presentation on historical tales and creation mythology from peoples within the Basin of Mexico. His paper about the relations of mythology to history and the human body was built on his recent rare achievement, *The Human Body and Ideology.*

Another working group, consisting of Henry B. Nicholson, Robert Bye, and Jose Cuellar, focused on the "Octli Cults: Then and Now." This group addressed a number of issues, including the problem of understanding continuity and change in the use of octli from Tetzcoco to Los Angeles, and raised the question of how we come to know ancient ritual practices of drinking given the impact of colonialism on the evidence and the fact that we are so involved in the present. Nicholson presented a detailed summary of his intensive research on the octli cults including rich descriptions of the costumes of octli gods and their significance. This was followed by Bye's presentation on the ethnobotanical perspectives of pulque. In his presentation he identified the process of fermentation in plants, which resonated with our concern for change and metamorphosis in ritual life. This was especially true in his identification of the different capacities of pulque both to nurture and to transform life in the forms of visions and ritual prayers. The theme was carefully relocated to the present-day use of pulque, tequila, and pulquerías by Cuellar (Dr. Loco), who surveyed historical patterns of drinking in Mexican and Chicano communities and drew our eyes to the issue of drinking and social conflict in contemporary times. The relationship of conflict, the control of conflict, and the ceremonial nature of conflict were all addressed by Cuellar, whose work also raised, by implication, the political significance of the extreme numbers of drinking establishments in certain Mexican and Mexican-American communities.

Elizabeth Boone's presentation on migrations and pilgrimages indicated a watershed in the ability of working group members to learn from one another. Her discussion of ritual and pictorials showed, in a novel fashion, how metamorphosis and movement in time and space was artistically depicted by the Mexica. She noted how she had initially recognized significant distances between Aztec art historians, archaeologists, and historians of religions in their approaches to Mexica culture and religion, and had wondered if a fruitful discourse would develop between different disciplines. Her innovative interpretations of pre- and postcontact pictorials demonstrated that she had creatively integrated what was originally strange to her work.

On Thursday, we went back into the field under the guidance of Robert Bye and Edelmira Linares, who escorted us to the community of Santa Catarina del Monte where we spent the day with a Nahuatl-speaking family involved in the contemporary cult of pulque. This enabled us to reflect again on continuity and change in a ceremonial landscape.

On Friday morning Felipe Solís, then curator of the Sala Mexica at the Museo Nacional de Antropología, presented an illustrated lecture on the new investigations at Mt. Tlaloc, where he, Richard Townsend, and others are doing a survey, excavation, and interpretation of this supremely important mountaintop site. Their work related the forms of the smaller objects (pottery and sculpture) to the form of the mountain, and suggested that we focus more on the feminine symbolism at Mt. Tlaloc and other sites.

Jorge Klor de Alva enlarged our understanding of the Mesoamerican and colonial concept of "body." In Klor de Alva's work, the body becomes a ceremonial center as well as a political entity, especially during the colonial process. In the complicated atmosphere of the sixteenth century, as seen in Klor de Alva's work, the Nahua world of bodies has a prolific series of references including the mind, the *altepetl,* the *cofradía,* the mountain, and the family. The European colonial experience aimed to control, snatch away, and transform the entire native body and conceptions of the body, to replace them with European conceptions of body and social world.

In response, Cecelia Klein developed the "hermeneutics of suspicion" theme evident in both Cuellar and Klor de Alva, to ask us to sharpen our methodologies and heighten our skepticism concerning how much we were projecting contemporary ideas onto the Nahuas of sixteenth-century Mexico and the colonial period.

Our conference continued with Doris Heyden's concise study of Tezcatlipoca's festival, focusing on the juxtapositions of dryness/rain and the transformation of seasonality in Aztec ritual. Jane Day responded by asking both Carrasco and Heyden to consider further the substratum of shamanism or at least shamanic elements underlying so much of the Toxcatl materials.

The Mexico City conference ended with Lawrence G. Desmond's entertaining research on "Chichen Itza and Uxmal, 1878–1989: A Photogrammetric Comparison." Desmond's contributions to the history of the Mesoamerican Archive, as well as to the history of photography in Mesoamerican ceremonial centers, are unique and deeply appreciated.

While all of these presentations are not included in this volume, the Mesoamerican Archive contains a complete audio archive of all proceedings from the 1979, 1987, 1988 and 1989 conferences.

This book has been divided into three sections. Part I, "New Discoveries at El Templo Mayor, Tlatelolco, and Mt. Tlaloc" presents three essays describing and interpreting new evidence from the center of the Aztec ceremonial landscape and one focusing on the great "center out there," Mt. Tlaloc. Eduardo Matos's chapter contains a tentative interpretation of the meaning of the "chueco" chac-mool and indicates how archaeology can assist in clarifying debates, such as the "hot" and "cold" debate of López Austin and George Foster, which have been largely carried on in relation to ethnohistorical sources. Juan Román Berrelleza presents his recent research on the skeletal remains found at Tlatelolco and presents a hypothesis on the ceremonial and symbolic uses of children in the Ehecatl-Quetzalcoatl cult. Salvador Guil'liem Arroyo explores the rare, painted mural found on the Templo Calendarico at Tlatelolco, relating the imagery to the ethnohistorical descriptions from the sixteenth century. Part I is completed by Richard Townsend's report of the Mt. Tlaloc investigation.

Part II, "Aztec Ceremonial Landscapes," focuses on the spatial, symbolic, and ritual dimensions and the deities of the ceremonial landscape that stretched from Tenochtitlan to Chalco, Zacatepec, Tepeyac, Aztlan, and even Mictlan. Here we offer Davíd Carrasco's interpretation of a metamorphic vision of place in Toxcatl; Anthony Aveni's concentrated description of Atl Caualo and its archaeoastronomical implications; Johanna Broda's prodigious overview of a number of ceremonial places; Elizabeth Boone's illumination of migration, myth, and performance in a wide range of pictorials; Alfredo López Austin's comparison of Tetzcocan myths of half-men who descended from the sky; Henry Nicholson's consolidation of the octli cult; and Doris Heyden's work on Tezcatlipoca and Toxcatl as a cipher of transformations in seasons of the landscape. While some of these chapters concentrate on specifics, all of them show the benefits of the serious, interdisciplinary discussions carried on not only during the summer conferences in Boulder, but throughout the last several years in Mexico, at Colgate University, at Dumbarton Oaks, the University of Chicago, and many other places. They reflect what has been called the "Archive on Wheels," another example of a metamorphic vision of place and scholarship.

Part III, "Changing Voices," contains responses to the chapters in the first two parts and reflects both original research and dialogue with major ideas of the conference. Part III addresses such issues as the earth as an eating landscape in Philip Arnold's chapter, responding to Aveni's work; the ceremonial landscape as a spectral world, a world of visions and mirrors of society and symbolism in Lawrence Sullivan's response to Broda; local knowledge as a test of theory in Peter van der Loo's dialogue with Long and Turner; and shamanism as the primordial landscape of the Tezcatlipoca cult in Jane Day's response to the ideas discussed by Heyden and Carrasco. Jorge Klor de Alva's work on modern anthropology and the colonization of mind and bodies raises critical questions about method and theory in the study of ceremonial landscapes of all types.

A special feature of this book are the rarely seen photographs of new discoveries at Tlatelolco, including the new chac-mool from the Templo Mayor, the mural on the Templo Calendarico, and the ritual remains from the excavation in front of the Ehecatl Temple.

While we celebrate this book as the product of the interaction of place, dialogue, and ideas in the Mexico City conference, it is clear that new challenges have appeared. As we complete a decade of collaboration among the Proyecto Templo Mayor, the Museo del Templo Mayor, and the Mesoamerican Archive and Department of Religion at the University of Colorado, it is not so much that we have achieved something excellent but rather that we have worked to prepare ourselves for new questions, harder work in the field and libraries, sustained discussions, and, perhaps, significant discoveries. And this is best, for as one writer on transformations, sacred spaces, alignments, and moving places wrote, "The readiness is all."

DAVÍD CARRASCO
MEXICO CITY AND BOULDER

NOTES

1. Carlos Fuentes, *Where the Air Is Clear* (New York: Farrar, Straus, and Giroux, 1960), pp. 4–5.
2. Participants in the 1979 conference at the University of Colorado included José Arguellas, Pedro Armillas, Johanna Broda, Davíd Carrasco, Edward Calnek, José Cuellar, Wilfred Gingerich, Richard Hecht, Doris Heyden, John Hoag, Alfredo López Austin, Eduardo Matos Moctezuma, Henry B. Nicholson, Esther Pasztory, Payson Sheets, Paul Shankman, William B. Taylor, and Paul Wheatley. Also participating from the Department of Religious Studies were Frederick Denny, Ira Chernus, Robert Lester, and Rodney Taylor.
3. A more detailed description of the developments leading up to this publication appear in *The Imagination of Matter: Religion and Ecology in Mesoamerican Traditions*, ed. Davíd Carrasco (Oxford: BAR International Series no. 515, 1989). A number of original articles by participants included in that work helped set the stage for the formation of this volume.

Aztec Ceremonial Landscapes

Part I

New Discoveries at El Templo Mayor, Tlatelolco, and Mt. Tlaloc

1

Notes on the Oldest Sculpture of El Templo Mayor of Tenochtitlan

Eduardo Matos Moctezuma

The oldest stage of the Templo Mayor that we have discovered so far is the one we call Stage II (see Figure 1.1). According to our tentative chronology, this stage corresponds approximately to the year A.D. 1390, the period before the Mexicas liberated themselves from the rule of Azcapotzalco, under whom they were subjugated. In trying to find elements that would permit us more positively to elucidate our chronology — which we still consider subject to revision — it was proposed that we dig a trench in front of each one of the stairways that lead to the upper part of the Stage II area of the temple, where the *adoratorios* dedicated to Tlaloc and Huitzilopochtli are located. These trenches were two meters wide and were dug in the center of each stairway. The stones that formed the stairs were dismantled, numbered, and photographed, and were to be replaced once the excavation was finished.

I will not cover here the details of the work done during the months of January through April 1989, but rather will focus on a significant discovery that occurred when the trench on the Tlaloc side was dug. On January 20, 1989, the archaeologist Teresa Gracia Franco unearthed a stone head facing west, standing on the south end of a stone slab in the filling of *tezontle* rock and mud that forms the nucleus of Stage II, just above the phreatic level. The head was attached to its base with stucco.

What immediately attracted our attention were the head's unusual features: The nose was contorted toward the left and the mouth had a

Funds for this work were provided by the Mesoamerican Archive and Research Project of the University of Colorado, Boulder, directed by Davíd Carrasco. This chapter was translated with the assistance of Joseph Richey and Anne Becker.

Figure 1.1. An Early Stage of El Templo Mayor (Stage II, c. A.D. 1390). This is the northern side of the temple, ruled by Tlaloc.

marked grimace toward the right (see Figure 1.2). Immediately, it reminded us of some stone and ceramic faces that we had studied in 1970 and that were identified as possible representations of facial paralysis (see Matos 1970), an illness that occurs for various reasons, among them a traumatism or a severe chill. It affects the facial nerves and muscles, paralyzing half of the face. When the affected individual tries to eat, talk, or laugh, there is a very characteristic expression on one-half of the face. If the excavated head was made to represent a paralysis, it is important to describe, however briefly, some of the characteristics of illnesses and their relation to certain gods of the Nahua pantheon.

One of the studies that has shed bright light on the relations among the human body, illness, society, myths, cosmovision, and certain beliefs of the Nahuas, is without a doubt Alfredo López Austin's, *Cuerpo Humano e Ideología.* In Chapter 8, he writes of a debate with George Foster concerning whether the concepts of "hot" and "cold" forces in medical treatment were pre-Columbian or European. López Austin shows that the Mesoamerican world conceived of the dichotomy of "hot" and "cold" and made it part of its cosmovision prior to European contact. Foster believes

Figure 1.2. Face with Possible Facial Paralysis

that the hot/cold dichotomy is a derivative of the European world. I am inclined toward the position of López Austin because his arguments are solidly based in Mesoamerican evidence. It is in the discussion about the hot/cold dichotomy that archaeological representations of sicknesses and the contexts in which they are found can be of help, particularly in the case of the figure we are examining.

Let us look at the context in which it was found. The head, because of its characteristics, must have belonged to a chac-mool. The excavations of the Proyecto Templo Mayor, have taught us the significance of the place that these sculptures occupied. The chac-mool found in front of the adoratorios to the god Tlaloc in Stage II (see Figure 1.3) reveals an intimate relationship between this sculpted figure and the cult of water. The ritual and symbolic relationship between Tlaloc and chac-mool is obvious, and if there are any doubts, we also have the Mexica chac-mool found in 1943 (today in the Mexica Room of the Museo Nacional de Antropología), whose characteristics show a direct association with the water god.

Figure 1.3. Detail of the Excavation. Note the positions of the two chac-mools

But returning to the head we recently discovered: there is no doubt that it represents this type of sculpture. It has a striking similarity to the chac-mool of Stage II and was attached to the end portion of the slab that may have represented the body of chac-mool. Further, the pathological characteristics of the chac-mool head appear to be associated with the god Tlaloc. This is not unusual because some gods, according to their attributes, are related to determined illnesses; for example, Tlaloc, the water god, is linked to illnesses such as dropsy. Therefore, it would not be strange that he should also have a strong relation to an illness such as facial paralysis, which may be caused by a severe chill. It is reasonable to ask if this illness is being represented. We believe so; such an obvious pathology and its causes would not have gone unnoticed by the Mexicas. Further research could compare this example with other representations of the same illness to search for similarities and differences.

On the other hand, the presence of a sick figure allied with the water god in the Templo Mayor is significant, in light of the fact that Huitzilopochtli, the god of war, who is also associated with a physical deformity, was found in the same building. Huitzilopochtli is a god with, as the chronicles say, a "skinny" foot — a foot that has suffered a real illness. The same pathology occurs with Nanahuatzin, the boil-covered god, who throws himself into a bonfire in Teotihuacan in order to become the sun at the creation of the Fifth Age. For a sick god to become the sun in one of the main Nahua myths illustrates that illness had a major religious significance in the Nahua world.

Again I would like to underline my support for the aforementioned position of López Austin in relation to the "cold" and the "hot," dual concepts that were present in the Templo Mayor. The northern half of the building is ruled by Tlaloc, who is associated with water, humidity, cold, and so forth — feminine characteristics. The opposite elements related to masculinity (the sun, heat, the sky, the eagle, and so on), occur on the other side of the temple, which corresponds to Huitzilopochtli.

The purpose of these brief remarks is to share some ideas that emerged with the discovery of this sculpture, the oldest that has yet been found in the Templo Mayor. Further interpretation is ongoing and will be published in the future.

References

López Austin, Alfredo

1984 *Cuerpo humano e ideología: Las Concepciones de los antiguos nahuas.* 3 vols. Mexico City: Universidad Nacional Autónoma de México.

Matos Moctezuma, Eduardo

1970 *Parálisis facial prehispanica.* Mexico City: Instituto Nacional de Antropología e Historia.

2

A Study of Skeletal Materials from Tlatelolco

Juan Alberto Román Berrelleza

Recent excavations carried out at the archaeological site of Tlatelolco, under the auspices of the Proyecto Templo Mayor and the University of Colorado, Boulder, recovered a number of offerings consisting of diverse materials and archaeological objects. Three successive seasons in the field were necessary for complete extraction of this abundant and complex collection of offerings, with the final season concluding in April 1989.

The study of the newly obtained objects and the respective data presents an invaluable opportunity to deepen our knowledge and comprehension of some religious ideas, ceremonies, and rituals practiced by the Tlatelolcas not long before the Spanish conquest. Rather than attempt to present final results (which would be difficult given how recently these excavations have been completed), I will delineate the general compass points that have directed the research and thereby establish our working hypothesis and achievements until now.

The origin of the Tlatelolcas, like other events of their history, including the founding of their city, has provoked and continues to provoke controversy among different specialists in the study of Mexican society (Orozco y Berra 1960, vol. 3:147; Martínez del Río 1944:5). I will not enter into the controversies that Tlatelolcan history has caused among investigators; I will say only that Tlatelolco was a neighboring city to Mexico-Tenochtitlan, populated by people of Nahua affiliation, with very similar, if not identical, cultural and religious traditions. Because of traditional and political conflicts, Tlatelolco was militarily defeated and almost destroyed by its neighbors, under whose domination it remained until the arrival of the Spaniards in 1521 (Duran 1967:253–65; Barlow 1987).

Figure 2.1. Sculpted Stone Representation of Ehecatl-Quetzalcoatl. All photographs are by Salvador Guil'liem Arroyo and Zúñiga Amézquita.

Figure 2.2. Temple of Ehecatl-Quetzalcoatl. This view looks from south to north over the temple in which the offerings were deposited. Note the excavated trench on the right side.

The investigation currently in progress centers on the study of the skeletal remains of some thirty-eight individuals who formed part of different offerings. The majority were young children. This deposit was located at the front of the platform of the principal façade of Temple R, dedicated to the cult of Ehecatl-Quetzalcoatl, as represented by the presence of the sculpted image of this deity and the architectural characteristics of this building (found in the southeast corner of the archaeological site at Tlatelolco; see Figures 2.1 and 2.2). To carry out the analysis and interpretation of the discovery, we have adhered to archaeological field information that correlates with the data provided by ethnographic sources and other studies related to the subject, all of which will be compared to the information obtained in the laboratory. For this reason, is it best to give a brief description of the offerings discovered.

For the most part, the offerings consisted of globular ceramic urns of varied sizes. Inside, small infant skeletons were found along with such diverse material as copper rattles, conch shells, snails, obsidian blades, pieces of wood, blue pigment, and bird bones, among other things. On some occasions, a wide variety of objects were placed outside of the urns — zoomorphic and anthropomorphic representations as well as dishes,

Figure 2.3. Detail of Offerings in Urns. Note the ceramic lids.

plates, and vessels of the same ceramic material. The majority of the urns had flat ceramic lids (see Figure 2.3). Another mode of offering was the burial of infants and adults alike directly in the earth beside objects and materials similar to those described above (see Figure 2.4). In addition to these types of offerings, the discovery of one offering of a textile and another of an incense burner should be added to the list.

The chronology of exactly when these materials were deposited has not yet been established, because the analysis of the ceramics and the information obtained from the structures of the building has not been concluded. But tentatively, the first data revealed by this analysis places the date of the deposit at some time shortly before the Spanish conquest. Given the location and context of these offerings, it is very probable that their deposit corresponded to a ceremonial and ritual complex dedicated to Ehecatl-Quetzalcoatl. It is possible that these ceremonies included sacrifices in honor of the deity.

It is important to mention several pre-Hispanic religious concepts that relate to this type of sacrifice, because it is through these concepts that some of our hypotheses about the significance of the discovery are built.

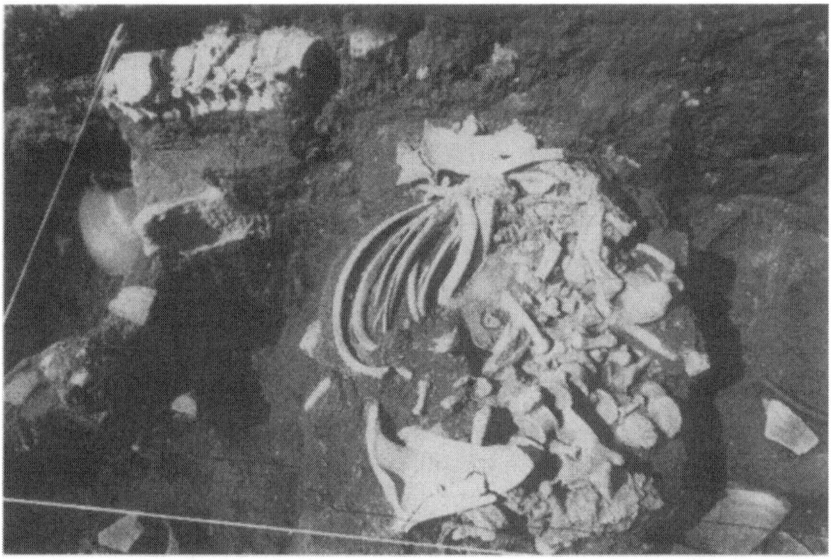

Figure 2.4. Detail of Skeleton. The body in this case was placed directly in earth.

From ancient times, agricultural groups have practiced propitiatory rites related to the magical security of the fertility of the land and the control of atmospheric phenomena. It can be said that these customs constituted the core of the annual cycle of ceremonies and the principal concern of the entire society. In this way, the yearly calendar of eighteen annual festivals was a cycle of structured ceremonies related to agricultural work. For example, during the dry season, five of the ceremonies were devoted to petitioning the water gods for rain: Tlaloc, Chalchiuhtlicue, the Tlaloque, and Quetzalcoatl (Sepúlveda 1973:9–10.) Although Quetzalcoatl had originally been a cultural hero (Piña Chán 1985; Graulich 1988), in later times he was considered the god of wind. For the Aztecs, the invocation of Ehecatl was the most important dimension of Quetzalcoatl. As Lord of the Winds, which precede the rain, Ehecatl-Quetzalcoatl was considered the announcer who "swept the road for the water gods" (Sahagún 1975: 32). In addition, the god of wind was thought of as having a quadruple form corresponding to the four cardinal points. On the other hand, this god formed part of the *tepictoton* or Tlaloque, who were gods that resided in the mountains, assistants to Tlaloc, the principal rain god. In this form, Quetzalcoatl, under his invocation Ehecatl, clearly belongs to the Tlaloc complex (Nicholson, 1957:232–36).

It is already widely known that the Tlaloque received young children in the ceremonial petitioning for rain; thus it should not seem strange to find the remains of children, probably sacrificed in the temple dedicated to Ehecatl-Quetzalcoatl at Tlatelolco. But why did the Aztecs prefer to use children for this type of sacrifice? Did the children selected for sacrifice exhibit any special characteristics?

Some existing facts appear partially to answer these questions. First, it must be remembered that in pre-Hispanic times, infancy was considered an age when individuals were exposed to many great dangers, natural as well as supernatural. But it was also an age of such purity that children could communicate with the gods, and they were protected by a series of magical and religious resources from earthly contamination and harmful forces that could destroy this purity. In this way, the children could retain their ability to communicate with the gods and obtain their favor as was necessary (López Austin 1984, vol. 1:324). Probably for these reasons infants were chosen to be offered to the gods.

Regarding the second question (the special characteristics of the children), physical anthropology has brought forward facts that help elucidate this aspect. During a previous excavation at the Templo Mayor of Tenochtitlan, there was also an opportunity to investigate a sacrificial offering of children. It was observed that half of the sacrificed individuals had various skeletal pathologies; that is, signs of disease that left traces in the bones, as is the case with tooth decay and lesions caused by anemia from iron deficiencies (a condition known as porotic hyperostosis), among others (Román 1986).

In the examination of the skeletal remains of the individuals recovered at Tlatelolco, we observed vestiges of these types of diseases, as well as other ailments (see Figures 2.5–2.8). In our opinion, this pattern at both Tenochtitlan and Tlatelolco indicates that these were children whose health conditions were precarious and who had little chance of survival.

This is particularly relevant if we briefly analyze the cyclic concept of the world prevalent in pre-Hispanic times, whereby nothing could be wasted. In the Mesoamerican cosmovision the universe integrated a broad range of natural forces and divine energies in eternal movement. This movement had to be put in perfect order to avoid energy loss that could create a state of imbalance and cause the destruction of cosmos, society,

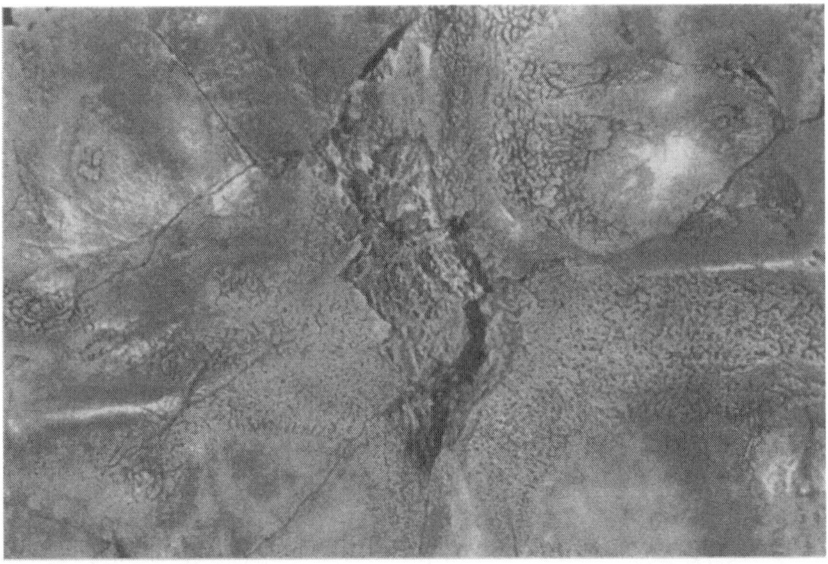

Figure 2.5. Detail of Internal Portion of Occipital Bone of an Infant. The bone clearly shows lesions caused by iron deficiency anemia.

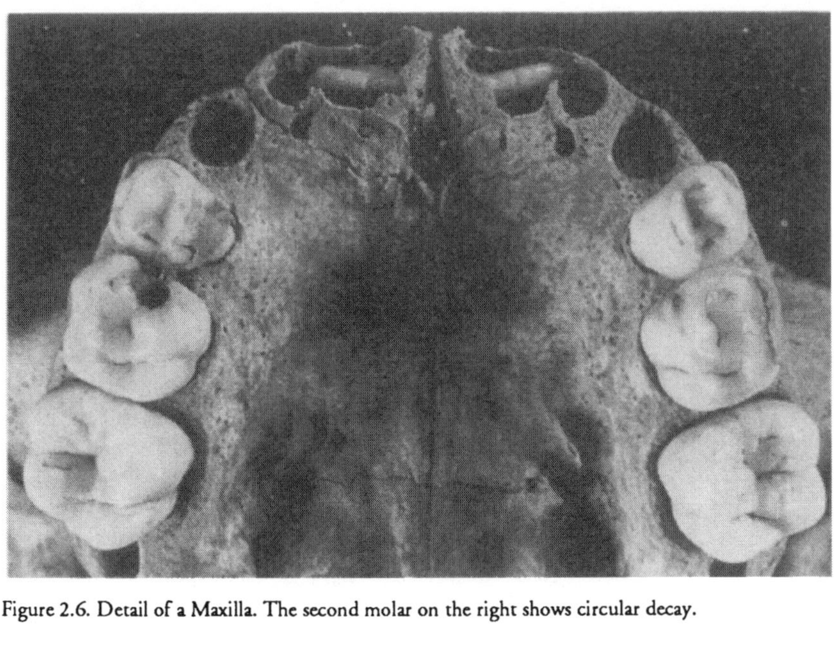

Figure 2.6. Detail of a Maxilla. The second molar on the right shows circular decay.

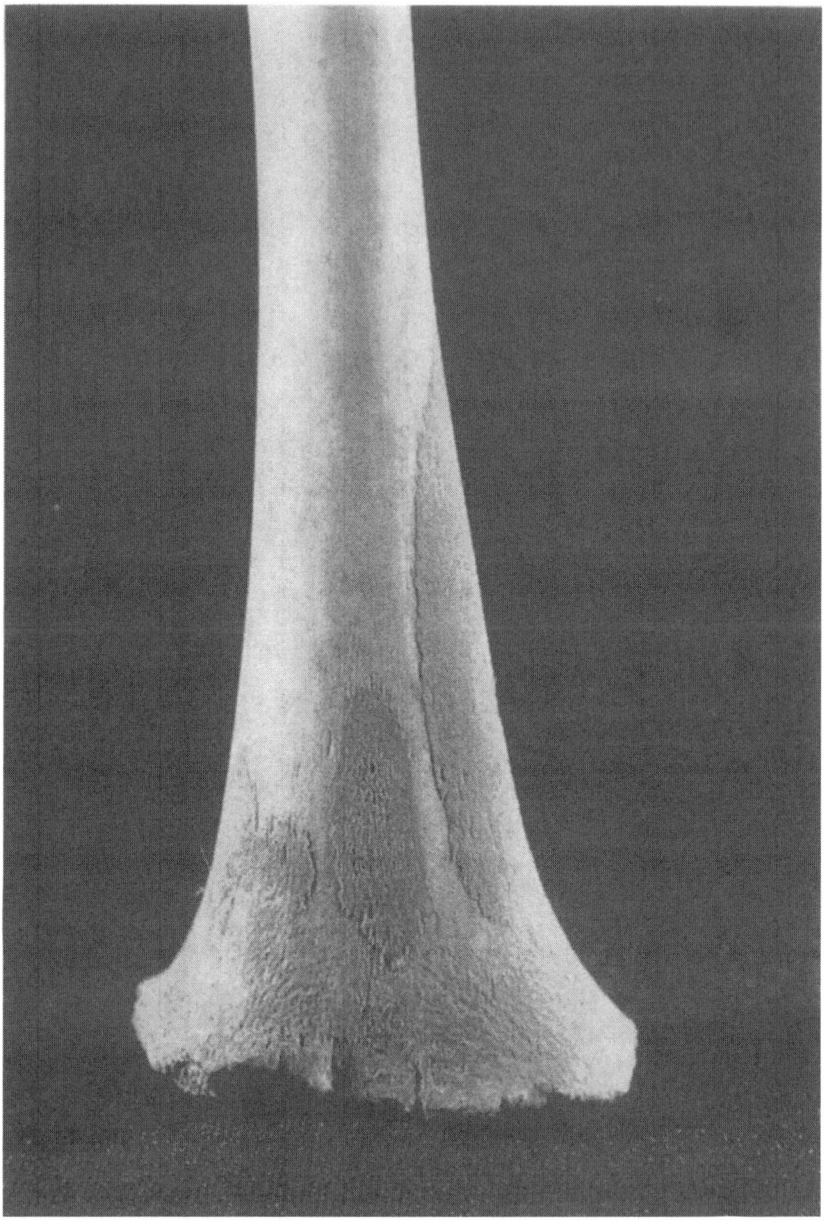

Figure 2.7. Detail of a Young Individual's Right Femur. The distal (or lower) end, seen here from the front, shows traces of a nonspecific infection.

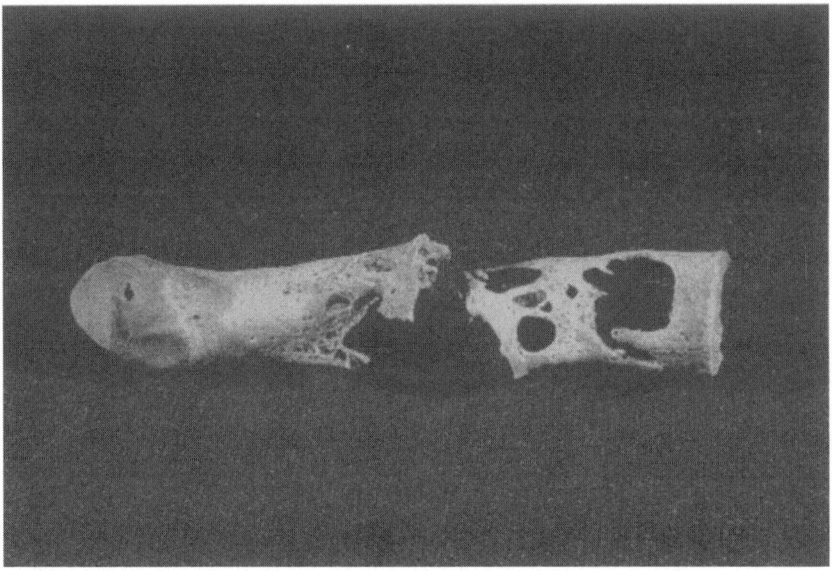

Figure 2.8. Detail of a Toe Bone. The loss of bone caused by an advanced infection is apparent.

and humans (Duverger 1983). The society operating within this cosmological view sought to maximize its limited resources. Within this universe, there existed individuals who possessed a sizable charge of energy and who could be ritually utilized if there were an imbalance between the beneficent and destructive forces, as would be the case when a drought destroyed crops and threatened agricultural stability. In a similar fashion, an individual dying a natural death could be considered a waste of energy, an imbalance, in that the energy was lost, or time was lost in reintegrating the person's energy into the cosmic cycle. The society and the cosmos required that this energy be recycled as rapidly as possible to avoid harmful disequilibrium.

So, if an individual of young age possessed the purity as well as the ability to communicate with the gods, and suffered from precarious health conditions putting his life in danger, the society was faced with the threat of a waste of vital energy. The response was to sacrifice the individual in order to bring a message to the gods — that is, establish a means of communicating with them through the children and the petitions that in one way or another would benefit the entire society. This functioned to conserve the energy contained in the subject by utilizing it to maintain the equilibrium between the world and the universe. In my view, the possible ritual treatment of children at the Ehecatl-Quetzalcoatl temple represents this cosmovision and this attempt to maintain social and spiritual equilibrium between the beneficent and destructive forces.

These are, in general terms, the initial interpretations of the discoveries at Tlatelolco. But the physical anthropological findings are only one aspect of the research and analysis. It is necessary to integrate the research from archaeologists, ethnographers, historians of religions, and other specialists, in order to develop an interdisciplinary understanding of the events in Aztec life that left for us these material remains.

Note

Translated with the assistance of Joseph Richey and Anne Becker.

References

Barlow, Robert H.
1987 *Tlatelolco: Rival de Tenochtitlan*, ed. Jesús Monjarás-Ruiz, Elena Limón, and María de la Cruz P. Mexico City: Instituto Nacional de Antropología e Historia–UDLA.

Durán, Diego
1967 *Historia de las indias de Nueva España e Islas de Tierra Firme*, ed. Angel María Garibay K. vol. 1. Mexico City: Editorial Porrúa.

Duverger, Christian
1983 *La flor letal y economía del sacrificio azteca.* Mexico City: FCE.

Graulich, Michael
1988 *Quetzalcoatl y el espejismo de Tollan.* Occasional Publications no. 1. Instituut Voor Amerkanistiek. Belgium.

López Austin, Alfredo
1984 *Cuerpo humano e ideología.* 3 vols. Mexico City: Universidad Nacional Autónoma de México.

Martínez del Río, Pablo
1944 Resumen de los trabajos arqueologicos. *Tlatelolco a través de los tiempos.* vol. 1. Memorias de la Academia Mexicana de Historia. Mexico City: Academia Mexicana de Historia.

Nicholson, H. B.
1957 Topiltzin Quetzalcoatl of Tollan: A problem in Mesoamerican enthnohistory. Ph.D. diss., Harvard University, Cambridge, Mass.

Orozco y Berra, Manuel
1960 *Historia antigua y de la conquista de México.* Vol. 3. Mexico City: Editorial Porrúa.

Piña Chán, Román
1985 *Quetzalcoátl: Serpiente emplumada.* Mexico City: FCE.

Román Berrelleza, Juan Alberto
1986 El sacrificio de niños en honor a Tláloc (La ofrenda No. 48 del Templo Mayor). Thesis. Escuela Nacional Anthropología e Historia, Mexico City.

Sahagún, Fray Bernardino de
1975 *Historia general de las cosas de Nueva España.* Mexico City: Editorial Porrúa.

Sepúlveda, Maria Teresa
1973 Peticion de lluvias en Ostotempa. *Boletin del I.N.A.H.* 4, no. 2a (January–March):9–20.

3

Discovery of a Painted Mural at Tlatelolco

Salvador Guil'liem Arroyo

As part of the investigation of the Great Temple Project under the direction of Eduardo Matos Moctezuma, a series of archaeological explorations were initiated in 1987 at the ceremonial site of Tlatelolco in what is called the Plaza de Tres Culturas. This excavation was supported by funds from the University of Colorado, especially the Mesoamerican Archive, under the direction of Davíd Carrasco. The temples in the southern sector were emphasized, such as the temple dedicated to Ehecatl and the Templo Calendárico, also called Temple of the Glyphs. I will concern myself with the latter.

The Templo Calendárico was discovered during a project in the 1960s led by Francisco González Rul. He tells us that this discovery was one of the factors that prevented the destruction of the remains of the southern half of the archaeological precinct where the construction of a reflecting pond was planned. Later, in 1988, Francisco Hinojosa Hinojosa made different exploratory digs in the temple where he located a substructure.

The building is formed by two superimposed rectangular bodies oriented toward the west. *Trecenas* (a thirteen-day sequence) of the divinatory calendar (a 260-day cycle) appear on the northern, eastern, and southern façades. The glyphs are comprised in a panel of stone and tezontle castings. On the northern façade, the trecena is ordered from west to east. The trecena begins with 1 Cipactli and ends with 13 Acatl. The second trecena appears on the eastern façade and is ordered north to south; it begins with 1 Ocelotl and ends with 13 Miquiztli. The third trecena appears on the southern façade and is ordered east to west, begining with 1 Mazatl and ending with 13 Quiahuitl.

Figure 3.1. Photograph of El Templo Calendárico

The principal façade is formed in its lower body by front steps interrupted by by beams and a center pedestal. In the upper part there is a stairway formed by four steps demarcated by beams. The temple rests on a tiled floor that surrounds it and is interrupted in the front by an access platform belonging to a substructure. On top of the access platform, in the center, rested a circular structure made of slabs, 3.2 meters in diameter. This structure also supported the central pedestal. Eduardo Matos and I questioned the function of this structure in relation to the buildings; it could have been an offerings container or a charnel house. The question warranted exploration of the interior. We dismantled the circular structure, first lifting the weight from the central pedestal and the platform. In moving the slabs from the northern half, the first piece of a mural was located. Immediately, a restoration specialist was called in from the Dirección de Restauración del Patrimonio Nacional of the Instituto Nacional de Antropología. Armando Soto was designated to supervise the consolidation and restoration of the mural, which was slowly and carefully uncovered according to the needs of conservation.

Figure 3.2. Drawing of the Mural on the Principal Façade of El Templo Calendárico at Tlatelolco. The painted mural is located on the wall between the two stairways.

The mural consists of two fundamental parts. The upper part reveals a calendrical trecena, only the central part of which was rescued. In the extreme upper right we can clearly make out the glyph 7 Miquiztli. Continuing to the left, we can distinguish three blocks whose glyphs are not fully visible. The accompanying numerals can hardly be seen. The extreme left is occupied by the Itzcuintli glyph accompanied by part of its numeral.

The vestiges of paint allow one to conclude, without a doubt, that it deals with the fourth trecena of the *tonalpohualli,* which begins with 1 Xochitl and ends with 13 Malinalli. From the information, it can be deduced that the building has a sequence of a fifth of the divinatory counting (260 divided by fifty-two). This sequence begins in the northwest corner and goes to the northeast, then toward the southeast, later continuing to the southwest, and concludes in the northwest.

In the lower part of the mural (see Figure 3.2), two profiles appear facing one another in the classic genuflecting posture of the pictographic codices. They are inside a red receptacle that is outlined by a red band. The larger figure occupies the southern half of the scene and has hands held in front; the upper hand holds a tool made of bone used in autosacrifice, and in the other there is a priest's bag. He has coarse hair and is

Figure 3.3. The Primordial Pair Oxomoco and Cipactonal. Compare this image from the Codex Borbonicus with the figures in the mural from Tlatelolco.

adorned by a small headdress, wears a breastplate and beaded necklaces, and from his mouth emerge markings that signify speech.

The other figure, smaller in size, also has coarse hair adorned with a simple headdress. One hand is held above the other, but what it holds cannot be distinguished — nor can the other details of the garments because of damage to the painting. Again in front of the mouth are markings that signify speech. The emblem of Itzpapalotl appears between the figures, and above the larger are, possibly, some numerals.

The total scene of the mural referred us back to the pictographic sources in search of clues to help identify the two figures. The painted trecena, although incomplete, is clearly one-fourth of the tonalpohualli. Regarding these two personages, there are a series of elements that identify them with panel 21 of the Codex Borbonicus (see Figure 3.3), and these are:

- Two persons in genuflection (a typical posture in the codices) face to face

- The figure on the right that lifts a bone tool and holds a priest's bag in the other hand; in the codex, both elements are held by a single hand
- The figure on the left that lifts the hand in front
- The coarse hair of both figures
- The missing teeth of both figures, signifying old age
- The fact that both figures are found in the lower part of a red receptacle

The emblem above the figures may repesent Itzpapalotl, who is not found in the Codex Borbonicus. We know, however, that Itzpapalotl is identified with the god Oxomoco according to the Codex Telleriano-Remensis's second part, panel 22. Also, Francisco del Paso y Troncoso identified the figures of panel 21 in the Codex Borbonicus as Cipactonal and Oxomoco. He wrote: "Both, as is well known, were masters of the divining arts and, according to tradition maintained by the Indians, were the inventors of the calendar, for this reason they are situated in the middle of the figures revealing one of the more complicated computations" (del Paso y Troncoso 1981).

Fray Bernardino de Sahagún noted the following concerning their powers:

> Of these wise men only four remained with these people: Oxomoco, Cipactonal, Tlaltetecuj, Suchicaoaca. After the others were gone, the four had a consultation whereat they said: "There will come a time when there may be light to rule this republic. But while our Lord God may be absent things change, to be able to rule themselves well, etcetera . . . everything will be in order, because the wise men brought their paintings wherever they governed."
>
> For these reasons they invented the judiciary, astrology and the art of interpreting dreams. They composed the counting of days, nights, and hours, the different seasons that were conserved while the Toltecs, the Mexicas, the Tepanecas, and all the Chichimecas governed. [Sahagún: 1985].

Similarly, "La Historia de los Mexicanos por sus Pinturas" (1941) also mentions these personages associated with the creation of the marking of time:

> Then they made a man and a woman. The man they called Oxomoco, and the woman Cipastonal, and they were sent to till the land and spin

and weave. And from them were born the macehualtin [commoners] and so they did not become idle and without work, they gave her certain grains of corn for curing and divining and casting spells. And so they are used today by women. Then they made the days, and put them in months, giving each month twenty days, and so they had eighteen months, or 360 days in the year, as they would say later.

In Coatlan, Morelos, Oxomoco and Cipactonal are identified by Krickeberg (1969) and show similar characteristics to the mural and to the Codex Borbonicus: one genuflecting before the other; coarse hair; the hands out in front; and Cipactonal holding a tool of bone in front of the symbol for the day. In the case of the other person, Oxomoco, the headdress seems to be representative of Itzpapalotl.

All the previous data seem to be in such agreement that they allow for the formulation of a plausible hypothesis: These discoveries show that the temple is indeed a temple that justifies the name Templo Calendárico, and seems to be dedicated to the *tonalamatl,* composed of four trecenas (fifty-two days). The deities that appear in the principal façade were, according to the ethnohistorical sources, the inventors of the divinatory calendar. In effect, Oxomoco and Cipactonal, the original pair, appeared in ancient documents as divine personages or as gods, connected to the origin of the calendar.

Note

Translated with the assistance of Joseph Richey and Anne Becker.

References

Codex Borbonicus
1981 Borbonicus Codex. Mexico City: Siglo XXI.

Historia de los mexicanos por sus pinturas.
1941 Historia de los mexicanos por sus pinturas. In *Coleccion de documentos para la historia de México.* Vol. 1, *Relaciones de Texcoco y de los señores de la Nueva España.* Juan Bautista Pomar and Alonso de Zurita. Mexico City: S. Chóvez Hayhoe.

Krickeberg, W.
1969 *Felsbilder Mexico: Felsplastic und Felsbilder bei den Kulturvölkern Altament OO.* Berlin: Dietrich Reimer Verlag.

Paso y Troncoso, Francisco del
1981 *Descripción, historia y exposición del Códice Borbónico,* Mexico City: Siglo XXI.

Sahagún, Fray Bernardino de
1985 *Historia general de las cosas de Nueva España.* Vol. 10, ch. 29. Mexico City: Porrúa.

4

The Mt. Tlaloc Project

Richard F. Townsend

The project to survey and map the Aztec temple on Mt. Tlaloc was successfully carried out in April 1989 by the project directors Richard F. Townsend of the Art Institute of Chicago and Felipe Solís of the Museo Nacional de Antropología in Mexico. We were assisted by the archaeologist Alejandro Pastrana and the archaeologist and mapmaker Hernando Gómez Rueda, both from the Instituto Nacional de Antropología e Historia de México. Two graduate students from the institute also assisted.

The archaeological site lies at an altitude of 13,500 feet above sea level, on the barren summit of Mt. Tlaloc, between the Valley of Mexico and the Basin of Puebla. Because of its remoteness the temple had never been adequately surveyed and little was known of its chronology and architectural iconography. Yet, the temple is partly described in a detailed account, in Diego Durán's sixteenth-century *Book of the Gods and Rites and the Ancient Calendar,* of the annual rainmaking rites performed by Aztec kings. We believed that an investigation of this place would find answers to a series of outstanding questions about religious thought and imagery in the Aztec Empire. What would the Mt. Tlaloc temple tell us about the imagery of architecture and sacred geography? How did the building function, and what do the rites say about the idea of kingship among the Aztecs and their neighbors? What underlying mythic themes might be revealed by an investigation of this site? Would the Mt. Tlaloc temple cast light on a structure of cultural connections between the Aztecs and their predecessors in the long history of civilization in the Valley of Mexico? After an initial planning meeting at the museum, we decided to carry out the work at the site in three field sessions.

Mt. Tlaloc is part of a complex chain of volcanic heights extending north from the snowcapped peaks of Ixtaccihuatl and Popocatepetl. The best approach is via Texcoco to the village of Tequexquinahuac, and then east by a dirt road winding up into the forested ravines of the rugged mountain massif. The way was easily passable to our rented VW van. The road is paralleled in its upper reaches by a fifteenth-century Aztec aqueduct, which still brings springwater from the high sources to the villages of the Texcocan plain. We established camp in the shelter of fir trees at about the 11,000-foot level and spent the remainder of the first afternoon prospecting for the best possible route to the summit. Topographic maps and aerial photographs were helpful, for the approach to the upper section of the mountain is traversed by impressive fault escarpments and ancient lava flows.

The climb next morning took three and a half hours. Toward the summit the coniferous forest gives way to a progressively colder, bleak, and barren zone of basalt, ash, and coarse grass. The summit is not a peak but rather a small, ovoid plateau, elongated and irregular in elevation. The height affords a dramatic view of Ixtaccihuatl and Popocatepetl, the range country of the north- central plateau. Approaching from the east, we found the entrance to a long processional way much destroyed, but the remains show that they originally reached approximately three meters high. The corridor between them, measuring some three meters wide, extends about half a city block in length. In former times, the visitor would have seen nothing of the spectacular landscape once inside the corridor.

The western end opens into a spacious rectangular precinct, also enclosed by a high surrounding wall. There is evidence of a processional way around the inner perimeter, but no significant building remains are presently seen inside. The surface of the enclosure is somewhat flat and covered with grasses. Several large boulders project upward from the matrix of the mountain. The only visible construction within the precinct is clearly of recent date, consisting of a crude stone shelter piled around and over a natural boulder toward the center of the quadrangle. This is a small shrine where evidence of candles, copal incense, and bottles with seed grains testify to the use of the site by villagers today. A cross surmounts this feature, and other crosses are placed on the rubble of the western precinct wall.

Toward the eastern side of the quadrangle, a rectangular pit was cut into the solid rock of the mountain, on an axis with the entrance from the processional way on the western side. This pit measures approximately three by one meter and is presently filled with rubble up to about 2.5 meters below the top.

According to the accounts written by Diego Durán, the sacred enclosure in Mt. Tlaloc was the site of a royal pilgrimage by the kings of Texcoco, Tenochtitlan, Tlacopan, and Xochimilco. The pilgrimage was made in April or May at the height of the dry season, to call forth rain from the mountain and to initiate the season of regeneration and agriculture. Durán mentions that the precinct had contained a finely made temple of impermanent materials — probably a hut of thatch. He also mentions several idols, the principal of which was named Tlaloc, surrounded by others named after the other peaks of the mountain range. These were the focus of the complex rites. Today, no trace of carved idols can be found among the rubble. But as our surveying proceeded, we began to understand the subtle iconography of the precinct yard, and how its features correspond to Durán's descriptions.

The location of the boulders within the quadrangle provided the critical clue. Allowing for a certain irregularity, it was apparent that four are located at the intercardinal points, two others rise on the eastern and western points, and the rock enclosed by the present shrine occupies the central position. This cosmological geometry recalls a famous page from the Codex Borgia, depicting Tlaloque standing at the intercardinal points and another, vertical Tlaloc in the central panel of the page. The protruding boulders are the most visible features of the enclosure on Mt. Tlaloc. We believe that the top of the mountain was modified in antiquity to remove other rock formations that might have interrupted the cosmological symmetry. In other words, the remaining natural boulders are the "idols" of which Durán spoke. The interior of the temple was an animistic microcosm of the Mt. Tlaloc range, which is a primary source of rain and springwater for the eastern Valley of Mexico. In keeping with this abstract schema, the rectangular rock-cut pit must surely correspond to an *omphalos,* an earth-navel leading down to Mt. Tlaloc's interior. There is curious affinity between this walled yard with its projecting rocks and the famous rock-and-gravel garden enclosures of Japan.

As the surveying proceeded, we also gathered several bags of pottery shards and other artifacts from the surface and from within the shallow burrows left by pothunters at the site. There is evidence of some looting, but the quadrangle is by no means completely despoiled. Upon studying our collection several days later in the museum, we found that about 80 percent of the shards were of fifteenth- and early sixteenth-century manufacture, from Texcoco or Tenochtitlan. But there were also the remains of mold-made figurines from the thirteenth-century Valley of Mexico, at least one sizable fragment of a tenth-century Toltec vessel, pieces of slate pectorals with a rust-encrusted side, possibly the remains of a type of iron pyrite mirror pectoral made at Teotihuacan, and two legs of pottery vessels that may be of Formative Period date. Other remains included tiny turquoise mosaic fragments of a kind used to ornament ear spools, masks, and other items, two jadeite and serpentine beads, and numerous obsidian blade fragments from the Cerro de las Navajas mines in Hidalgo. A careful analysis of these remains has yet to be made. The collection suggests that while the temple enclosure is of fifteenth-century origin, the site itself may have seen ritual use for some fifteen hundred years. Curiously, we found no shards of the Spanish colonial period.

On subsequent field sessions we continued to refine the map of the precinct. The question of the original height of the enclosure walls emerged. Why was it so important for these walls to have been built to a three-meter level? In ancient times the visitor would have seen nothing but the interior landscape and the sky. Only upon reemerging from the long processional way would the sweeping view of the central highlands be visible. It seemed, therefore, apparent that this relationship between interior and exterior space was manipulated as part of the iconography of the site. What was the purpose of the long processional way? Why was the precinct not entered directly through an opening in the western wall? Why should the ancient kings as chief ritualists be obliged to walk down the way in rank order, before reaching the inner quadrangle? These questions are central to the imagery of the temple in its setting and to the meaning of the ritual action.

Answers began to appear when we remembered painted pages from the sixteenth-century Codex Borbonicus and the Codex Tolteca-Chichimeca, respectively depicting an earth deity in the act of parturition, and a mountain with a womblike interior as the birthplace of the Aztec tribes. These documents plus other well-known references from the sixteenth-century ethnohistorical sources characterize the earth in female terms. From this point of view the Mt. Tlaloc temple enclosure was a diagrammatic womb of the earth, containing the source of water and regenerative forces. Upon entering the processional way, the kings, bearing offerings and sacrifices, fertilized the interior microcosm. Several weeks later the first clouds of the rainy season would be seen to collect around the summit of Mt. Tlaloc. Soon, powerful thunderstorms would begin to form from condensation brought by warm, moist air flowing from the Gulf of Mexico. In the ensuing rainy season these storms blow down and out across the Valley every afternoon. The imagery of the rites, the architectural setting, and the natural landscape forcefully conveyed ideas of regeneration and expressed a concept of kingship embedded in the natural cycle. Indeed, the long pilgrimage of the kings to the mountaintop and its source of life, and their return with a boon to the cities of the Valley suggest the enactment of an ancient cosmogonic myth. It may well be that many myths, unrecorded as "stories" by the Spanish friars, were nevertheless encoded in the meticulously described ritual events.

Another important aspect of our work in the Mt. Tlaloc range was to explore the area of springs, located in an alpine valley at an altitude of approximately 11,000 feet. These springs are year-round sources of water for the aqueduct that continues to supply villages of the Texcocan region. These springs and the surrounding heights are named in Los Títulos de Tetzcotzingo, an important fifteenth-century document recording Netzahualcoyotl's decrees of land and water rights in the Texcocan area. Concerning ritual and symbolic matters, we found a stone bowl carved into the matrix of a streambed boulder below one of the higher springs. This was an offering place to the waters, mythologically personified by the female deity Chalchiuhtlicue. The offering place in the streambed, like the Tlaloc boulders in the temple, portrays the animistic, topographic origins of certain Aztec deities. Durán's description of the Tlaloc rites contains a concluding section on the rites of Chalchiuhtlicue, which will be discussed in future published work. The final visit to the Mt. Tlaloc temple was devoted exclusively to photography in an attempt to record the features of the site in diverse lighting conditions.

Note

Our present plans for concluding the project call for another field session. Archaeological test pits will be excavated at selected places within the ritual precinct, under the supervision of Alejandro Pastrana and Hernando Gómez Rueda. This aspect of the project has yet to receive full official approval. It is our plan to prepare a monograph with essays by the major participants that will describe the site, outline the significant topographic and hydraulic features of the Mt. Tlaloc range, discuss the chronology indicated by pottery shard collections, discuss the Tlaloc and Chalchiuhtlicue imagery, and interpret the imagery and ritual functions of the temple.

Part II

Aztec Ceremonial Landscapes

5

The Sacrifice of Tezcatlipoca: To Change Place

David Carrasco

In a series of sharp, critical essays aimed at shifting the direction of the discipline of the history of religions, Jonathan Z. Smith urges a focus on the category of place rather than sacred space. In his new book, *To Take Place: Toward Theory in Ritual*, Smith describes his enterprise as "a matter of theory: the issue of ritual and its relation to place." Smith begins with his favorite quotation from Claude Lévi-Strauss, "All sacred things must have their place," and goes on to demand that we choose to concentrate on the refinements of ritual that carry "more of the social and verbal understanding of place than does the more familiar substantive sacred space in writings by so-called phenomenologists or historians of religion. It is this former sense of *place* [emphasis in original] in relation to the 'microadjustments' of ritual that supplies the focus for these inquiries"(1987: xii).

Smith's agenda includes a sustained critique of the model of sacred space developed by Mircea Eliade in his voluminous publications. Eliade's model of "centre place" treats the world as oriented by a quintessential axis that becomes the primary mode of human symbolism, integrating the cosmos. In such works as *Myth of the Eternal Return, Patterns in Comparative Religions,* and *The Sacred and the Profane,* Eliade has forcefully illuminated the power and meaning of the symbolism of the center. In his model, the center is the place where an opening exists between the planes of existence, resulting in the founding of worlds and their organization around this point of communication with supernatural, transcendent beings. According to Eliade, there are two basic attitudes toward this center. On the one hand, it is acessible to humans who experience it and symbolize it in cities, temples, trees, dwellings, and in certain human beings. On the other hand, the center is guarded by a labyrinth that impedes access to its power, mystery, and authority. Eliade (1958:381) writes in his chapter "Sacred Places": "The labyrinth could be defending a city, a tomb or a sanctuary but, in every case, it was defending some magico-religious space that must be made safe from the uncalled, the uninitiated."

Smith, beginning in his article "The Wobbling Pivot" in which he asks "whether one can pay such attention to the center without giving equal attention to the periphery," has progressively worked to show that Eliade's notion of the "centre" is "not a secure pattern to which data may be brought as illustrative; it is a dubious notion"in the study of religion. On the way to this challenge, Smith has put forth two alternative views of place. The first he calls a

> locative vision of man and the cosmos [that] is revealed in a variety of descriptions of the places in which men may stand. The world is perceived as a bounded world; focusing on the etymological roots, the world is felt to be an *environ*ment, an *ambi*ance. That which is open, that which is boundless is seen as the chaotic, the demonic, the threatening. The desert and the sea are the all but interchangeable concrete symbols of the terrible, chaotic openness. . . . Order is produced by walling, channeling, and confining the waters [1978:134].

Opposed to this map of boundaries is Smith's utopian map of place, which receives less attention but equal passion in a series of statements regarding Albert Camus's *The Rebel*, Alexander the Great's "testing of boundaries and seeking to transcend all limits," and the category of exile in Judaism. Smith's utopian view of landscape is perhaps best represented in his tentative use of the Dionysian pattern of Euripides' *The Bacchae* to illuminate the "White Night of Jonestown." In both of these ceremonial performances, one in Greek theaters, the other in a South American forest, the participants "obliterate distinctions . . . and under the power of a utopian vision of the world relentlessly and restlessly [go] testing the boundaries of the cosmos and seek[ing] to transcend all limits" (1978:201).

In fact, all three of these models of spatial ordering illuminate aspects of Mesoamerican religions. Some cities were situated around temple precincts symbolizing cosmic mountains and the World Tree, which were perceived as openings to the celestial and subterranean realms. Also, space *and* time, especially time, were measured according to a rigorous, locative model. As Maarten Jansen and others have shown, certain dates in Mesoamerican calendars are intimately related to, or locked into, specific places and communities. And we have a few outstanding cases of rulers such as Moctezuma Ilhuicamina who challenged traditional, locative conceptions of imperial space and broke through resistant frontiers to remap the Aztec Empire into a utopian scheme. Smith is well aware of the spectrum of social and symbolic places, as the chapter titles of *To Take Place* show. He repositions the category of place: "In Search of Place," "Father Place," "To Put in Place," "To Take Place."

In a recent series of explorations into the ceremonial patterns of Aztec religion, another conception of spatial order and transformation that is less fixed, more dynamic and momentary has become apparent to me. Sacred space and ceremonial landscapes in Aztec ceremonies expand and retract, meander and transform, link and fold into one another in a "metamorphic vision of place," or, to add to Smith's spectrum, the motion and movement of Aztec rituals suggest the title "To Change Place." Deity impersonators, pilgrimages, processions, and mock battles alternate, change, and move beyond static conceptions of sacralized space and social place. The performances of the Mexican calendar link up, cross, and change territories where the sacred dwelled. In the festival of Toxcatl, dedicated to the protean god Tezcatlipoca, we are presented with an arresting example of this "metamorphic vision of place." It is a vision of place in which change and transformation are the sustained pattern. People change places, the places are transformed by hierophanies, and the humans are momentarily and ultimately changed. It is my tentative suggestion that this metamorphic vision of place reflects a total worldview reflected in such diverse manifestations as the Myths of the Suns, the career of *hombre-dioses* such as Topiltzin-Quetzalcoatl, and the linguistic achievements of Texcoco's poet philosophers. As a means of exploring this notion, let us begin with a description of Toxcatl during which the *teotl ixiptla*, or image of the god Tezcatlipoca, Lord of the Smoking Mirror, was sacrificed during the month of May.

The Ceremony of Toxcatl

In the month of Toxcatl (dry season), the people celebrated a festival for the "god of gods," Tezcatlipoca. One of the final acts was the sacrifice of a captive warrior who was chosen on the basis of his perfect physical features, one "who had no blemishes upon his body." This warrior had been changed into a teotl ixiptla, or image of Tezcatlipoca, and received extraordinary care and public attention as he lived for one year in "all luxuries" while being trained in music, singing, speaking, and walking. For a short time prior to his ritual death, the image was provided with four wives for sexual pleasure and ritual union. At the end of this year, the Tezcatlipoca ixiptla was sacrificed on the top of a temple in the ceremonial center of the city of Chalco. His heart was extracted and offered to the sun, he was beheaded, and his skull placed on the *tzompantli,* or skull rack.

At first glance, this short description indicates the extraordinay importance of the human body of the ixiptla and the cultivation of the enemy warrior into an exemplary cultural image. A more sustained view shows the importance of his movement through a ceremonial landscape, mapped, marked, and renewed by his actions, as well as the perception of social hierarchies in the experience of the participants.

Toxcatl was considered the "most important of all festivals" and called a "debt payment" or *nextlaoalli.* The god Tezcatlipoca was "given human form" through the ritual technique of choosing the most physically attractive male from among a special group of captive warriors who served as the yearly supply for this ceremony. This group was supervised and maintained by a special corps of guardians. It was imperative that all impersonators of Tezcatlipoca slould have a "fair countenance, of good understanding [and should be] slender, reedlike, long and thin, like a stout cane, like a stone column all over." An extensive ritual description of the requirements for the god's "human form" includes the following:

> He was like something smoothed, like a tomato, like a pebble, as if sculptured in wood; he was not curly-haired . . . he was not rough of forehead . . . he was not long-headed. . . . He was not of swollen eyelids: he was not of enlarged eyelids, he was not swollen-cheeked . . . he was not of downcast face; he was not flat-nosed: he did not have a nose with wide nostrils: he was not concave-nosed . . . he was not thick-lipped, he was not gross-lipped, he was not big-lipped, he was not a stutterer, he did not speak a barbarous language. He was not buck-toothed, he was

> not large-toothed, he was not ugly-toothed. . . . His teeth were like seashells . . . he was not cup-eyed, he was not round-eyed; he was not tomato-eyed; he was not of pierced eye. . . . He was not long-handed; he was not one-handed: he was not handless; he was not fat-fingered. . . . He was not emaciated; he was not fat: he was not big-bellied; he was not of protruding navel; he was not of hatchet-shaped navel; he was not of wrinkled stomach; he was not of shrunken stomach . . . he was not of hatchet shaped buttocks. . . . For him who was thus, who had no flaw, who had no (bodily) defects, who had no blemish, who had no mark, . . . there was taken the greatest care that he be taught to blow the flute, that he be able to play his whistle; and that at the same time he hold all his flowers and his smoking tube [Sahagún 1981:67].

The captive who best approximated this negative description of perfection was chosen and carefully trained in several Aztec arts including music, smoking, flower holding. But he was not just a stationary, imprisoned paragon of beauty and culture, for "very great care was taken that he should be very circumspect in his discourse, that he talk graciously, that he greet people agreeably on the road if he met anyone." This last point is vital for understanding Tezcatlipoca's relation to the ritual landscape because his image was allowed to go wandering throughout the city for a year with his public entourage. During these promenades he greeted people who considered him "our lord. There was an assigning of lordship; he was importuned; he was sighed for; there was bowing before him: the commoners performed the earth-eating ceremony before him" (Sahagún 1981, II:68).

At an appointed time during his year-long public displays and contact with the populace, Tezcatlipoca was taken before the *tlatoani* (overlord or king) Moctezuma, who ceremonially, "repeatedly adorned him: he gave him gifts; he arrayed him; he arrayed him with great pomp. He had all costly things placed on him, for verily he took him to be his beloved god" (Sahagún 1981, II:69).

Sahagún's informants provide the details of this further transformation into the ruler's god: His head was pasted with eagle down and popcorn flowers; he was arrayed with "the flowery stole." Golden shell pendants were placed on his ears and turquoise mosaic plugs were inserted in the lobes; a shining seashell necklace and white seashell breast ornament were draped on his neck and chest; a snail shell lip pendant was inserted in his lip. Hardly an area of his body escaped transformation. Golden bracelets covered his upper arms while turquoise bracelets covered "almost all his forearm." A net cape of wide mesh with a fringe of brown cotton thread hung above his costly breechcloth, which reached to the calves of his legs. His legs were covered with gold bells above obsidian sandals with ocelot skin ears. This living image of physical, cultural, and imperial splendor presented himself in the pathways of the city once again, where the citizenry beheld the ruler's "beloved god."

Then, during the twenty days prior to the sacrifice two major transformations took place. The image shed these luscious ornaments and his hair was cut into the style of a seasoned warrior, a style called *tochyacatl* with only a forked heron-feather ornament with a quetzal-feather spray attached to his head. He was given four wives and "for only twenty days he lived lying with the women, that he lived married to them." The symbolism of this ceremonial coupling is meaningful as each of these wives is also a teotl ixiptla representing the goddess Xochiquetzal, Xilonen, Atlatonan, or Uixtociuatl. The five of them sang and danced in public for five days and distributed foods and gifts to people at a series of specific locations including Tecanman; then at a place where the image of Titlacauan was guarded; then at Tepetzinco in the middle of the lagoon; and on the fourth day at Tepepulco. Following this series of visits and distributions of gifts, the Tezcatlipoca ixiptla was taken by boat — with the women consoling him, encouraging him — to a place called Acaquilpan or Caualtepec. After arriving back on land "near Tlalpitzauhcan," the women separated from Tezcatlipoca, who was now followed only by his servants and guardians.

The entourage returned to the mainland and in a surprising maneuver traveled more than fifteen miles to the ceremonial center of Chalco south of Tenochtitlán. Abandoned by his entourage, the image proceeded to a small temple called Tlacochcalco, which, according to Sahagún's text, "he ascended by himself, he went up of his own free will, to where he was to die." As he ascended the temple, he broke his flutes and whistles on the steps. Then, the scene speeded up as the offering priests seized him, "threw him upon his back on the sacrificial stone: then cut open his breast, he took his heart from him, he also raised it in dedication to the sun" (Sahagún 1981:71). The ixiptla's body was carefully lowered from the temple and his head severed from his body, emptied of its contents, and eventually hung on the skull rack. Then, according to Sahagún's informants, this journey from imprisonment to lavish deification to death on the stone had the meaning: "And this betokened our life on earth. For he who rejoiced, who possessed riches, who sought, who esteemed our lord's sweetness, his fragrance — richness, prosperity — thus ended in great misery. Indeed it was said: 'No one on earth went exhausting happinesss, riches, wealth.' "

THE CEREMONIAL LANDSCAPE

The ceremonial life of Aztec cities was as much a theater of the human physique as it was a form of rhetoric and ideology. To put the matter differently, Aztec sacrificial rites were exuberant forms of rhetoric expressed through imagery about the human body as it moved through, changed, and mapped out a ceremonial landscape that was concentrated and dispersed, local and imperial, depending on the particular festival. The relation of the human body to the cosmos in Nahuatl culture has recently been illuminated by Alfredo López Austin in *The Human Body and Ideology,* in which he writes: "There is a whole complex of ideas by which the universe was conceived as a projection of the human body and inversely explained human physiology in relation to the general processes of the cosmos. For this reason a knowledge of the concepts about the human organism is indispensable to anyone who wishes to penetrate the complicated cosmological thought of the Mesoamericans" (1988, vol. 1:8).

In a sense, López Austin's work challenges Mesoamerican specialists and historians of religions to explore together the fuller relations of the ritual use of the human body to the larger ceremonial order of Aztec religion; for Aztec ritual moved and transformed human experience through colorful, florid, visual displays of images of highly energized relationships between temples and mountains, between social groups, between distinct levels of social status, and between humans and their gods. While static and nonhuman images played important roles in linking up these elements of society, it was the living human images of deities, power hierarchies, and nature's forces moving through the landscape that played a central role in the Aztec theater-state. The decoration, movement, and changes of the human body and its most potent parts, including the head, the heart, hair, and blood, constituted a significant portion of the nexus of ceremonial life. And from a slightly different point of view, the eyes were the most important organ. Seeing and movement through the ceremonial landscape were the crucial actions by which to know the cosmos and its interrelated parts.

There is no doubt that all the senses were alert and tuned to the ritual expressions in Tenochtitlan's great ceremonial landscape. The songs were heard, the beat was pounded with feet and interpreted with muscular movements, the blood was smelled and the gods were touched, and sometimes eaten. As Lawrence Sullivan has shown in his study of South American performances, "synesthesia," or the unity of the senses, was the avenue through which knowledge about the cosmos or unity of the world was communicated. In writing about how these unities are learned, Sullivan contends that what sets performance apart from brute behavior is, in part, a "quality of knowledge" experienced in ritual action. The atmosphere necessary for acquiring this quality of knowledge is the experience of synesthesia,

> usually defined as a phenomenon in which one type of stimulation evokes the sensation of another. For example, the research of Marlene Dobkin de Ríos proves the ways in which the hearing of sound, under the influence of sacred plants results in the visualization of colors. Synesthesia translates from the new Latin into quasi-down-home as 'unity of the senses'. . . the point is that performance displays the symbolic expression of synesthesia as it is imagined in a culture. In so doing, it renders perceptible a symbolism of the unity of the senses. The symbolic experience of the unity of the senses enables a culture to entertain itself with the idea of the unity of meaning [Sullivan 1986:8].

Sullivan's approach to synesthesia through a focus on ritual sound offers a valuable lead for new insights into the understanding of Mesoamerican ritual power. But in Aztec ceremonial life, as demonstrated in the ceremony of Toxcatl, synesthesia, or the perception and understanding of unities, was achieved as much by visual experiences as by hearing the gods. The senses were integrated, and the world became meaningful in large part through *seeing* the still and moving images that marked and linked up the wide-ranging ceremonial landscape in and around the capital. People came to Tenochtitlan and moved through its ritual topography in part to see the processions, mock battles, human sacrifices; to see the images of gods and deity impersonators; to gaze at the sacred places where they were concentrated; to see humans changed into gods; and to see other human beings seeing the divine in ceremony and visions.

Here, I want to consider through a focus on one major ceremonial performance, how the human body as both actor and observer combined to organize the senses so that the culture could entertain itself with the idea of unity of meaning and a view of hierarchical differences. On one side of this ceremonial performance we have the human body encapsulating a divine force and adorned with sacred images moving, changing, and linking up a ritual landscape. On the other side we have the participants and observers seeing a cosmology and social world come to life through the movements and changes of a divine image. My intention is to build on Sullivan's approach by following Rhys Isaac's (1982:10) view of a cultural landscape as a terrain or living space that has been subjected to the

> requirements of a conscious and unconscious design. . . . A society necessarily leaves marks of use upon the terrain it occupies. These marks are meaningful signs not only of the particular relations of a people to the environment but also of the distribution of control and access to essential resources. Incised upon a society's living space appears a text for the inhabitants — which he who runs may read — of social relations within the world.

I will explore the design that the Aztecs placed on their living space, and develop a portrait of a ceremonial landscape by using two elements of Isaac's description: (1) the marks and meaningful signs on the landscape, consisting of the temples, neighborhoods, and palaces that were visited and linked into a ceremonial whole by the movement in the ceremony — these marks are largely transformations created by humans; and (2) "he who runs" or in Tezcatlipoca's case he who processed — that is, the images and series of transformations that the Tezcatlipoca ixiptla underwent. In this way we will see both a spatial landscape and a landscape of social relations symbolized in the transformations in the mode of being of Tezcatlipoca's ixiptla. This combination will help provide a perspective through which to view the Aztec attempt at a unity of meaning as well as the expression of the force of the social hierarchy with its uneven access to power and privilege. The ceremony of Toxcatl reflects neither an axis mundi nor a locative vision of place, but rather a vision of place organized by powerful transformations, metamorphoses; a vision of place in which the terrain of the sacred is not concentrated, limited, or restricted to one or several locations. In a manner reminiscent of the paths marked by meandering footprints in the codices, Tezcatlipoca's movements alter our line of vision and mingle places in striking combinations. This metamorphic vision of place is best represented in the tranformations that Tezcatlipoca's ixiptla underwent. He was a capricious god who changed places and changed forms.

This ceremonial landscape was connected by the physical movements and contact of people traveling through the land. As the texts describing Atl Caualo and Toxcatl show, this landscape consisted of particular places in the lakes and in the mountains plus the social markers of roads and temples and neighborhoods. The ritual cycle ensured that there was a constant, organic flow from the center of the *altepeme,* (city-state), through the *calpultin* (corporate groups), and out into the natural landscape. These paths often led back into the ceremonial centers of local communities.

A cursory review of just four of the yearly ceremonies reveals both a tendency to saturate space beyond the ceremonial center and a tendency to reconcentrate people, goods, and symbols within the axis mundi.

In the year-opening ceremony of Atl Caualo, the participants visited seven distant and distinct shrines on surrounding hillsides where children were left for sacrifice. The ritual covered over 120 kilometers in a variety of directions. The subsequent ceremony of Tlacaxipeualiztli covered a ritual map that was not as wide-ranging but was meant symbolically to saturate the whole ceremonial world: "The captor went everywhere. He went everyplace, he omitted no place, nowhere did he forget in the calmeca, in the calpulcos. On the lips of the stone images, on each one, he placed the blood of the captive" (Sahagún 1981:54). In the ceremony of Uey Tocoztli, the action crossed the various calpultin and *calmecac* of the city and spread to the fields and various ceremonial structures in different locations. And in the ceremony of Etzalcualiztli, the participants visited different locations in the lake (Temilco, Tepexicoztoc) where special reeds were gathered, then moved to the ruler's palace in the ceremonial center, outward again to local schools, then out to Tetamacalco and Totecco at the water's edge, then out into the lake to Pantitlan and finally back to Tetamacalco. This spatial breadth is also reflected in the ceremony of Tepeilhuitl during which the women who were sacrificed "were representative of the mountains (ixiptlaoan tetepe) . . . Tepexoch, . . . Matlalcueye, . . . Xochtecatl, . . . Mayahuel (ixiptla of the maguey) and Milnauatl" (Sahagún 1981, II:132).

We are fortunate to see a map of the metamorphosis of ceremonial place in the New Fire ceremony held on the occasion of the ending of the fifty-two-year calendar cycle. This ceremony, also called the Binding of the Years, began in the capital from which processions left, in public view, for the Cerro de la Estrella over twenty kilometers south of the main ceremonial center. Following an all-day procession of priests, deity impersonators, musicians, and warriors, the entourage arrived in the darkness at the summit of this ceremonial mountain where, following ceremonial preparations, the "new fire" was started in the chest of a sacrificed warrior. This fire was taken down the mountain, retracing the route of the procession into the center of the capital, and placed in the holder of the statue of the god Huitzilopochtli. Then, it was taken to all the communities in the empire where it ignited the new fires (or time period) locally. This fiery display ignited the imperial landscape as well as the new time period.

This dynamic pattern challenges the static conception of sacred spaces and the direct-line map of pilgrimages (which appear in our books) by emphasizing the strenuous and powerful physical demands that place pilgrims and celebrants in a wide-ranging, heterogeographical territory. In the New Fire ceremony, all the senses were challenged — through walking, climbing, singing, censing — but most important were the eyes; the fire was seen in the darkness symbolizing a new age.

TEZCATLIPOCA: THE LORD OF EVERYWHERE

The clearest expression of the pattern of the metamorphosis of place is in the cult, symbolism, and ceremony of Tezcatlipoca. In Sahagún's Book 1, titled "The Gods," Tezcatlipoca is called "a true god, whose abode was everywhere — in the land of the dead, on earth, and in heaven." Tezcatlipoca's omnipresence is elaborated in the eleven prayers dedicated to him found in Book 6 of the Florentine Codex. Thelma Sullivan, the distinguished Nahuatl scholar, describes Tezcatlipoca this way (1974:86):

> The nature and powers of Tezcatlipoca are nowhere more sharply etched than in these texts. There are, first of all, the names by which he is invoked: Tloque Nahuaque, literally "Lord of the Near, Lord of the Close," figuratively the supreme lord, the lord who is everywhere, in

> everything, upon whom all depend. Other names are: Yohualli Ehecatl, "Night, Wind," that is, invisible and impalpable; Moyocoyatzin, "Capricious One"; Monenequi, "Tyrannical One"; Titlacahuan, "Our Master" (literally "we are his slaves"); Teimatini, "Knower of People"; Techichihuani, "Adorner of People"; Yaotl, "The Enemy"; Necoc Yaotl, "The Enemy on Both Sides"; Moquequeloa, "The Mocker"; Ipalnemoani, "Giver of Life" (literally "by virtue of whom one lives"); and Teyocoyani, "Creator of Man." They bespeak awesome and frightening powers, an arbitrariness against which man is powerless.

While this series of names speaks to a variety of powers, my eyes are drawn to the spatial reach of Tezcatlipoca, who is near and close, takes the form of the wind, is the enemy on both sides, and knows people wherever they are. In a sense, there is no escaping Tezcatlipoca.

The omnipresence of Tezcatlipoca is also expressed in his ritual mirror that enabled the god or his priest to "see all that took place in the world." His vision spread out to penetrate everywhere; but this ability was anchored in a specific spot — namely, the mirror called Itlachiayaque (place from which he watches; Durán, 1977:99) And from this place his vision could not only stretch into places far away but also penetrate into the interior of hidden things. Consider this prayer from Book 6 of the Florentine Codex: "O master, O our lord, O lord of the near, of the nigh, O night, O wind: thou seest, thou knowest the things within the trees, the rocks. And behold now, it is true that thou knowest of things within us; thou hearest us from within. Thou hearest, thou knowest that which is within us: what we say, what we think; our minds, our hearts. It is as if smoke, mist arose before thee."

In a sense, we see that the god's knowledge of humans and nature is acquired through a synesthesia. First he sees the things within the trees and then he hears the things within the human mind and heart. This saturation of space is transformed into the power to create a sense of direction in space through the playing of Tezcatlipoca's flute. Ten days before the festival, the image plays the flute "in the four directions so all would perform the rite of eating the earth and of begging the gods for things they coveted." In this preparatory ritual, sound creates a sense of space and its cosmic organization. The centrifugal quality of the god's vision and sound is extended to the space and character of warfare and of other gods who dwell both near and far from the human community.

> On hearing the flute that day, brave and courageous men, all the old soldiers implored the gods, in rare anguish and devotion to be given victories against their enemies and strengthened to bring back many captives from war; these men prayed to God of all Created Things, to Lord by Whom We Live, to Sun, to Quetzalcoatl, to Tezcatlipoca, to Huitzilopochtli, to Cihuacoatl. All the principal divinities adored by the natives [Durán 1977:107].

In this evocation of warriors, the pattern of center-periphery is explicit; the flute of Tezcatlipoca prepares them to go out of the city to war and to bring back to the city captives. The flute also stimulates them to ask for divine help from gods who are spatially near, Cihuacoatl, associated with the earth, and those who are spatially far away, the sun and divine forces that are everywhere, the God of All Created Things.

The clearest display of the metamorphosis of place is in the route or ritual randomness of Tezcatlipoca's wandering during the year. As in most festivals, the action began in or near the walled ceremonial center when Tezcatlipoca's image was chosen from a special collection of secluded enemy warriors. Following special training to become a living image of the god, Tezcatlipoca was given the freedom (with guards and retainers) to walk throughout the city. His handsome form, idealized further by the lavish ornaments and training, displayed the beauty and majesty of this god before the thousands whose daily work and movements were interrupted by the entourage. We can imagine the ostentatious impression this retinue, with the ixiptla at the center, made — stopping all traffic and drawing all eyes upon it as the group followed a patterned and random series of routes.

The spreading presence of Tezcatlipoca was heralded, according to Diego Durán's account, by the ritual censing of all homes. At the start of the month of Toxcatl, all homes in the community were entered by a priest who perfumed them with incense "from the threshold . . . to the last corner" including each object in the house, announcing the onset of the time and atmosphere of Tezcatlipoca. Having permeated domestic space and public neighborhoods with sound and smoke and the living image of the god, Tezcatlipoca proceeded to the palace of the tlatoani Moctezuma. This movement crossed not only geographical, domestic, and public space but also hierarchical space as the god's image joined with the office and person of kingship. In the adornment ceremony, the teotl ixiptla was transformed into the ruler's version of the god.

Toward the end of the year-long ceremony, Tezcatlipoca visited four designated ceremonial locations, as though to transform the apparently random sense of space into an ordered integration of ritual precincts, associated with the four directions his flute sounded out. Then the ceremony moved off land and out into the lake, reflecting the "everywhere" conception of the god of gods. He is present not only on the land but in the waters that nurture and threaten it. When the ceremonial entourage returned to land, it headed in the direction of Chalco to the south.

Chalco, according to Chimalpahin, was organized into four communities oriented in cardinal directions. Tlacochcalco was the main center of the Chalcan kingdom, and there the image ascended the temple, moving upward in space, closer to the celestial forces, and was sacrificed. Yet the movement of this illustrious body did not cease at the sacrifice. Not only was the body carried down the steps, but more importantly the head was severed, emptied of its contents, and carried to the skull rack where Tezcatlipoca's gaze met the eyes of countless onlookers. In spatial terms, the teotl ixiptla saturated space with Tezcatlipoca's music, mirror, and living image before returning to a ceremonial center to undergo his final transformation.

Living Images of Transformation

Some of the most potent vehicles for the communication of religious meaning and social hierarchy are the images, icons, and sacred objects utilized in ritual communities and ceremony. Scholarship has focused on a rich spectrum of imagery including sculpture, costume, masks, wall paintings, sand paintings, pottery, amulets, and architecture. For instance, some of the most extensive entries in the recent *Encyclopedia of Religion* are the fourteen articles on iconography, defined as a "program in art history that exposes the different meanings of images vis a vis the beholder." This intense focus is as it should be because imagery, perceived through visual experiences, has been determined to be "an essential instrument in the development of human consciousness."

This emphasis on the beholder's experience and link between image and consciousness relates to what I call the experience of "ortho-visus"; that is, seeing divine images in dramatic appearances according to an authoritative norm. The ceremony of Toxcatl suggests that ortho-visus, in this case seeing how Tezcatlipoca's images and powers saturate the world, is a potent trigger in the experience of synesthesia. The role of seeing the divine through images in the world is essential to truly knowing the divine. Moses saw the burning bush, the disciples saw the resurrected Jesus, Black Elk saw the rainbow teepee, the Hindu worshiper sees Kali. This experience of seeing the divine takes a powerful reversal in the case of Tezcatlipoca's statue in Tenochtitlan, which, according to Doris Heyden's research, had obsidian mirrors for eyes. But most studies of imagery and iconography, at least if the *Encyclopedia of Religion* is representative, focus on still, immobile, nonhuman images of the divine. The beholder sees the divine image solidly in place or on display. An outstanding example of this approach is found in Diana Eck's study *Benares: City of Light,* in which she shows how pilgrims go to the sacred capital for *darshana,* defined in popular terms as "not sight seeing but sacred sight seeing" or beholding the divine and being in its presence. Eck's study includes the observation of Mark Twain that the collection of divine images embodying Hindu gods were a "wild mob of nightmares."

As a means of approaching what I believe to be special in Aztec religion — namely, the major role played by living, human, perishable images of deities — allow me to draw a picture of a distant but relevant cultural pattern of seeing the divine. Specifically, let us turn briefly to a Catholic pattern of sacred sight seeing as described in the chapter "The Palace of the Virgin" in Otto von Simson's *The Gothic Cathedral.* We find here a classic example of how seeing the divine in a material image causes a metamorphosis in the community that views it.

On the night of June 10, 1194, a huge fire destroyed a large part of the town of Chartres, including the entire cathedral except for the west façade. The main relic of the cathedral, the tunic that the Virgin Mary was said to have worn on the night of Christ's birth, which for centuries had drawn pilgrims from all parts of Europe, was also believed destroyed. This devastation, according to Simson (1956:161),

> kindled the deepest human emotions. The historian has every reason to take such emotions seriously. They provide the impulse without which great collective efforts are impossible and unintelligible. In Chartres, the grief over the destruction of the ancient shrine prompted, soon after the calamity had occurred, the resolution to rebuild it more splendidly than it had ever been before. The general mood during those days can perhaps alone explain the almost incredible effort that produced within the brief

span of one generation the cathedral that we admire today as the loftiest example of medieval art.

The townspeople, according to a number of records of the day, felt that the disaster indicated that the Virgin had abandoned her shrine and fled in a moment of divine wrath. But in response to the deep mood of despair, the church leaders dedicated three years of revenues to rebuild the church. Then, on the feast day chosen to inaugurate the rebuilding, a miraculous event occurred:

> Before this crowd . . . the cardinal of Pisa repeated his plea with an eloquence that brought tears to the eyes of his audience. And, by what seemed to be a happy coincidence, at this very moment the bishop and chapter appeared carrying in solemn procession the Sacred Tunic, which contrary to general belief had, safe in the cathedral crypt, survived the conflagration undamaged. The wonderful occurrence caused an incredible impression. Everyone pledged the possessions he had salvaged to the reconstruction of the sanctuary. The medieval temper as we can often observe, was given to sudden changes from despair to joy. In Chartres it was now suddenly believed that the Virgin herself had permitted the destruction of the old basilica because she wanted a new and more beautiful church to be built in her honor [Simson 1956:163].

There are a number of rich meanings in this orchestrated miracle of the Virgin's reappearance, but I wish to emphasize only one: It is the seeing of the divine image returning and traveling through the human community that brings about a radical emotional change as well as generous financial offerings. We have a synesthesia of the senses and the pocketbook! But even here, as in Eck's work, the emphasis is on inanimate objects filled with the divine. In Aztec religion, the divine presence in terrestrial objects takes place most significantly in human beings called *teteo imixiptlahuan* (human images of the gods). Many ceremonies involved human beings in whom the god became encapsulated. López Austin (1988, vol. 1:377) sums up this view of how the human body is filled with the nature of divinities when he writes of deity impersonators as

> teteo imixiptlahuan, . . . men possessed by the gods, who, as such, died in a rite of renewal. The idea of a calendric cycle, of a periodic returning, in which the power of a god was born, grew, decreased, and concluded

> made it necessary in a rite linking the time of man to mythical time that a god would die so his force might be reborn with new power. It was not men who died, but gods — gods within a corporeal covering that made possible their ritual death on earth. If the gods did not die, their force would diminish in a progressively aging process. Men destined for sacrifice were temporariliy converted into receptacles of divine fire, they were treated as gods, and they were made to live as the deity lived in legend. Their existence in the role of ixiptlatin, or "images," could last from a few days up to four years.

The narratives of Aztec ceremonies show us a rich series of images, flowing, jerking, moving, and immobilized in the landscape. In fact, Aztec ceremonies and the city itself were landscapes "made of images." The seminal image in the ceremony of Toxcatl was the ixiptla of Tezcatlipoca. In order to appreciate the power of this living image who linked up the ceremonial landscape I will discuss two of the "scenes" of Tezcatlipoca's appearances: (1) the static ceremonial stage consisting of his temple and stone ixiptla; and (2) the series of transformations that the human image of the deity underwent.

The Ceremonial Stage

References to Toxcatl emphasize that it contains the "most splendid ceremonies," which carried colorful, lavish images throughout the city. The stationary focus of this splendid ceremony was Tezcatlipoca's temple, "constructed with such a profusion of figures, sculpture and work in stucco that it gave pleasure from any point of view. . . . Within its walled enclosure were many chambers, some occupied by the dignitaries of the temple, since there existed a hierarchy" (Durán p.111).

This hierarchy of temple space was paralleled by a hierarchy of costume, although commoners and lords alike displayed themselves in lavish, even ostentatious dress. "All crowned themselves with headdresses or miters made up of small painted wreaths, beautifully adorned like latticework." And children became living images of Tezcatlipoca when the priests "took the infants, dressed them in the garb and insignia of the idol, smearing them with divine pitch and feathering their heads with the plumes of quail or turkey" (Durán 1977:110). Durán notes that the children were "offered" to Tezcatlipoca, meaning that their lives were dedicated to his service. At the upper end of the hierarchy, the "lords or chieftains" displayed their superior position by hanging "little figures of gold or stones or many other finely worked things" on their headdresses. But the most lavish costumes were given to the god.

On the nineteenth of May, "the lords came to the temple carrying a new attire and gave it to priests so the idol could be clad in it." The stone image of Tezcatlipoca was dressed in jewels, bracelets, and feathers stored in boxes "more reverently than we put away sacerdotal vestments . . . so carefully stored that they served no other purpose than that of being adored as if they had been the god himself"(Durán 1977:100). However, this image was not normally seen by the common eye. Tezcatlipoca was hidden away from sight in a lavishly decorated inner room "hung with splendidly worked cloth in the Indian manner, in different colors and designs, all covered with feathers so favored by these people in their decorations and garments." The inner chamber with an altar and Tezcatlipoca's image was hidden by a "veil or with a finely worked door covering" and in this way was kept closed off and dark, and the idol hidden: "No one dared enter this place, with the sole exception of priests appointed to serve the cult of the god." The altar was a gorgeous sight, "as tall as a man . . . covered with the most elegant, most finely wrought richest mantles ever woven or embroidered." Then, at the right moment, after "special ornaments were added, such as featherwork, bracelets, sunshades — all the best that could be given to him" — the veil was lifted in a hierophanic drama "so that Tezcatlipoca could be seen by all."

Tezcatlipoca's Transformations

What is very important for an understanding of the "sense of unity" encapsulated in this ceremony is the series of changes that the teotl ixiptla underwent. As he changed places, he linked up the marks and locations of the spatial landscape. As he changed his identity, he revealed a powerful spectrum in Aztec experience. In other words, the image of Tezcatlipoca was alive, not only in the sense that a human being was the public image, but in the changes he underwent at different stages of the year-long ceremony. The ideal person who started the ceremony was changed into the cultural paragon of Aztec society. Although it is nowhere stated as such, the impersonator was akin to a human "flower and song," an excellent aesthetic form on the earth, manifesting divine powers in a human body, costume, and arts. After parading before the populace he was changed into the ruler's god, the lord of the palace, and then again paraded before the eyes of the people who are humbled in his presence. Then, in a remarkable reversal, he is striped of his divine adornments, both the ones bestowed by Moctezuma and the human ornaments in the forms of women who are ixiptlatin of goddesses. Another transformation is signaled when he breaks his whistles and flutes on the steps, for he has returned to the image of the warrior, akin to the battlefield status he held before his capture.

Studies of iconography and image do not afford us much help in understanding this series of transformations. Rather, it is in the genre of theatrical studies that we can directly approach the meaning of these changes.

Richard Schechner, studying transportation and transformation in theatrical performances, discusses the diversity of performances and the processual structure in which images reject, replace, erase, and superimpose themselves on other images during the history of a theatrical form. But even within a single performance, there are two general types of changes that the images undergo. First, there are transportation performances in which a performer is "taken somewhere" — that is, "goes to another time/space reference, personality reference, geographical reference — but in the end returns to where he started; namely, the "ordinary world." Second, there are transformation performances in which a performer's social and symbolic identity is permanently changed, as in an initiation rite. In the end there is no return to the previous identity, for when one "cools down," one is in a new place, location, relationship with the cosmos.

Schechner's categories are helpful but must be adapted in order to clarify the changes in Tezcatlipoca's impersonator. As the ritual of Toxcatl shows, the performers underwent a series of transformations leading to an ultimate transformation of the Tezcatlipoca ixiptla. This emphasis on a real, final transformation is important because the radical nature of Aztec human sacrifice in general and Toxcatl in particular represents a most convincing example of what historians of religions call a "change in the mode of being." And more importantly, Toxcatl as a whole presents through this series of transformations in the human image, an image of the whole society, or at least an image of the whole male society, acting out its idea of perfection ("the perfect embodiment of a quality"). This image of perfection consists of a series of metamorphoses moving through the scheme: warrior→perfect body→cultural paragon→king's god →sexual potency→seasoned warrior→sacrificed deity.

An Ultimate Transformation

It is in the rapid series of movements that demarcate the actual sacrifice that we find the meaning of the year-long ceremony. As in the case of most human sacrifices, the act of killing occupies a very small portion of the ceremony and its description. There are three outstanding moments in the ceremonial killing of Tezcatlipoca: the ascent of the temple; the offering of the body parts; and the Aztec comment on the significance of the sacrifice.

We are told that the teotl ixiptla "went up of his own free will, to where he was to die" (Sahagún 1950–1982, II:71) and that on each of the steps, "he shattered one of the flutes that he had played as he had walked, all during the year" (Sahagún 1950–1982, II:10). This ascent toward his death is marked by astonishing self-control and a commitment that is hard to believe. In fact, we know from descriptions of other sacrifices that the captives sometimes attempted to run away or swooned and fainted on the steps of the pyramid. (In some sacrifices of young women there were elaborate efforts to distract and fool the victims about their impending death; those divine images were in fact not perfect victims going along of their "own free will.") But the implication, at least by Sahagún's informants, is that this individual was the perfect "god within a corporeal covering," ascending the temple without aid or coercion. The point is that Toxcatl was designed to display the perfect sacrifice of the perfect ixiptla, who was the perfect physical image of an enemy warrior who had been enculturated into Aztec ceremonial style.

The ideal sacrifice is accomplished in the remarkably simple description of the actual killing. Diego Durán's (1977:107) informants report that "four of the sacrificers seized the victim by the feet and the hands while the priest opened his chest and extracted his heart, raising it with his hands as high as he could, offering its steam to the sun." Then, a special distinction is expressed in Sahagún's (1950–1982, II:70) report: "For in this manner were all (these) captives slain. But his body they did not roll down, rather they lowered it. Four men carried it. And the severed head they strung on the skull rack." While other victims were also killed in this manner, Tezcatlipoca's impersonator's body was exceptional in that it was not rolled down the stairs as was typically done in other sacrifices. Rather, he was carried carefully away to where his head was severed and then carried to the skull rack.

My argument that this sacrifice was meant to be the perfect sacrifice becomes enlarged: The entire ceremony is the image of the perfect life and ideal death of the warrior in the Aztec world, a contention reflected in the short paragraph within Sahagún's text, which constitutes a rare Aztec interpretation of their ritual: "And this betokened our life on earth. For he who rejoiced, who possessed riches, who sought, who esteemed our lord's sweetness, his fragrance — richness, prosperity — thus ended in great misery. Indeed it was said: 'No one on earth went exhausting happiness, riches, wealth' " (1950–1982, II:71). This remarkable commentary represents in miniature a revered linguistic form in Aztec culture; namely, the ***huehuetlatolli,*** or "rhetorical orations of the elders." This complex linguistic form has many characteristics but the relevant one is the commitment to formal, even lavish expressions of "oughtness" in conduct and social relationships. The huehuetlatolli were rhetorical orations delivered on ceremonial occasions telling how life should be lived, acted out, gestured, from generation to generation. Often these ideals were expressed using the dual form of speech ***in xochitl, in cuicatl,*** flower and song. In this Aztec interpretation we see the expression of a profound duality: "This is how one must live; this is how one who lives in this fashion must die." We are told that it is acceptable and even desirable to live in riches, esteeming Tezcatlipoca and his sweetness, his fragrance, his wealth. But it is also the cosmic law that a person, especially the warrior who becomes Tezcatlipoca, must undergo an elaborate initiatory elevation and humiliation, must die a perfect death and be displayed on the skull rack. In fact it appears that Tezcatlipoca becomes the model for all humans as "no one on earth went exhausting happiness, riches, wealth."

A Hierarchy of Meaning

In this performance and ceremonial landscape, the Aztecs are showing that Tezcatlipoca's perfect life and ideal death represents through synesthesia, their way of entertaining themselves with one unity of meaning in their world — a meaning stated as: "Tezcatlipoca occupies all places always; humans occupy Tezcatlipoca's place on earth for a year at a time." The Aztec community learns and relearns this message each year. Yet, we cannot ignore what has been everywhere present in some form; namely, the pervasive message of social and symbolic hierarchy and the concomitant meaning that access to the message of Tezcatlipoca's power, riches, and sweetness is not the same for all. We are faced with a performance that illustrates Stanley Tambiah's contention that synesthesia reveals both ontology and hierarchy, a oneness of meaning and a symbolism of ranking and differential access to happiness, riches, wealth — a juxtaposition emphatically performed in urban society. This combination of ontology and hierarchy is made clearer when we follow the clue of this huehuetlatolli fragment from Book 2 of Sahagún to the extensive prayer dedicated to Tezcatlipoca spoken by a priest on behalf of the commoners in Book 6.

The prayer begins with a lavish pouring forth of formal addresses to the god, followed by a portrayal of the condition of how "the common folk endure suffering, endure fatigue, live in want on earth. Poverty, misery, uselessness prevail. They escape nowhere; indeed they are in dire need as they go seeking sustenance, going through all the forest, all the desert. And here, in truth they glory in their thin intestines; their viscera go stuck to their sides; go rumbling. Verily they go skin and bones, like a skeleton." This pathetic image of poverty takes on a spatial image as "they become all thin. They continue all to run about. They go about weeping, sighing. Truth they go about in great affliction. The entire day, the entire night they are ranged about the fire." The priest who speaks this prayer then asks compassion of Tezcatlipoca for the common folk in this fashion:

> Show mercy, have compassion for thy common folk. May thou honor them . . . with a little of thy freshness, thy tenderness, thy sweetness . . . for in truth they struggle for it. May they a little through thy grace raise their head. May they through thy grace know repose for a little time. Through thy grace may the common folk have what is necessary for their bones, their bodies. May they through thy grace dream, may they see in their dreams. May they for a little time keep it for thee. Perhaps it will be taken, removed and hidden, concealed. That which was only for a little time, even as the flower which one hath smelled, hath marveled at.

What is outstanding in this parallel statement of the sacrificial gloss discussed above is that misery in life for the common people is to be relieved with a "little" riches, which "for a little time" will give some happiness and provide a limited access to the sweetness of Tezcatlipoca. The hierarchy of access is further expressed in the priest's promise to Tezcatlipoca that if the commoners try to act above their social place they will suffer terribly: "If perhaps the people I now present before thee should become arrogant, these very same will discover, will earn as their reward, their merit, torment, pain, misery and blindness, paralysis. They will not be esteemed, will not be glorified; and they will be incapable on earth. Truly this thou wilt have in store for them. And that is also the time when they will sob, they will be terrified" (Sahagún 1950–1982, VI:9).

The problem of unity/hierarchy deserves further investigation. The text and its interpretations suggest a redirecting of terms toward an expansion of categories to join a ***hierarchy of meaning*** to a ***unity of meaning*** when exploring synesthesias in urbanized societies. For while Tezcatlipoca may have been the Lord of Everyplace, it appears that in the spirit of his metamorphic powers, people did not have the same access to his powers in every social, geographical, or sacred place.

It is appropriate to recall the thematic context for our common deliberations, namely, the nature and character of ceremonial centers in Mesoamerican traditions. In the past we have focused on the spatial order and symbolic alignments of Aztec urbanism with its dynamic tensions between centers and peripheries. Now, we are striving to combine that focus with new research into the ceremonial landscapes organized and imprinted by performance. My discussion here has attempted a rethinking of the theme of the ceremonial center by focusing on the exceptional festival of Toxcatl. While it seems correct to view the ceremonial landscape of the Mexicas as defined by both sacred spaces and locative places, the landscape of Tezcatlipoca, incompletely described here, with its prodigious, moving displays of a god's image among humankind, seems as much inhabited by shape-shifters, mosaics, magic, and metamorphosis as by axis mundis and bailiwicks. A broad study of the sources indicates that not just ritual but most of Mexican social life can be viewed as performances of transformations communicating an urbanized, hierarchical way of life. These public performances mirrored and gave life to the ceremonial landscape and helped the world breathe with meaning.

This tie among the ceremonial city, metamorphosis, and hierarchy is reflected in the passage describing the crisis felt by the community on the death of a tlatoani. The priest, speaking of the lost ruler, prayed to Tezcatlipoca: "And the city, will it perhaps here in his absence be mocked? Will it divide? Will it scatter? Truly he came spreading his wings, his tail feathers over it; truly he spread himself over it" (Sahagún 1950–1982, VI:23).

Selected References and Bibliographical Remarks

Carrasco, D.

1989 The king, the capital and the stars: The symbolism of authority in Aztec religion. In *World archaeoastronomy*, edited by A. F. Aveni. Cambridge: Cambridge University Press.

1989 *The Imagination of Matter: Religion and Ecology in Mesoamerican Traditions*, Ed. Oxford: B.A.R. International Series, 515.

1987 *The Great Temple of Tenochtitlan: Center and Periphery in the Aztec World*, with Johanna Broda and Eduardo Matos Moctezuma. Berkeley: University of California Press.

Dumont, L.

1980 *Homo hierarchicus: The caste system and its implications*. 2d ed. Chicago: University of Chicago Press.

Durán, D.

1977 *Book of the gods and rites and the ancient calendar*. Translated and edited by F. Horcasitas and Heyden. Norman: University of Oklahoma Press.

Eck, D.

1982 *Banaras: City of Light*. Princeton: Princeton University Press.

Eliade, M.

1958 *Patterns in comparative religion*. New York: World Publishing.

Heyden, D.

1988 Black Magic: Obsidian in symbolism and metaphor. In *Smoke and mist: Mesoamerican studies in memory of Thelma D. Sullivan*, edited by J. K. Josserand and K. Dakin. BAR International Series 402. Oxford.

Hvidfeldt, A.

1958 *Teotl and ixiptlatli*. Copenhagen: Muksgaard.

Isaac, R.

1982 *The transformation of Virginia, 1740–1790*. Chapel Hill: University of North Carolina Press.

Jansen, Maarten E.R.G.N.

1988 Dates, deities and dynasties: Non-durational time in Mixtec historiography. In *Continuity and identity in native America*, edited by M. Jansen, P. van der Loo, and R. Manning. Leiden: E. J. Brill.

López Austin, A.

1988 *The human body and ideology: Concepts of the ancient Nahuas*. 2 vols. Salt Lake City: University of Utah Press.

Sahagún, B. de.

1950–1982 *Florentine Codex: A history of the things of New Spain*. Translated and edited by A.J.O. Anderson and C. E. Dibble. 13 vols. Santa Fe: School of American Research and the University of Utah.

Simson, O. von

1956 *The Gothic cathedral*. Chicago: University of Chicago Press.

Smith, J. Z.

1978 *Map is not territory: Studies in the history of religions*. Leiden: E. J. Brill.

1987 *To take place: Toward theory in ritual*. Chicago: University of Chicago Press.

Sullivan, L.

1986 Sound and sense: Toward a hermeneutics of performance. *History of Religions* 26, no. 1.

Sullivan, T.

1974 The rhetorical orations or huehuetlatolli, collected by Sahagún. In *Sixteenth-century Mexico: The work of Sahagún*, edited by M. Edmonson. Albuquerque: University of New Mexico Press.

Williams, R. L.

1989 The visual arts, the poetization of space and writing: An interview with Gabriel García Márquez. *PMLA* 104, no. 2.

Wilson, P. J.

1988 *The domestication of the human species.* New Haven, CT: Yale University Press.

During the process of writing this chapter, I consulted and learned from five works on ceremonial centers, landscape, and place. The first was Rhys Isaac's Pulitzer prize-winning study *The Transformation of Virginia, 1740–1790,* which combines a patient capacity for observation with a sensual awareness of the geographical and cultural landscape of tidewater Virginia. It is rare to read a work that unites and utilizes with such skill "several strategies of presentation" in relation to sacred space and place. Isaac (p. 6) writes of his approach:

> If this work has a distinctive contribution to make, it lies in the results of a search for means of access to the alien mentalities of a past people. Considerable effort has gone into experimenting with strategies of presentation that would serve to explicate ways of life. Devices appropriated from both art and social science were found to afford the most serviceable mirrors of reality. The theater supplies a concept of dramaturgy, suggesting a way of looking at the important communications included in patterns of action. Social life, in its routines as well as in its convulsive processes of change, is viewed as a complex set of performances. Not only words but also settings, costumes, and gestures all carry their messages in the incessant exchanges of interaction. The authority system can be seen expressed in the assignment of roles. Crucial power struggles occur over the definitions of the situation — the "scenes" to be enacted, their meanings, and the forms of action appropriate to them.

In fact, Isaac does achieve extraordinary interpretive results with this combination of approaches. His narrative stimulated me to suggest a new way of seeing the ceremonial landscape in the Valley of Mexico. His approach gives a solid context for studies of synesthesia by portraying the shapes and arrangements in the landscape that continually arouse the senses.

A rare work that lends support to my emphasis on both ceremonial centers and ortho-visus is *The Domestication of the Human Species* by Peter J. Wilson. Wilson rethinks a number of major assumptions about domestication, human settlement, architecture, and social theory, and he proposes that there were "two major events wherein the relation between the senses and the environment were put under stress and rendered problematic" in the preurban history of human species: (1) the shift from an arboreal to a savanna environment, which resulted in a new "visual order" for humans; and (2) the domestication of space through the innovation of building permanent structures for humans to dwell within. He writes that "the domestication of plants and animals follows the domestication of human beings and is inspired by it." The implications of Wilson's work for the study of synesthesia, ceremonial centers, and social integration are rich. He argues that it is "visual attention which is of primary importance to the operation of drives, instincts, emotions, feelings and bodily processes of human beings and thence to the survival and well-being of the individual and the species."

As I argue here, it is the visual experience, the seeing of the ceremony and images of the divine, that stimulates the integration of the senses most persuasively and leads to new knowledge or a special quality of knowledge. Wilson's argument begins with a discussion of how "primates are exceptional for highly developed visual sensitivity," especially valuable for "navigational demands." In movement through the landscape it is the visual order that enhances and organizes the attention, communication, and expressions of human beings: "Seeing is thus a more complex process than the other sensory modes, and its product is far removed from its stimulus — that is, what we 'see' is distant literally and qualitatively from the object. Seeing, on which human beings rely so extensively, is, in fact, perceiving." Wilson notes that "sight and sound" are similar in their detachment from the sources of their stimulus.

What is also important is the fact that domestication of the human species (i.e., new relationships between itself and nature and between humans and humans brought about by permanent settlements that encourage secrecy, hospitality, intimacy) has a major effect on visual perception and "on all the activities that depend on vision or involve it," and primarily social life.

In both *Quetzalcoatl and the Irony of Empire* and *The Great Temple of Tenochtitlan: Center and Periphery in Aztec Traditions* (with J. Broda and E. Matos) I have asked a similar question: What changes in the nature of religion and in the nature of the human are stimulated or triggered in the urbanization of the human species? The focus on the ceremonial city that orders the agenda of the Mesoamerican Archive at Boulder is a means of probing this question. Wilson's claim is that "domestication changes human nature."

Another insightful source for future work on both the visual ordering of synesthesia and the ceremonial center is Raymond L. Williams's "The Visual Arts, the Poetization of Space and Writing: An Interview with Gabriel García Márquez." Not only do we get a new element in synesthesia — that is, the relation between seeing and writing — we also see some interesting parallels between the literary universe and ceremonial space, reminiscent of Mircea Eliade's work on the literary imagination and religion. García Márquez notes how his most helpful aids to writing were "portraits, family albums, photographs." Williams points out how García Márquez showed him, during the interviews, some of the nineteenth-century drawings of Colombia by Charles Saffray and Edouard André. The author of *Cien Años de Soledad* remarks about one: "But then I discover a detail that reveals an entire world to me. The detail could be something I see in a painting. Perhaps the fighting cock in this drawing could give me the solution for an entire novel. It's just something which happens to me. I'm totally passive and it's like a flash. . . . It is always something that I see. It is always, always an image, with no exceptions" (Williams 1989:132).

This seeing of images brings about a metamorphosis in the writing of his novels; that is, the structure is changed and developed. García Márquez notes (Williams 1989:134): "When I was writing the *Autumn of the Patriarch* there was a point at which I was struggling a lot. I had a certain idea about the palace which eventually would appear at the beginning, but I just couldn't get it right. Then I came across this picture [of a palace stairway in India] in a book, and the photo solved my writing of the novel. It was the image that I needed." García Márquez goes on to discuss images from his life experience and their impact on his writing; then he discusses three ways in which he uses imagery to "poeticize space" and bring about a dramatic metamorphosis in his work: First, he mixes people from different time periods and restaurants from different countries into individual scenes within his novels; second, the human presence in space holds surprises for the writer as well as the reader.

> One of the most emotional experiences I have had as a writer relates to all this. It happened in *Love in the Time of Cholera*, with the family of Fermina Daza, when she is a child. I was creating all her life inside the house where she lives with her father and her spinster aunt, and the house is a copy of the one that is now the Oveja Negra bookstore in the Plaza Fernández Madrid in Cartagena. I was working on the first draft. I had the girl, her father, her aunt and her mother, but the mother always seemed extra. I just didn't know what to do with the mother. When they were at the dinner table, I could see the father's face perfectly, and I could see the faces of the girl and the aunt perfectly, but the mother's face was always blurred. I imagined her one way and then another way. I made her like so-and-so but she remained a constant problem and I didn't know what to do. She was ruining my novel. . . . And then suddenly one day, thinking that I was stuck on a dead-end road, I realized that what had happened was that the mother had died when the girl was born. And this was the reason the aunt was there, because the father had brought her to the household to raise the child when the mother had died. . . . It was a precious experience for me, and it explains how the character of the mother began to live the very moment I discovered that she had died. So she is always a presence in the house and the characters speak of her as someone who had died, who has left her mark on her daughter. This also explains why the father is so lonely and has the type of personality he has.

Equally relevant for my discussion of seeing, ceremonial space, and the urban world is García Márquez's device of mixing the time periods of life in a city such as Cartagena. He notes that "in *Love in the Time of Cholera* I used a trick when they go up in a balloon and pass over the ruins of Cartagena. Do you remember that? They see the old city of Cartagena abandoned. As an almost poetic image, it's beautiful, and the use of this image gives an idea of how things can be handled in literature" (p. 138). Williams, the interviewer, observes, "Once again, the poetization of space." García Márquez replies: "Exactly, and just when I have them convinced that this is Cartagena, then I take them through an abandoned Cartagena. It's a doubling of the city. Let's say its the same city in two distinct periods, two different temporal spaces" (p. 138).

The fourth work that aided me was Michael Sallnow's *Pilgrims of the Andes*, a marvelous interpretation of "miraculous landscape" of certain traditions of Andean pilgrimage, revealing how the cosmos is ordered by elaborate movements through space. This work would be especially helpful for comparison with contemporary Mesoamerican pilgrimages.

Within by own Nahuatl studies, I found James Lockhart's "Postconquest Nahua Society and Culture Seen Through Nahuatl Writings" pushing my thought in the direction of "local knowledge." Lockhart notes that we can glean an understanding of self-definition among the Nahuas by discovering certain patterns that "pervade the whole corpus" of Nahuatl documentation. The outstanding spatial and social notion of self-definition was "the altepetl . . . an entity . . . partially defined by its tradition of ethnic distinctness, partially by its possession of a certain territory, and partially by its dynastic ruler, the tlatoani."

But, what is most relevant for this study is Lockhart's claim that "one could often find the semblance of a central settlement in an altepetl. The residence of the tlatoani, the site of the kingdom's main temple, and its central marketplace often coincided, leading to a settlement cluster in that vicinity." A more complex view of this settlement cluster emerges as Lockhart (p. 13) notes:

> The cluster, however, had no separate name and no juridical identity or organizational unity. Different segments of it belonged to different constituent parts of the entity. These named parts, called calpolli or tlaxilacalli, comprised an ideally symmetrical whole (often but not always in groups of 2, 4, and 8); each part was separate, equal in principle and self-contained, with its own territory, subethnic identity, and subrulership. The parts were arranged in a fixed order of rotation according to which all mechanisms of the altepetl operated. This order of the parts, indeed, defined the whole at a level even more basic than the rulership. Where the Spanish view included three types of entities — pueblo, cabecera, and sujeto — Nahuatl documents recognize only two: the altepetl, being the whole, and the calpolli or parts. The Spanish view emphasizes urban nucleation and a stepped hierarchy; the Nahua view emphasizes a symmetrical arrangement and rotational order. Through indigenous-language sources it becomes clear that the Spaniards operated under a partial delusion, and modern scholars have followed them in it. Over the course of the colonial period the altepetl underwent many modifications, but, half undetected by Spanish authorities, it retained its basic principles of organization.

These principles of organization extend, according to Lockhart, to the Nahuatl songs from the second half of the sixteenth century that, like the altepetl, "relate similarly to a central theme but never refer directly to each other, and therefore in variant versions the pairs are often found differently arranged, although the overall numerical scheme remains the same, and the integrity of each pair is maintained." This same pattern is found in preconquest art and postconquest religious architecture, in the annals genre, and in home complexes. It appears that a continued focus on the nature and character of the ceremonial center does indeed provide, as I noted in the introduction to *Imagination of Matter: Religion and Ecology in Mesoamerican Traditions*, a very revealing analogy for the development of both theory and empirical research in Aztec studies.

6

Mapping the Ritual Landscape: Debt Payment to Tlaloc During the Month of Atlcahualo

Anthony F. Aveni

> We are not to picture ancient cities to ourselves as anything like what we see in our day. We build a few houses; it is a village. Insensibly the number of houses increases, and it becomes a city; and finally, if there is occasion for it, we surround this with a wall.
>
> With the ancients, the city was never formed by degrees, by the slow increase of the number of men and houses. They founded a city at once, all entire in a day; but the elements of the city needed to be first ready, and this was the most difficult, and ordinarily the largest work. As soon as the families, the phratries, and the tribes had agreed to unite and have the same worship, they immediately founded the city as a sanctuary for this common worship, and thus the foundation of a city was always a religious act.
>
> — Fustel de Coulanges (1864:134)

Orientation to the Problem

Working with other colleagues in the Mesoamerican Archive at Boulder, Colorado, over the past few years, I have tried to raise questions about the establishment of the great cities of Mesoamerica:

1. Were the great centers of ancient Mesoamerica preplanned (most particularly, Tenochtitlan and Tlatelolco)?
2. Given the evidence in the ethnohistorical and archaeological record, together with the field study methods of archaeoastronomy, to what

degree is it possible to specify that planning took place?
3. What motivating forces beyond the old dichotomy between economic determinism and religious interests can be posited to explain why Mexican centers were arranged as we find them?
4. Did ideas about organization, planning, and arrangement change and evolve? Can one perceive continuity and tradition in city planning?
5. What function did the mathematically (geometrically) expressible activities of astronomy and calendar play in the planning, and what was the relationship of the calendrical activity in the center to that in the periphery?
6. What role did cosmogony or mythology of foundation play in determining the layout of the city?
7. What was the modus operandi for laying out the city?
8. Can the development of the state be traced through the development of its astronomical and calendrical systems?

As these studies have proceeded and as they have been presented in papers that Calnek, Arnold, Broda, Townsend, and I read at annual conferences and in a paper that two colleagues and I (Aveni, Calnek & Hartung 1988) published, two realizations have emerged:

1. To understand the arrangement and planning in the ceremonial space of Tenochtitlan, one must become familiar with the *land*scape and the *sky*scape of both the city and the space in the Valley of Mexico that surrounds it.
2. One must appreciate that in Mexican mythology, prescriptions for ritual action in the urban center took place in the theater of this environment. Certain ritual events were required to take place in both the proper *spatial* and *temporal* order.

We have adopted these two realizations as attitudes or orientations that guide us in our studies for very specific reasons:

- The strong presence of a locative element in the foundation myth, which tells about situation and directionality of elements of the built and natural environment
- The spatial-temporal relationship between the shrine on Mt. Tlaloc (Durán 1971:155) on the visible horizon of Tenochtitlan and the Templo Mayor; furthermore, the connection of the axis between them and the solar orientation calendar

- General statements by Durán and other chroniclers on the importance of directionality, cosmic axes, the quadripartite division of the city, and the directions or doorways where the sun appears and disappears

All three of these points have previously been documented in some detail (Aveni, Calnek & Hartung 1988). At issue in the present discussion is the degree to which the Mexican imperial state sought to regulate the timing (and spacing) of the rites to the gods.

Tracking the Atlcahualo Ritual

In "The Environment as Ritual Theater: Tenochtitlán and Its Spatial Asides" (Aveni 1988), I made another attempt to climb up onto and survey the stage that once held the Mexican performers. In the two winter seasons preceding the 1988 annual meeting of colleagues at the Mesoamerican Archives, I attempted to locate, visit, and provide descriptions of the actual places mentioned in one of the sets of rituals described in Sahagún (1950–1982, II:ch. 20 appendix) in which there is reason to think that the Mexicas proceeded to make their sacrifices or debt payment to Tlaloc in a highly ordered manner. These places lie in the landscape surrounding the temple precinct. My goal here is to map out physically the ritual in the space-time framework encompassing the temple.

As first steps toward this goal, I would like to describe each of the places that Sahagún mentioned as involved in the ritual that took place in the month of Atlcahualo; and demonstrate by what manner and in what time frame each of the steps was carried out. Each of the sites is located at the boundary between earth and sky (the horizon) as viewed from the Templo Mayor.

Sahagún's text begins:

> Twentieth Chapter, which telleth of the feast day and the debt-payment which they celebrated during all the days of the month, which they named, which they said was Atl caualo or Quauitl eua.[1]
>
> It was (the month of) Quauitl eua (when) this feast day came, and when it took place, then the feast day was celebrated for the Tlalocs.
>
> There was the paying of the debt (to the Tlalocs) everywhere on the mountain tops, and sacrificed banners were hung. There was the pay-

> ment of the debt at Tepetzinco or there in the very middle of the lake at a place called Pantitlan.
>
> There they would leave the rubber-spotted paper streamers and there they would set up poles called *cuenmantli,* which were very long. Only on them (still) went their greenness, their sprouts, their shoots.
>
> And there they left children known as "human paper streamers," those who had two cowlicks on their hair, whose day signs were favorable. They were sought everywhere; they were paid for. It was said: "they are indeed most precious debt-payments. (The Tlalocs) gladly receive them; they want them. Thus they are well content; thus there is indeed contentment." Thus with them the rains were sought, rain was asked.
>
> And everywhere in the houses, in each home, and in each young men's house, in each *calpulco,* everywhere they set up long, thin poles, poles coming to a point, on each of which they placed paper streamers with liquid rubber, spattered with rubber, splashed with rubber.
>
> And they left (the children) in many (different) places.

Evidently, the child sacrifice represents a calling up of the water, the initiation of the process of fertilization, for the text continues:

> According to the accounts of some, they assembled the children whom they slew in the first month, buying them from their mothers. And they went on killing them in all the feasts which followed, until the rains really began. And thus they slew some in the first month, named Quauitl eua; and some in the second, named Tlacaxipeualiztli; and some in the third, named Tocoztontli; and others in the fourth, named Ueitocoztli: so that until the rains began in abundance, in all the feasts they sacrificed children [Sahagún 1950–1982, II:ch. 4].

It is in this twentieth chapter on the ritual of debt payment to Tlaloc that Sahagún is *specific* about exactly where and in what order the procession takes place. Following Sahagún's statement further and examining various maps of both the ancient and modern city, it at once becomes evident that: (1) the first deposition place in the ritual lies Tenochtitlan-north (not true or astronomic north) of the Templo Mayor; and (2) the succeeding places where the children were deposited fall in clockwise order about Tenochtitlan's mountainous periphery (see Table 6.1 for details). But, can specific environmental detail be documented? What are the

Table 6.1. Tlacateuihtin (Human Banners) Sacrificed in Atlcahualo

Place	Direction/ Distance from Templo Mayor	Sacrifice	Time	Color/ Adornments	Sex	Possible Sky Event
Quauhtepec	4.5°, 17.5 km	Quauhtepetl	Morning(?)	Brown	Male	North (within 1.5° of orientation of North Avenue)
Yoaltecatl	23°, 7.5 km	Yoaltecatl	Morning(?)	Black Striped with Red	Male	
Tepetzinco	83°, 5 km	Quetzalxoch Tepetzintli	Morning(?)	Blue Blue(?)	Female	Sunrise twenty days before the spring equinox
Poyauhtlan	83°, <5 km	Poyauhtecatl	Morning(?)	Stripes of Liquid Rubber	Male	
Pantitlan	>95°, 10 km	Epcoatl	Morning(?)	Mussel Shells	Male	Sunrise in Atl Atlcahualo(?)
Cocotl	128°, 36 km	Cocotl	Morning(?)	Red-Brown	Male	
Yiauhqueme	246°, 15 km	Yiauhqueme	Morning(?)	Brown	Male	December solstice sunset

visible mountains and discernible sky events that might have served as spatial and temporal points of reference in the conduct of this ritual? What is the visual perspective like from each of these sacred places? By confronting such questions we might be able to develop a processual model for the conduct of the ritual.

Concerning the first point — that the ritual sequence begins at the north — we note that in a number of cases in Mesoamerica (e.g., Teotihuacan, Tenayuca, and Ihuatzio in the Mexican highlands, and at Copan in the Mayan region) a prominent mountain can be found to the north of a ceremonial center. At Copan the text of Stela B portrays the cosmic mountain as the place of origin of the ancestors of the Lord 18 Rabbit who is depicted, as if in a dream state, paying a visit to his ancestral home. Recently, glyphic identifications of north with up and south with down have been posited (and debated) by the epigraphers of Mayan glyphs (Closs 1988).

Of the relationship between Teotihuacan and Cerro Gordo, Tobriner (1972:105) has written: "Only the northern vista is marked by a large mountain which gives it a dramatic effect; the Teotihuacanos emphasized this effect by building the Pyramid of the Moon, which mirrors the mountain in its positioning and trapezoidal shape. These purely visual observations illustrate that the Teotihuacanos were very much aware of Cerro Gordo when they planned their city."

I believe that the Tenochtitlan north-south axis may have had some cosmological meaning quite different from the astronomical north-south axis (the meridian) about which Western European societies reckon the passage of time. The same may be true at Teotihuacan, where we have already demonstrated the existence of separate sets of grid axes: true NSEW and Teotihuacan NSEW, which is skewed 15.5° clockwise from the cardinal directions (Aveni & Hartung 1979).

On my second point — that the ritual sequence moved in a clockwise direction — I will not dwell except to state that it is counter to the usual direction relative to which one follows the flow of time in the calendrical diagrams in the codices. Let us next examine each of these point locations one at a time as we follow Sahagún's description of the rite.

Sahagún says: "(First was) at Quauhtepec, and its same name, Quauhtepetl, went with the one who died there. His paper vestments were dark green." (Of Quauhtepec, Sahagún's Spanish text says: "Es una sierra emjnente que está cerca del tlatelulco.") In January 1989 Johanna Broda made arrangements to take us to the top of this site, which had already been mentioned and located in an eighteenth-century map attributed to Bobán. Indeed, the modern community below and to the west of this peak still retains the name of that hill. Cerro Cuauhtepec, highest peak in the Guadalupe Range (elev. 3,000 m; called Pico Tres Padres on most topographic maps) lies 17.5 kilometers along the direction 4.5° azimuth from true north as reckoned from the Templo Mayor (or -2° as reckoned from either the N-S axis of the temple or the North Avenue out of the ceremonial center). Celebrants could have embarked from the northern edge of the ceremonial precinct in canoes and proceeded seven kilometers to the north shore of the lake, disembarking somewhere between Tenayuca and Ticoman, or they could have proceeded out along the northwest causeway (today, Calzada Vallejo), then ascended from the southwest via any number of sinuous paths on a climb of approximately ten kilometers (as measured along a straight line) to the summit (see Figure 6.1 and Table 6.1, Quauhtepec). It took us about two hours, having proceeded from the barrio of Cuauhtepec where we had abandoned our vehicles (we could locate it precisely by taking compass bearings to the nearby peaks: Santa Clara, Chiquihuite, Tenayo, Picacho, and Cerro Gordo.)

I shall forgo any attempts to romanticize about the nature of what we experienced as we climbed upward out of the urban zone, except to say that the ecology took on a decidedly different aspect, perhaps rather close to the way it was in precontact times, from what lay extant on the floor of the valley behind. One is reminded of the Velasco paintings that hang in Mexico City's Museo de Bellas Artes (see, e.g., *El Valle de México,* 1878). At a point just a few hundred meters short of the summit we found a number of ruined multichambered structures that occupied an area of several hundred square meters. These now-shapeless masses were built out of rough-cut, partially worked flat stones, much like those that composed the huge ceremonial enclosure and access way at Mt. Tlaloc. This is the area surveyed and marked on one of Sanders, Parsons, and Santley's (1979) maps (called Tontepec on the González Aparicio [1973] map). Upon a large rock outcrop at the summit stood a cross of structural steel approximately ten meters high. There can be no doubt that this place lay on the visible skyline of the valley as viewed from the Templo Mayor, for the precinct would be distinctly visible to the south were it not for the presence of the ever-lingering smog. Turning to the north one can distinctly

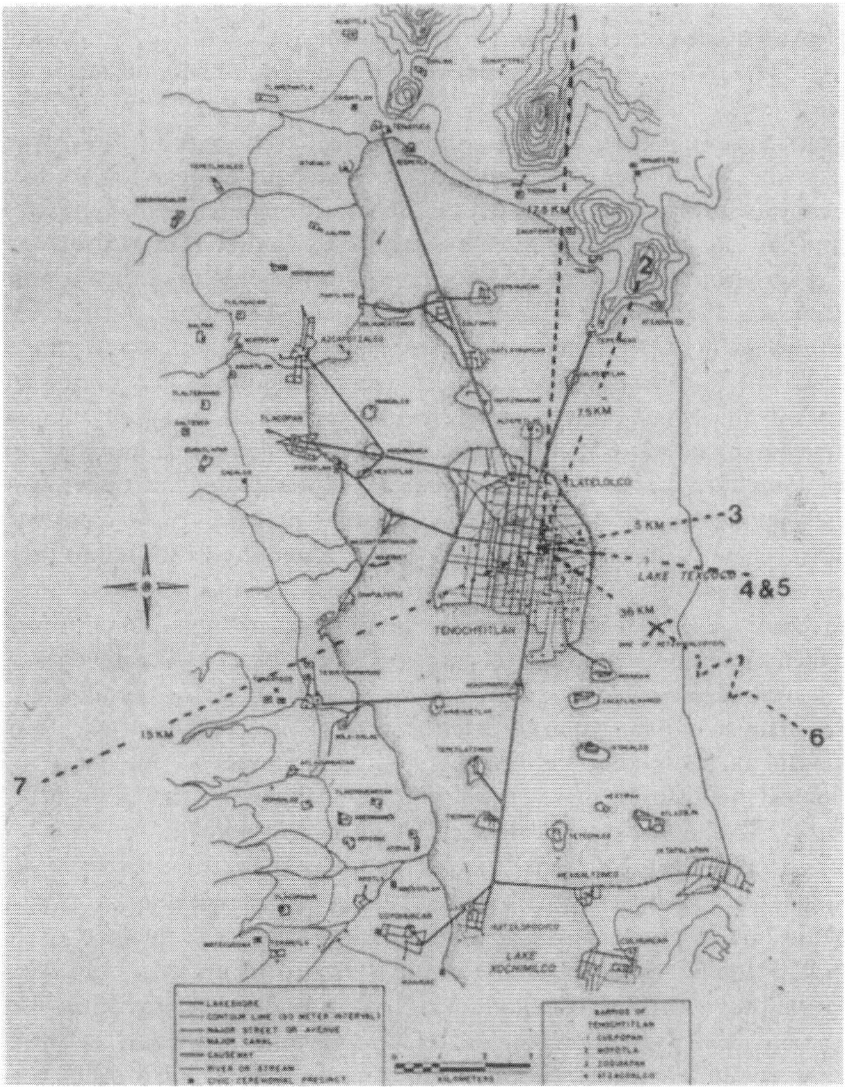

Figure 6.1. Places of Child Sacrifice. The map shows the directional lines leading to the sites, as best these sites can be determined, where child sacrifices took place during Atlcahualo. Adapted from Sanders, Parsons, and Santley, *The Basin of Mexico: Ecological Processes in the Evolution of a Civilization*, vol. 2, map 11 (New York, 1979), by permission of the authors.

perceive Teotihuacan with Cerro Gordo behind it, along with several other peaks that are not visible from downtown Mexico City.

"The second place where one died was the top of Mount Yoaltecatl. Its same name, Yoaltecatl, went with the 'human paper streamer.' His vestments were black striped with chili red." (Sahagún's Spanish text explains: "Es una sierra emjnente, que está cabe quadalope.") We arrived at this location, called Yoaltecatl on the González A. map (see Figure 6.1 and Table 6.1), in January 1988 by entering through the Parque Nacional Tepeyac from the road passing north beyond Indios Verdes, then toward the east in the direction of Pachuca-Teotihuacan. The summit (elev. 2,450 m) is a flat area several hectares in extent located 7.5 kilometers (distance) and 23° E (direction) from the north as reckoned along a straight line from the Templo Mayor. At least one ruined pyramidal structure and the remains of several other platforms are situated there, but much of the building stone has been repositioned in the construction of cattle pens and field boundaries, likely by the small population of peasants who now dwell in the area. (The very dense scatter of late Aztec sherds we found there would make this a logical place for the focus of the ritual, but more archaeological verification needs to be provided on this point.) Broda noted the existence of a possible access way that bears 214° (or 34° W of S). This appeared to lead down toward the direction of the Shrine of Guadalupe. We have not yet attempted to follow this access way down toward the shrine but we believe it will be important to do so. Perhaps coincidentally, the façade of the old shrine exhibits a similar bearing (201° or 21° W of S, the same as the Calzada de los Misterios).

To arrive at this second deposition point of the sacrificial victims one might have proceeded north-northeast along the Calzada de los Misterios, which marks the remains of one of the causeways across the lake, to the base of the hill upon which the shrine is located today, then in between the hills of Cerro Los Gachupines and Cerro El Guerrero, and finally up the latter hill to the summit of Yoaltecatl. One wonders whether the Shrine of Guadalupe and the site of the miracle of 1531 has an indigenous antecedent in this sacred place on the mountain skyline mentioned in the Atlcahualo ritual.

The third place (see Figure 6.1 and Table 6.1, Tepetzinco, elev. 2,280 m) mentioned in the ritual procession is well known to all visitors who pass into and out of Mexico City through its international airport. Sahagún reports: "The third place was at Tepetzinco. There died a girl called Quetzalxoch, (a name) which they took from Tepetzintli, which they (also) named Quetzalxoch. Her array was light blue." (The Spanish text adds: "Es aquel montezillo, que está dentro destra laguna, frontero del Tlatelulco.") Presently inaccessible because the Mexican government has established a military watchpost there, this island in the middle of the lake, called by the Spaniards El Peñol de los Baños, bears 83° (7° N of E) from the Templo Mayor at a radial distance of five kilometers. It also happens to mark the place where the sun rose twenty days after the vernal or twenty days before the autumnal equinox. Had we not already established through separate argumentation (Aveni, Calnek & Hartung 1988) a relationship between the location of the hills of the Cerro Tlaloc range and the sunrise position twenty days *before* the vernal equinox, as viewed from the Templo Mayor, we might have abandoned the calendrical significance of the direction to this hill as pure coincidence. In the solar orientation calendar employed by the Mexican state, it may have served to define the time one mesomonth on the opposite side of the equinox relative to that indicated by Cerro Yeloxochitl in the Tlaloc range. Also note that unlike Quauhtepetl and Yoaltecatl, Tepetzinco does not lie on the skyline proper, the distant mountains of the Tlaloc range being behind it.

Neither the fourth nor fifth places (see Figure 6.1 and Table 6.1, Poyauhtlan and Pantitlan) mentioned in the Tlaloc debt payment ritual can be precisely located because the city has been drastically modified and built up in the southeast, but there are modern place names in this region that are distinct reminders of where they lay:

> The fourth place was Poyauhtlan, just at the foot just in front of the mountain, at Teptezintli. Its name, Poyauhtecatl, went with the one who died (there). Thus he went adorned: he was painted with liquid rubber; he was touched with liquid rubber.
>
> The fifth place, there in the middle of the lake, was a place called Pantitlan. The one who died there went with his name, Epcoatl. His vestments, which he went wearing, were set with pearls. [The Spanish text: "Es un monte, que está en los termjnos de tlaxcalla, y alli cabe tepetzinco."]

Durán's lengthy passage on Pantitlan offers us little information that would enable us to pinpoint its location, except to say it was not a mountain. He tells us that Pantitlan was a drain in the lake near Tepetzinco: "Occasionally a tremendous whirlpool appears when the water is sucked down. In this way many canoes are in peril because of carelessness and lack of knowledge as they pass on the surface." He goes on to describe one of the Tlalocan sacrifices conducted there:

> When the great lords of the city arrived at that place, the great tree called Tota was taken and was thrust into the mud next to the spring or drain. Its branches were tied and it filled out again. Then (the people) took the child within the litter and slit her throat with a small spear (used for killing ducks) and her blood was allowed to flow into the water. Once (the blood) had flowed, she was cast into the waters, right into the whirlpool. It is said that the latter swallowed her so that she was never seen again. After the little girl had been cast in, the sovereigns came to make offerings, one after the other, and so did the lords. They offered as many rich things (such as jewels, stones, necklaces and bracelets) as had been given on the mountain. These were thrown into the lake in the same place where the girl had been cast. Here each year such quantities of gold, stones and jewels were cast that it was a marvelous thing to see.
>
> Today, some people think that the great treasure of Mocteczoma was thrown by the Indians into that spring [Durán 1971:164–65].

And later (166): "Some say that it was a drain. Others disagree, (saying) that it was a spring and that during the rainy season a great quantity of water burst forth, filling the entire City of Mexico and its canals with water."

Of Poyauhtlan Sahagún says: "Poyauhtlan: there fasted Mexico's fire priest and the fire priest of (the Temple of) Tlaloc, once yearly, at (the feast of) Etzalqualiztli. Both offered incense there at Poyauhtlan. And there was dying there; captives died there." Our best estimate of its location would place it somewhere to the west and possibly south of Tepetzinco — the end point of a canal at the south shore of the lake.[2]

Bearings and distances for both of these places, as best as we can give them in the absence of further data, are given in Table 6.1. In neither case could the sites have been positioned at the skyline, but as we locate them on the map the latter appears to lie in the direction of sunrise sometime during the month of Atlcahualo.

The journey to the sixth site (see Figure 6.1, Table 6.1, Cocotl), which is the most remote from Tenochtitlan, could have been made by canoe into the lake of Chalco. On the southeast shore of this lake in direction

128° and at a distance of thirty-six kilometers from the temple precinct lies an unnamed mountain above the village of Cocotitlan. Calnek has suggested that this hill is the best candidate for the hill of Cocotl mentioned by Sahagún: "The sixth place to which they carried (a victim) was to the top of (the hill of) Cocotl; he also went with its name, Cocotl. His array was varicolored, part chili-red, part dark green" ("Es un monte que está cabe chalco atenco"). This place is also mentioned in the conduct of the Chalcan war,[3] and it is cited on the González Aparicio map.

In January 1988 when we ascended the hill (elev. 2,360 m), we were sorry to see that a pyramid of considerable size (base dimensions 40 m on each side, height 5 m) was already being dismantled, the materials being carted off to be used in the building of houses in the community below, which already extended more than halfway up the summit.

Like the fourth and fifth places, the seventh (and last) (see Figure 6.1 and Table 6.1, Yiauhqueme) cannot be precisely located at the present time, but Calnek estimates that it lies near Santa Fe (Acolxochic) in the district of Tacubaya. Sahagún informs us: "The seventh place was the top of Yiauhqueme; likewise the 'human paper streamer' went with its name, Yiauhqueme. As to the clothing which he had with him, he was all dressed in dark green."[4] Concludes the chronicler: "These were the places where the debt-payments, the 'human paper streamers,' died."

Sahagún then begins a lengthy paragraph describing other aspects of the adornments, of the children to be sacrificed, following which the chronicler says:

> And when they were brought to the place of vigil, in the Mist House, there all night was to be spent in vigil. The offering priests and the *quaquacuiltin,* those who were old offering priests, made them keep the vigil. And if any of the offering priests avoided them, they would call them "the abandoned ones." No longer did one join others in singing; nowhere was he wanted; nowhere was he respected.
>
> And if the children went crying, if their tears kept flowing, if their tears kept falling, it was said, it was stated: "It will surely rain." Their tears signified rain. Therefore there was contentment; therefore one's heart was at rest. Thus they said: "Verily, already the rains will set in; verily, already we shall be rained on."
>
> And if one who was dropsical was somewhere, "There is no rain for us."

The Mist House (Atauhcalco) is described as "un oratorio que estaua junto a Tepetzinco de la parte del occidente"; i.e., situated on the side of Tepetzinco facing the Templo Mayor. Evidently, it was the staging area, the point of departure for the various color-adorned human paper streamers to the seven sacrificial sites on the periphery.

There in the chronicle the ritual associated with the sacrifice of children ends and there begins a description, also in the month of Quauitl Eua of gladiatorial sacrifice to Xipe Totec at his temple Yopico.

Answering Questions

In general, I have tried to experience something of the "asides" of Tenochtitlan by visiting and mapping out the sites that the chroniclers specify in their description of Mexica rituals. Specifically, I have explored the connections between the activities in the ceremonial precinct and the sites on the horizon in the Atlcahualo ritual simply because it offers us the richest description of named sites and because Sahagún, perhaps unwittingly, has supplied us with a spatial ordering of these sites. But how much order and what degree of specificity? Just how prescriptive were the Aztecs? To what extent was precise knowledge a part of their worldview?

Reviewing the comments from my presentations at the 1987 and 1988 Mesoamerican Archive conferences, I discovered that some of my colleagues were most bothered by this perceived problem of getting the order right, of making things correct and precise. "Is the problem ours or was it the Aztecs'?" they asked. When things did not match, was proximity good enough? Are the slight deviations ours or theirs; are we exploring our science or their ritual? What really happened when things did not fit? How did they deal with that? Did it matter to them; if so, in what way? What did a subtle shift of alignment mean to them? Does a rigidity in our scholarship make more rigid what in reality may have been flexible for them? Could the problem, if there were one, be expressed as a positivity, rather than a negativity, as we scientists tend to look at it; that is, must we see the problem as one related to mathematical or geometrical sophistication? These were some of the questions I was asked.

There should be no confusion between our methodology and that of the Aztecs'. If I use a surveyor's transit to acquire my data, I do not imply that they also must have used one. Humanists ought neither to be frightened nor offended by the second column of my Table 6.1. I use it to describe as accurately as I can where a place is, how it is situated relative to other known places, and what went on in the natural environment in and about that place. However, in using my instruments I am constantly amazed at how precisely a mountain or a sunset can be fixed without resorting to technological apparatus. Perhaps some of my colleagues misconceive the nature of "precision." Perhaps they view it as an exotic quality that lies far beyond the realm of nontechnological societies. Perhaps they need to get in touch with nature and the landscape. Indeed, "getting it right" may not loom as the impossible task they seem to imagine.

So much for our attitudes: now, what about those of the Aztecs? We need to remember that the rituals we are studying are those of a highly organized, imperial urban state in which there would have been much to be gained by "getting it right." After all, those priests were paid to do something! Ethnographic analogy does us little good here for just as the highly developed architectural, calendrical, and political practices of the Classic Maya were vastly eroded in the Postclassic and conquest periods, so too might we expect the conduct of the Aztec timing and spacing of ritual to become more flexible. Nonetheless, there must have been some adjustability, some autonomy in the timing of these rituals, for as the Mexica state developed, one needed to make different calendars that spoke to different interests in a compatible way.

What emerges from our still-incomplete mapping of the Atlcahualo ritual is some sense of the problem (for them) of physically incorporating the natural world into the space of the urban community. Careful observations of the natural world served as a vehicle for expressing the ideas of Mexica rulers concerning how they were related to the gods. They may not have been concerned with the orchestration of every odd contortion upon their ritual stage, and, therefore, we in turn must not feel unfulfilled should we fail to serve up a rational explanation for every deviated angle. Rather, our goal ought to be to explicate some sort of intelligible grand design. But in so doing, we will forever confront the question: When is a datum significant and when is it not? We shall cross each bridge when we come to it, armed ever with the belief that, like the Maya, the Mexica did want to get it right.

The function of the Atlcahualo rituals to Tlaloc in this grand design seems to have been to provide a scheme for making the debt payment to Tlaloc in the form of human sacrifice at the openings in the earth where the different qualities of water manifest themselves: the gushing spring of Pantitlan; the island of Tepetzinco surrounded by lake water; the various mountain waters, and so on.

There are other rites that specifically mention Tenochtitlan's asides (see, e.g., Broda 1971, esp. Tables 1–3), among them the Painal procession in the fifteenth month (Panquetzalitztli; Durán 1971:458), the Festival of the Hunt in honor of Camaxtli (at Zacatepec) in the fourteenth month (Quecholli; Durán 1971:146, 455), tributes to Chicomecoatl near the fall equinox in the eleventh month (Ochpaniztli; Durán 1971:229, 447), and another set of sacrifices to Tlaloc in the month Huey Tozoztli centering on May 3 (the day the sun crosses the zenith) (Durán 1971:156, 422).[5] Unfortunately, none of these rituals overtly posits the kind of orderly spatial patterning suggested in Sahagún's description of Atlcahualo, at least at first glance. Was the chronicler not attentive enough? Was he not given sufficient detail? Can Atlcahualo be the only month in which full attention was given to the peripheral sites? If so, why? We cannot begin to explore the answers to these questions until we ourselves step up onto the stages on which some of these other scenarios were acted out. This plan of action will provide us with plenty of fieldwork for the future in Mexico City.

Notes

In am greatly indebted to E. Calnek for his assistance in constructing Table 6.1.

1. In the taped proceedings of the 1988 Summer Conference of the Mesoamerican Archive, P. Arnold glosses Atlcauhualo as "water leaving" and Quauitl Eua as "pole raising."
2. E. Calnek, in the taped proceedings of the 1988 conference.
3. H. B. Nicholson, in the taped proceedings of the 1988 conference.
4. But see Book 2, Appendix (1950–1982, II:192): "Atempan: . . . there they assembled the human paper streamers . . . they left them . . . at Quauhtepec, above Yiauhqueme."
5. See D. Carrasco's discussion of the Toxcatl ritual to Tezcatlipoca (ch. 5 above).

References

Aveni, A.

1988 The environment as ritual theater: Tenochtitlan and its spatial asides. Paper presented at Mesoamerican Archive Summer Conference.

Aveni, A., E. Calnek, and H. Hartung

1988 Myth, environment, and the orientation of the Templo Mayor of Tenochtitlan. *American Antiquity* 53:287–304.

Aveni, A., and H. Hartung

1979 The cross petroglyph: an ancient Mesoamerican astronomical and calendrical symbol. *Indiana* 6:37–54.

Broda, J.
1971 Las fiestas aztecas de los dioses de la lluvia. *Revista Español de Antropología Americana* 6:245–327.

Closs, M.
1988 A phonetic version of the Maya glyph for north. *American Antiquity* 53:386–93.

Durán, D.
1971 *The book of the gods and rites and the ancient calendar.* Translated and edited by F. Horcasitas and D. Heyden. Norman: University of Oklahoma Press.

Fustel de Coulanges, N.
1864 *The ancient city.* New York: Doubleday.

González Aparicio, Luís
1973 *Plano reconstructivo de la región de Tenochtitlán.* Mexico City: Instituto Nacional de Antropología e Historia.

Sahagún, B. de
1950–1982 *Florentine Codex: General history of the things of New Spain.* 13 vols. Santa Fe: School of American Research and the University of Utah Press.

Sanders, W., J. Parsons, and R. Santley
1979 *The Basin of Mexico.* Vol. 2, *Maps.* New York: Academic Press.

Tobriner, S.
1972 The fertile mountain: An investigation of Cerro Gordo's importance to the town plan and iconography of Teotihuacan. In *Teotihuacan onceava mesa redonda.* Mexico City: Sociedad Mexicana de Antropología.

7

The Sacred Landscape of Aztec Calendar Festivals: Myth, Nature, and Society

Johanna Broda

The interdisciplinary study of pre-Hispanic Mesoamerica, combining ethnohistory, archaeology, archaeoastronomy, art history, and history of religions, has been a particularly fruitful field of research in the Valley of Mexico, historic heartland of the Triple Alliance and seat of numerous important city-states with distinctive ethnic affiliations and ancient cultural roots in the past.

The peculiarity of this geographical zone is that it was the main (or at least one of the principal) political and cultural centers of Mesoamerica, with a historical continuity extending from Preclassic times. It is to be expected that we should find here an extreme complexity in the relations among settlements, natural features, alignments, interactions, and symbolic forms — "a grand design" derived from an ancient tradition. These circumstances are enhanced even more by the fact that for no other region of pre-Hispanic Mesoamerica does there exist such an abundance of historical sources (from Indian codices and annals to Spanish and mestizo chronicles, from colonial archival and published documentation to contemporary fieldwork accounts and modern bibliography in general) (see Figures 7.1–7.4). Thus, it is possible effectively to combine the study of pre-Hispanic society and religion with historical accounts written by different ethnic groups of the Valley (that refer to the ways in which these Nahua groups conceived of their geographic and cultural space, their "ritual landscape," that is, their own ideological interpretation of this space). On the other hand, this historical documentation on pre-Hispanic

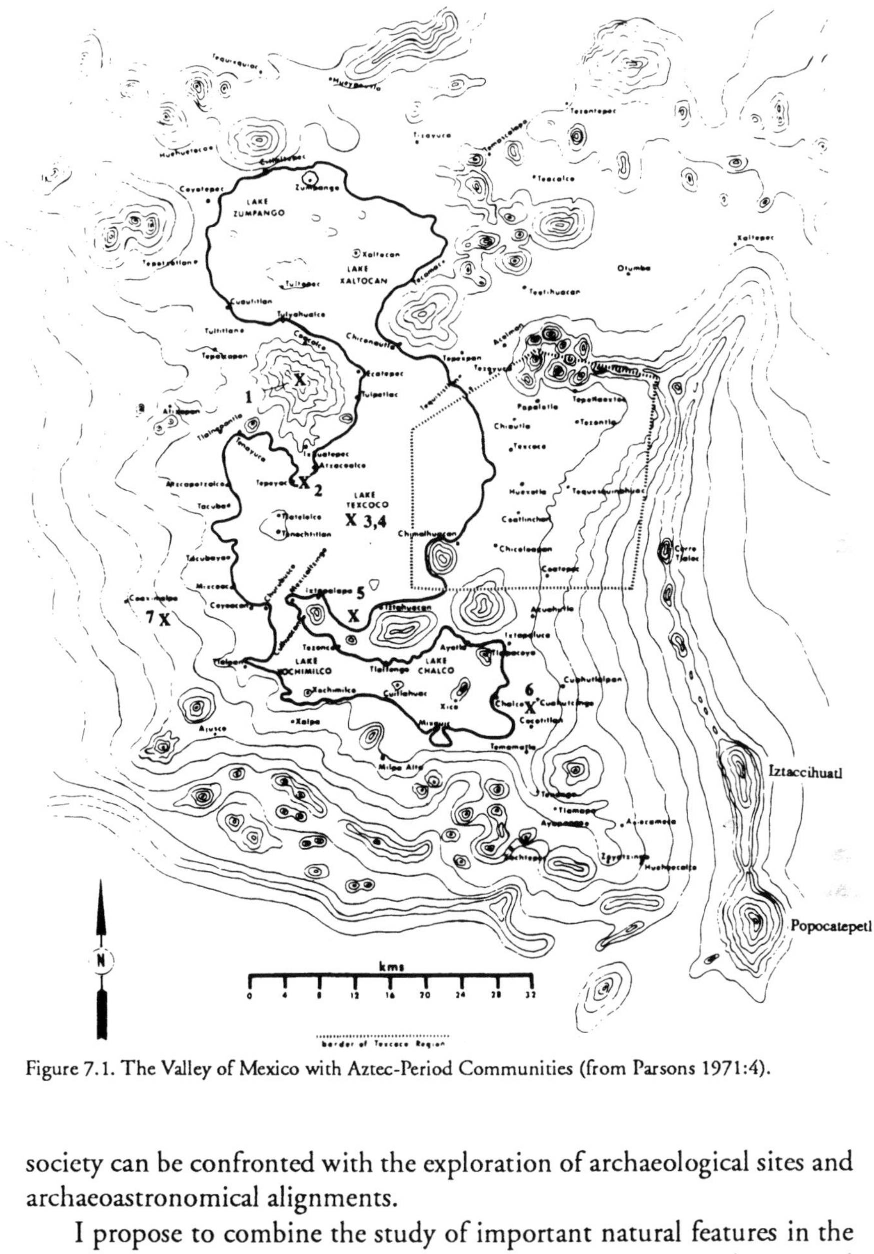

Figure 7.1. The Valley of Mexico with Aztec-Period Communities (from Parsons 1971:4).

society can be confronted with the exploration of archaeological sites and archaeoastronomical alignments.

I propose to combine the study of important natural features in the Basin (mainly mountains or water resources) that were used as sacred

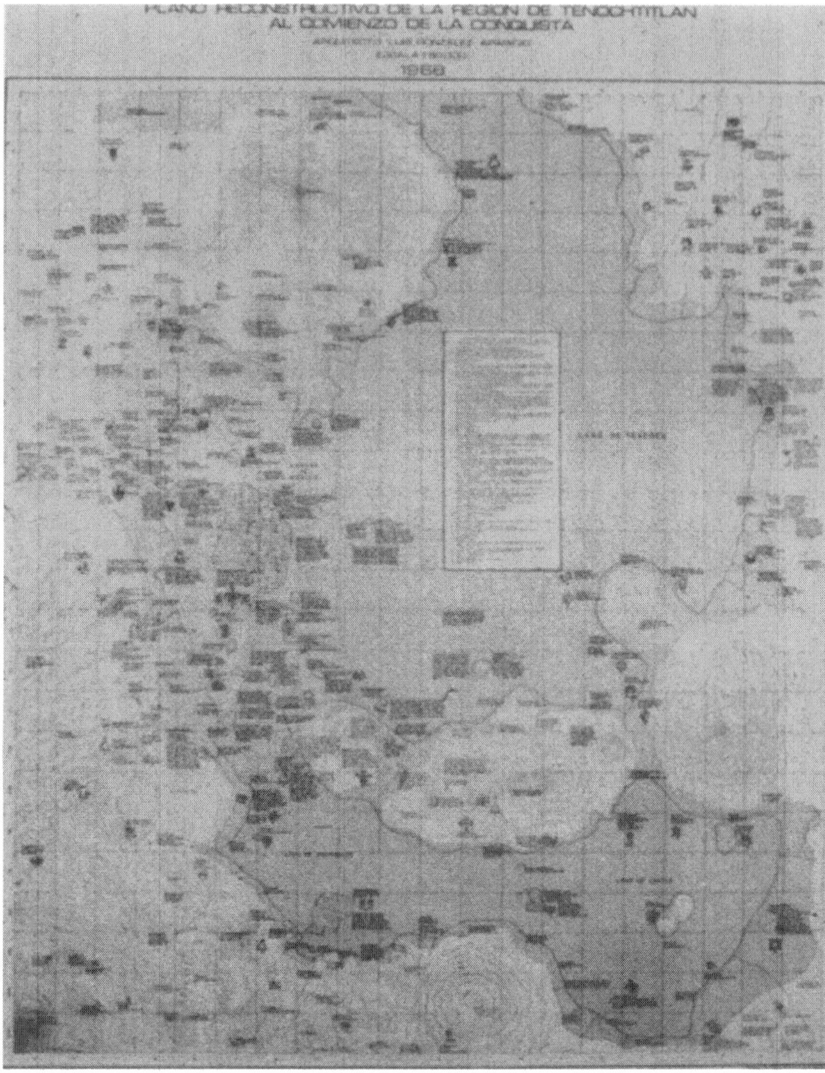

Figure 7.2. The Valley of Mexico on the Eve of the Spanish Conquest (from *Plano Reconstructivo de la Región de Tenochtitlan* by L. González Aparicio, 1973).

places (sanctuaries) with the study of the principal towns and their history. In this reconstruction of the Aztec vision of place, I propose to examine the archaeoastronomical alignments that may exist between the natural features connected to shrines and human settlements, taking into account the geographical and ecological setting and the former vegetation of these

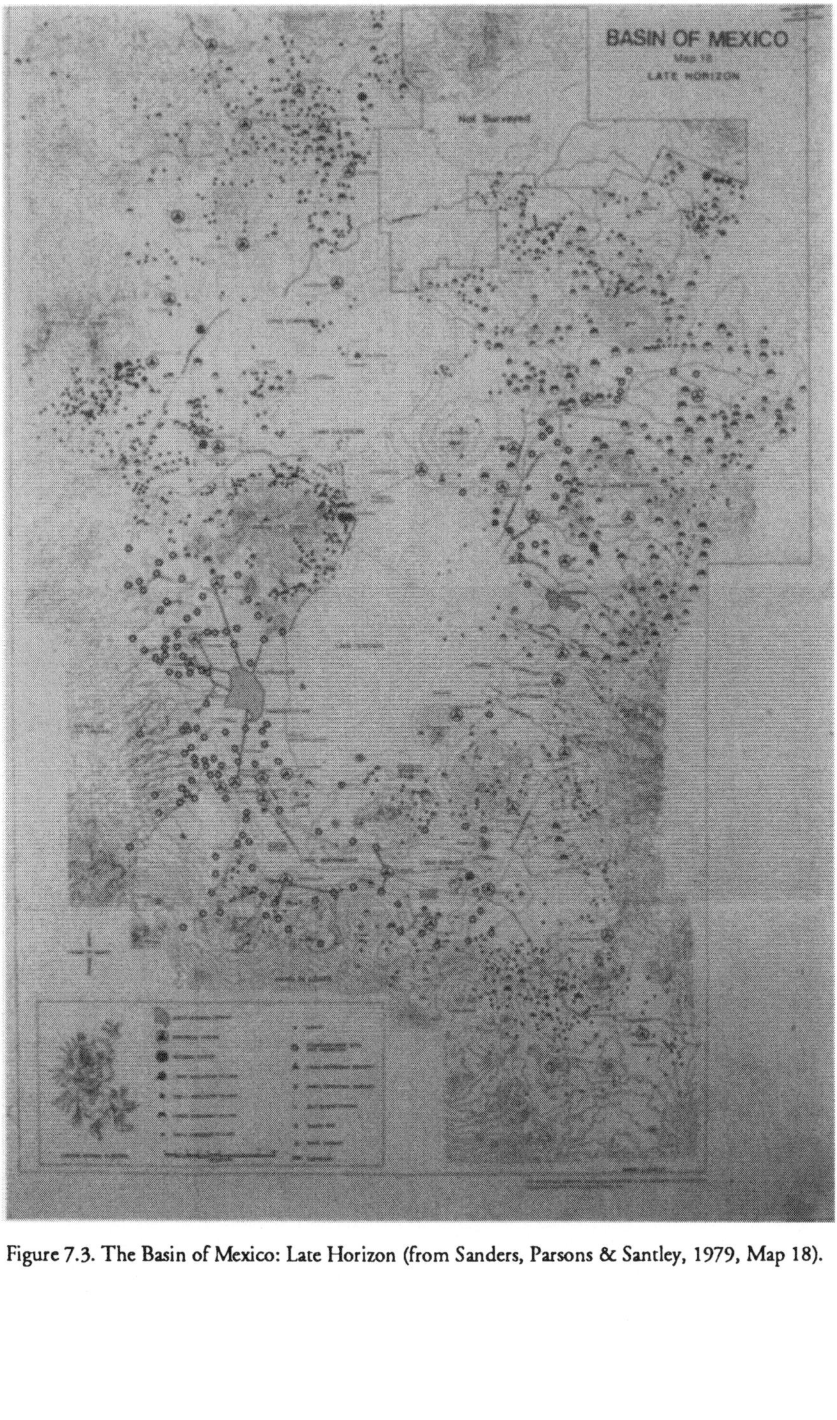

Figure 7.3. The Basin of Mexico: Late Horizon (from Sanders, Parsons & Santley, 1979, Map 18).

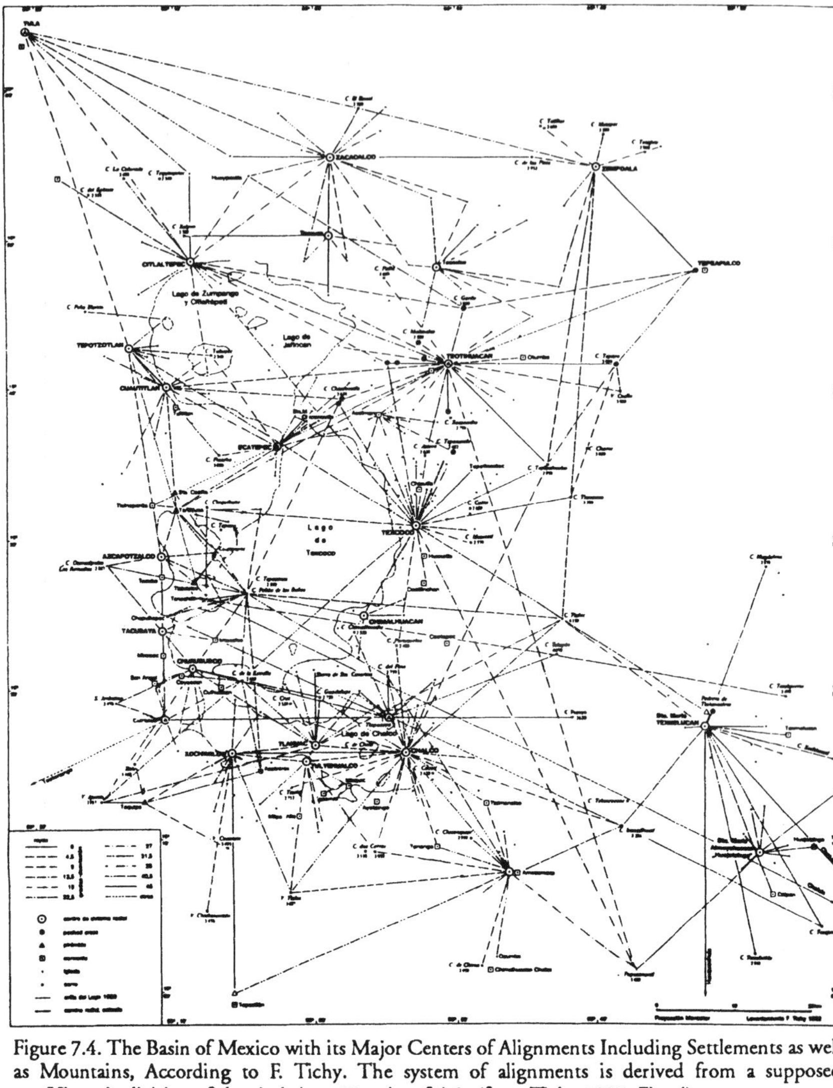

Figure 7.4. The Basin of Mexico with its Major Centers of Alignments Including Settlements as well as Mountains, According to F. Tichy. The system of alignments is derived from a supposed pre-Hispanic division of the circle into 80 units of 4.5° (from Tichy 1983, Fig. 4).

places. This is the outline of a rather wide project for the future. In this chapter I want to synthesize some of the research done so far, and concentrate on the analysis of the relation between myth, nature, and society in a series of specific Aztec calendrical festivals. The different sections of this chapter may seem to be rather wide apart; however, I hope to show that both strands of investigation cross-nurture one another.

1. Archaeoastronomical Fieldwork in the Basin of Mexico: The Mountain Cult and Site Alignments

One of the basic propositious of this study is that the mountain cult was a fundamental aspect of pre-Hispanic cosmovision and religion. I recognized this circumstance after analyzing the cosmovision implied in the offerings that were buried in the constructive phases of the Templo Mayor (Broda 1982, 1987a, 1987b). The mountain cult was intimately connected to the cult of rain, water, and the earth and is one of the oldest elements of pre-Hispanic religion, the roots of which go back to Preclassic times. The important observational elements that pre-Hispanic religion contained included not only the observation of the annual course of the sun and of certain planets and constellations, but this study should be extended to the notions of geography, climate, and the observation of nature in a wider sense (Broda 1989 and in press). This analysis can be concretely undertaken in the case of mountain worship by relating archaeological, ethnohistorical, and ethnographic records (Broda, in press). Authors that have contributed to the study of this subject in central Mexico are Charnay (1973); Lorenzo (1957); Townsend (1982); Ponce de León (1983); Iwaniszewski (1986b); Montero (1988).[1] Franz Tichy (1983) has done pioneer work in analyzing the archaeoastronomical as well as geometrical alignments that existed between the most important mountains and settlements in the valleys of Mexico and Puebla-Tlaxcala (see Figure 7.4). In general terms, the approach that I am proposing here has been greatly influenced over the years by Tichy's work. As a cultural geographer he has tried from the outset to combine the measurement of astronomical alignments with the study of cultural landscapes and has proposed innovative insights into pre-Hispanic calendrics and geometric units of measurement.[2] Any further research on the Basin of Mexico has to take into account his important contributions in this field.

The confrontation of pre-Hispanic Mesoamerican cultures with their natural environment (sky and earth) was a twofold dialectical one: Truly precise observation and correct prediction of natural phenomena were intimately fused with a magical attitude and an explanation of the cosmos in mythical terms. Thus, by cosmovision we understand those notions about nature and society that were combined into a coherent structural whole and were characterized precisely by this intimate fusion between the exact observation of nature, on the one hand, and myth, magic, and ritual on the other (Broda 1982, 1989, and in press).

The study of Mesoamerican cosmovision based on texts, iconography, and archaeology has been greatly enriched over the past fifteen years by the new, specialized study of archaeoastronomy whose main driving force has been Anthony F. Aveni, who has figured as the author and editor of an impressive opus in this field.[3] Archaeoastronomy has undertaken the systematic study of the orientation of pyramids and ceremonial sites, correlated with certain significant dates of the solar course as they can be observed on the horizon. This points to the fact that in ancient Mesoamerica time and space were deliberately coordinated in the landscape by means of the orientation of buildings and sites, an imposed order that was expressed in terms of the calendrical structure. Ancient Mesoamericans created a sacred landscape in which they tried to establish a harmonious, reciprocal structure among shrines, temples, settlements, and natural features such as mountains and water resources. Both archaeoastronomy and the history of religions can make important contributions to our understanding of these circumstances, which naturally must be based on a detailed analysis and profound knowledge of the historical and archaeological sources of ancient Mexico, as well as on actual reconnaissance of these sites.

Within the detailed study of Aztec calendar festivals that I initiated more than twenty years ago, I had naturally been aware of the fact that the principal source materials (Sahagún, Durán, Motolinía, Pomar, *Costumbres de Nueva España,* and so on) list concrete places (settlements, shrines, temples, mountains, springs) within their descriptions of the monthly ceremonies (Broda 1971, 1979). However, I had never before made a serious attempt to locate these places on the map of the Basin of Mexico and to study the directional, geographic, as well as symbolic implications of the interrelations among them. In this context, the Mesoamerican Archive meetings organized by Davíd Carrasco have stimulated new research over the past years. Forming part of the archive research group, Philip P. Arnold systematically studied the extensive archaeological reports of more than fifteen years of field surveys by Sanders, Parsons, Blanton, and others[4] that provide an exceptional point of departure for any future study because of the great detail and thoroughness of their information (see Figures 7.1 and 7.3). Arnold (1986, 1989) combines the approach of history of religion with the utilization of these archaeological reports and reaches some useful and interesting conclusions. Anthony F. Aveni and Edward Calnek, on the other hand, initiated, in 1988, a systematic field project of visiting the places (mountains) where the Aztecs brought child sacrifices during the month of Atlcahualo,[5] corresponding to February (Aveni 1988a, 1989a). Our joint visits to Yoaltecatl in January 1988 and to the Sierra de Guadalupe or Quauhtepec (Pico Tres Padres) in January 1989 were extremely stimulating for me and constituted the starting point to develop the above-mentioned wider project on the sacred geography of the Basin of Mexico, the first results of which are presented in this chapter.

There is a unique circumstance relating to this type of fieldwork: Practically all of these archaeological sites that were situated along the shore of the lake in 1519 have by now been engulfed and largely obliterated by the exorbitant growth of Mexico City, which from the 1960s on has expanded over most parts of the Basin. Since these mountains are "peripheral" places, they are situated mostly in poor areas of the megalopolis and are both unsafe and difficult to reach. The hardships of this type of fieldwork are not those usually faced by the anthropologist in inaccessible and isolated rural regions but consist in the difficulties of crossing highways, of finding one's way in slum areas dangerous and hostile because of their poverty. The inhabitants of these areas — some of them recent immigrants to the city — do not remember or never knew the old names and significance of these places.

If one finally manages to get to one of these mountaintops, the risks are not having any view at all due to the smog that densely fills the Valley of Mexico. However, one might also be lucky on rare occasions when propitious winds blow the contamination away and reveal a magnificent panorama, much more impressive than one could ever have imagined while one was submerged in the smog. If one is fortunate enough to get a glimpse of such a sight (and this might happen only a few days per year), one, however, is still able today to visualize the imposing view that these hilltop shrines of the Valley of Mexico conveyed to those who ascended to them. The flat bed of the lake (that can still be perfectly perceived today) permits one to view distances of thirty to fifty kilometers and offers panoramic sights of great beauty. The combination of lakes, distant mountain ranges, the high volcanoes to the southeast, and the towns distributed over the Valley with their imposing ceremonial architecture and precincts, must certainly have induced a spectacular vision, a fact that was recorded by Cortés and Bernal del Castillo in 1519.

It is the task of anthropological research to try to recreate in our minds the visual perspective that these places may have offered to the spectator in the sixteenth century and combine this analysis with our knowledge of the historical importance of these sites. Naturally, this attempt can remain only an approximation and must be free from the mystique of reconstructing the "true image of the pre-Hispanic past."

2. Myth, Nature, and Society in the Yearly Cycle of Festivals of the Aztec Calendar

"Myth, nature, and society" encompass a wide range of topics that can readily be applied to the complete cycle of Aztec calendar festivals and to the geography of the Basin of Mexico as a whole. However in this study I will necessarily concentrate on several specific festivals and on a series of concrete places, most of which are mountains. The festivals that I will refer to are (following Sahagún's sequence of months) I Atlcahualo, IV Huey tozoztli, VI Etzalcualiztli, VII Tecuilhuitontli, VIII Huey tecuilhuitl and XIV Quecholli.

In this book Aveni and Arnold deal extensively with the ritual landscape of I Atlcahualo (see chs. 6 and 14); I will discuss here several aspects of Atlcahualo from the perspective of my own research as well. However, on the other hand, I want to show in this chapter that the complexity of Aztec calendar festivals contained different ways of taking possession of the landscape of the Valley of Mexico. Besides the relation to nature, focusing on rain/maize, climate/agriculture as well as the cult of the lake and the sea that was implied in the festivals dedicated to the rain gods, we will deal here with ritualized political relations during the festival pair of VII Tecuilhuitontli/VIII Huey tecuilhuitl, when the Aztecs enacted in the context of the cult of maize, the sun, and the underworld an ideal reciprocal relationship of good government, or cosmic harmony between the king and his subjects. In these ideal reciprocal relations within a highly stratified ancient society the *macehualtin* (commoners) and the different groups of nobles, dignitaries, and warriors participated as well as the conquered towns of the Valley that had ethnic compositions other than Aztec. In the case of VII Tecuilhuitontli/VIII Huey tecuilhuitl, the ritual landscape expressed a desired political geography of cosmic harmony between the *huey tlatoani* (great lord) of Tenochtitlan and the subject towns, as well as within the hierarchical order of Aztec society itself.

Finally, I will discuss the month of XIV Quecholli that expressed yet another aspect of the great complexity of ritual relations implied in the

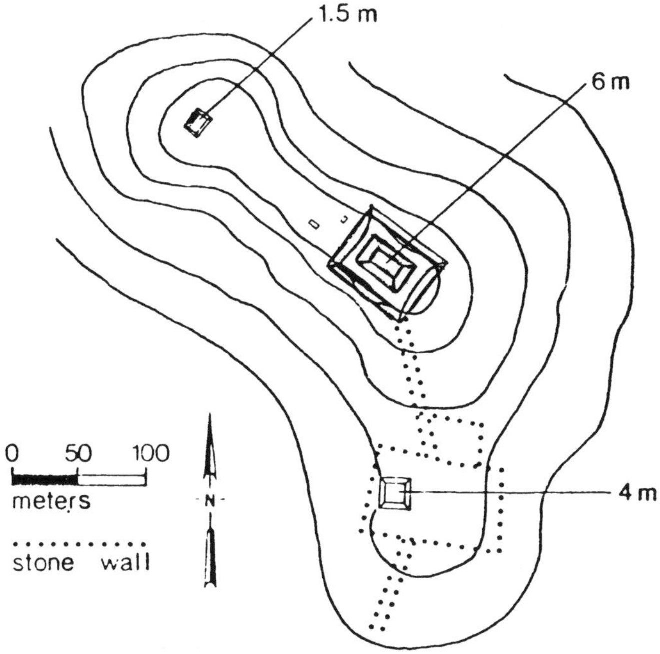

Figure 7.5. Plan of the Archaeological Site of Zacatepetl; Impressionistic Contours (according to Parsons et al. 1982:238, Fig. 39).

yearly festival cycle. Quecholli provides us a unique combination of references to the enactment of myth related to cosmovision as well as to history, all concentrated in the rituals taking place at one particular sacred mountain, Zacatepetl. Taking possession of landscape (i.e., of a particular mountain in a natural environment that still may be reconstructed to a great extent) was, in the case of Quecholli, completely immersed in myth. It was a particularly "dense" enactment of mythical elements combined with historical references that imply an Aztec interpretation of their early history, defining their Chichimec origins in their own ideological terms. Zacatepec (at the place of the *zacate* mountain), "where mountain grass is spread," "grass from under the pine trees," where "they come upon the grass" (*zacapan*)[6] was the sacred mountain par excellence. Amid a rough and rustic Chichimec environment, it was the place of hunting from the beginning of time and where the origins of cosmic warfare were dramatically enacted through particularly sanguinary rites.

In the yearly cycle of Aztec calendar festivals the interaction with nature was enacted in different ways; in all of them, however, a fundamental principle was that of reciprocity — reciprocity with nature and within the hierarchical structure of Aztec society. A reciprocal relationship between society and nature was established, a kind of treaty of cosmic harmony was negotiated. Human sacrifice, which formed one of the basic structural elements of ritual, was conceived as a magical act of reciprocity according to the principle of *do ut des* ("give that you may receive"). One of the main themes of the annual cycle of festivals was the agricultural or fertility cult. Human sacrifice in this context denoted an act of reciprocity with the deities that represented natural phenomena; that is, the gods of rain and the mountains, the goddesses of sweet and salty water, the maize deities, and the earth goddess. The natural phenomena that were "negotiated" were water, rain, and agricultural growth.

3. The Petition for Rain, Child Sacrifices, and the Mountain Cult

1. I Atlcahualo: Alignments and Cosmological Connotations

During the month of I Atlcahualo, corresponding to February, child sacrifices were brought to the rain gods as a petition for rain. These children that represented the rain gods were imagined as dwarfs and were magically related to the growth of the maize plant. These child sacrifices were *nextlahualli,* the "debt paid"(Broda 1971:272–76). The rain cult also was a mountain cult, a fact that is perfectly explicable in the logic of Aztec cosmovision (Broda 1987a, 1987b, 1989, and in press). Mountains — so abundant in the geography of Mesoamerica — were sacred places. They were imagined to be receptacles where the water was kept during the dry season to be let loose when the rains started. Therefore, the bodies of the children (sacrificed by decapitation) were thrown into deep caves or cliffs next to mountain sanctuaries (Pomar 1941:17; Broda 1971:275).

It is probable that the Aztecs conceived of the north as the direction from which the rains came (see Sprajc 1989:47).[7] In this sense it is interesting that the highest peak to which the priests ascended during I Atlcahualo in order to sacrifice a male child was the Quauhtepetl (eagle mountain), which was the biggest mountain range situated in the central part of the Basin. It had a strategic position, delimiting the northern boundary of the Lake of Mexico as seen from the island of Tenochtitlan-Tlatelolco. From the peaks of Cerro Quauhtepec, one sees not only the main part of the Valley of Mexico, but also its northern sections, which are hidden from other perspectives by Quauhtepetl's massif. Thus, it is a strategic point from which to view the former lake areas of Zumpango and Xaltocan, with Cuauhtitlan to the northwest and the Teotihuacan Valley to the northeast. The highest peaks of the Sierra de Quauhtepec reach up over three thousand meters (Cerro Picacho; Pico Tres Padres)[8] and just beneath Pico Tres Padres are the archaeological remains of the former Aztec sanctuary. Today, the site consists of heaps of roughly hewn stones that must have formerly been transported to the summit from farther below (Alejandro Robles, personal communication). The structures are not recognizable in their present state; only their location at the pass below the summit is evident, and an archaeological reconnaissance and consolidation of the site is badly needed.

On Table 7.1 I have listed the places where, according to Sahagún, children were sacrificed during I Atlcahualo. These places, which I have analyzed according to the sixteenth-century sources previously (Broda 1971:268–76, Table 1), have recently been explored in their geographical setting by Aveni, Calnek, Arnold, and myself (see chapters in this volume). The identification of these places on the map permits us to associate them with the cardinal directions, as can be seen on Table 7.1. This reconstruction of the cardinal directions as conceived by the Aztecs is to be taken in cosmological rather than exact geographical terms. N, S, and W are unequivocal. With respect to Tepetzintli, Poyauhtlan, and Pantitlan, I tend to identify them with the "Center" because they seem to have represented the central axis or heart of the lakes of Tetzcoco and Mexico. However, it might also be argued that these places were situated to the east of Tenochtitlan.

The seven places of sacrifice were located, following the cardinal directions, along the shore of the lake, with Tenochtitlan-Tlatelolco at the center: Two of these places formed part of the big northern sierra, the Quauhtepec; one was an important peak within the western range of mountains (Yiauhqueme); Cocotl was a conspicuous mountain situated at the southeastern fringe of the southern lake region, in the vicinity of Chalco Atenco; and to the east, three places lying at the very heart of the central lakes (Tepetzinco, Poyauhtlan, and Pantitlan), delimited an eastern demarcation separating, maybe, the domains of Tenochtitlan from those of Tetzcoco.

Table 7.1. I Atlcahualo: Child Sacrifices and the Mountain Cult

Cardinal Direction	Place-Name	Child Sacrifice
N	Quauhtepetl	Dressed in red color; name of the child: Quauhtepetl
N	Yoaltecatl	Dressed in black/red; name: Yoaltecatl
C (E)	Tepetzintli	Dressed in blue; name: Quetzalxoch (female)
C (E)	Poyauhtlan, to the E of Tepetzintli (there was an ayauhcalli)	Dressed in paper garments with stripes of rubber; name: Poyauhtecatl
C (E)	Pantitlan	Garments adorned with shells; name: Epcoatl
SE	Cocotl	Dressed in red/yellow; name: Cocotl
W	Yiauhqueme	Dressed in yellow; name: Yiauhqueme

The Center of the Lake and Eastern Demarcation as Seen from Tenochtitlan: Tepetzintli-Pantitlan. That the center and eastern demarcation should have been represented by three places denotes the importance of this direction. A female child called Quetzalxoch,[9] dressed all in blue, was sacrificed at Tepetzintli, a sacrifice of primordial importance and one of the rare cases for which we have a documented explanatory myth. The myth establishes a clear reference to the Aztec's ascent to power within the Valley of Mexico and their claim to assume the heritage of the Toltecs (Broda 1971:258, 276). Tepetzinco is called today El Peñón de los Baños and is a small but conspicuous hill right next to the modern airport of Mexico City. Recently, it was taken over by the army in order to protect the installations of the nearby airport. For this reason and due to recent urban growth, it has become extremely difficult to explore the area around the Peñón de los Baños. Formerly, it was a small island in the middle of the Lake of Tetzcoco and one of the most sacred places of the Valley. To the east of Tepetzintli there was a place called Poyauhtlan (place of the fog that is like smoke; Broda 1971:273, n. 22), where there was an *ayauhcalli* — a shrine dedicated to the rain gods — at which a male child named Poyauhtecatl was sacrificed. (Apparently there were four such *ayauhcaltin* in the Valley, but their exact location has not been established.) This place was also used in rites and sacrifices during VI Etzalcualiztli.

Finally, the importance of Tepetzintli was enhanced by its proximity to Pantitlan, the famous whirlpool (or drain) within the Lake of Tetzcoco that had an important Aztec sanctuary built around it (a kind of enclosure inside the water that was marked by flaglike banners, the *cuenmantli,* that were characteristic of the cult of the rain gods; see Sahagún 1950–1982, bk. II:42); Pantitlan means "amid the flags." It was such a dangerous place that Durán relates shipwrecks around it in the second half of the sixteenth century; these were caused by sudden and unexpected agitations of the waters as well as strong winds. It is not clear whether Pantitlan was only a whirlpool that swallowed the water or contained also a subterranean spring. According to Durán, during the rainy season water gushed forth at this place, while during the dry season it was thick, salty, and smelled bad (Durán 1967, vol. 1:88–91). Pantitlan probably was thought by the Aztecs to lead inside the lake and establish a subterranean connection with the sea (Durán 1967, vol. 1:91; Broda in press). The male child that was sacrificed at this place received the name of Epcoatl and his garments were decorated with shells (Broda 1971: 274), seemingly a clear reference to the sea.

Pantitlan-Tepetzintli were two prominent places of worship within the sacred geography of the Basin of Mexico. In terms of its axial relations to other sites, Tepetzintli, according to Tichy (1983:73 and 74, fig. 4), was even more important as a center of alignments than was the Templo Mayor[10] (see Figures 7.2 and 7.4). The main causeways of Tenochtitlan as well as the Templo Mayor itself were oriented in the direction of 7° N of W in which the sun sets on April 6 and September 6; on these days the sun rose behind Tepetzinco (7° N of E) as seen from Templo Mayor (Tichy 1983:74, fig. 6).

The Aztec migration legends also attribute an extraordinary importance to Tepetzintli. According to some of these traditions, Copil — the son of Huitzilopochtli's rebellious sister Malinalxochitl — led a conspiracy of the ancient city-states of the Valley against the Aztec newcomers at

Chapultepec and was slain in combat at Tepetzinco. Copil was decapitated and his head placed atop this small, rocky outcrop. His heart, on the other hand, became the foundation of the future site of the Templo Mayor (Aveni, Calnek & Hartung 1988:292; Tezozómoc 1949:63).

Although of very low elevation (2,300 m, or less than a hundred meters above the bed of the lake), Tepetzintli (lit. small hill [honorific form]) stuck out prominently from the lake bottom (a fact that can be perceived even today from a far distance; e.g., from Zacatepetl), and there were rock carvings on it just as there were on the boulders of Tepeyac[11] and of Tetzcotzinco near Tetzcoco (Townsend 1982:59). There were also springs that issued at Tepetzintli; the foundation legends call this place Acopilco, "in the place of the water of Copil" (Boehm de Lameiras 1986:316). These thermal baths still exist today and seem to have been so important in former times that Tepetzinco received the Spanish name of El Peñón de los Baños.

Interestingly enough, Tepeyac has also been associated since colonial times with an important spring of salty, curative water (Noguez, personal communication), while Tetzcotzinco, known as Los Baños de Netzahualcoyotl, used the canalized waters flowing down from the springs at Mt. Tlaloc to create (possibly ceremonial) ponds with panoramic views from the hillside. Thus, in the Basin of Mexico, mountains, springs, and caves formed salient features of worship and had their practical importance as well.

The North: Quauhtepetl-Yoaltecatl-Tepeyac. The northern direction within the rituals of I Atlcahualo was represented by the Sierra de Guadalupe and included the peaks of Quauhtepetl, Yoaltecatl, and Tepeyac.

We have identified above Quauhtepetl with the modern Pico Tres Padres where there are the archaeological remains of a former Aztec sanctuary at its summit. According to Sahagún, a boy dressed in red garments was sacrificed at Quauhtepetl (the eagle mountain).

Another male child was sacrificed at Yoaltecatl (the night dweller), today called Cerro El Guerrero, which is the mountain situated behind the hills of Tepeyac and Los Gachupines (the former name of Cerro Los Gachupines was Zacahuitzco). Yoaltecatl forms the southeastern edge of the Sierra de Guadalupe facing Lake Tetzcoco to the east (with the panoramic view of Mt. Tlaloc and Telapon on the eastern horizon) and the volcanoes and Ajusco to the south. Its broad, flat summit was occupied by an Aztec sanctuary totally destroyed today; the former existence of this sanctuary is indicated only by the (artificially?) flattened hilltop (of what seems to have been a large, rectangular plaza) as well as by the enormous quantities of rough, natural stones concentrated in this area, which today are used to delimit small plots for cultivation.[12] To the south of this flat area, there are the remains of the most conspicuous mound of Yoaltecatl — probably once the site of the main building of this sanctuary — with an evident concentration of delicate, first-quality Aztec ceremonial sherds;[13] however, the whole summit area is scattered with sherds that appear on the surface level of the cultivated land plots, testimony to the fact that Yoaltecatl must have been a very important ceremonial site. It offered a magnificent view over Lake Tetzcoco to the east, but the main viewing perspective was toward the Lake of Mexico with the twin towns of Tlatelolco-Tenochtitlan just ahead to the south. On the opposite southern side of the Valley the imposing Serranía del Ajusco caught the eye.[14]

The proximity to Tepeyac suggests an extraordinary importance of the pre-Hispanic site of Cerro Yoaltecatl. At the southern end of the summit, where the hill descends toward the Valley of Mexico, vestiges of what might have been a broad access causeway are recognizable (the causeway is marked at its eastern fringe by a row of erect stone slabs and its [artificially?] leveled surface is conspicuous). The traces of the access road are interrupted about halfway down the hill where the contour lines become steeper. It may once have continued, but, by whatever constructive techniques this might have been accomplished, all traces are now destroyed. The causeway's most conspicuous feature is its direction: It points exactly to the foot of Tepeyac where the oldest constructions belonging to the Basílica de Guadalupe are situated.[15]

This fact argues strongly in favor of postulating that in pre-Hispanic times the cult of the earth goddess Tonantzin had a shrine at the foot of Tepeyac that was closely linked to the sanctuary on top of Yoaltecatl. It is difficult to establish which one of the two sanctuaries was more important. Another striking circumstance connects the shrine of Tepeyac with Yoaltecatl. The derivation of the place-name is rather obscure, but it seems to be from *yohualli* (the night). However, in Book 6, Chapter 31 of the *Historia General,* Sahagún speaks of the supreme dual deity as Yoaltecutli-Yoalticitl, explaining that Yoaltecutli was the Lord of the Night while Yoalticitl was "la diosa de los baños" (1956, vol. 2:186); that is, the goddess of midwives, of the steambath, and of curing who was but another form of the mother goddess Toci-Tonantzin. Thus, the name of the mountain suggests a certain link with the cult of the earth and mother goddess. According to Noguez, next to Tepeyac there was an important spring, still functioning until recently, with medicinal, salty water. It must have been an important constituent of the worship of Tonantzin-Yoalticitl. In the colonial cult of the Virgin of Guadalupe, mothers with small children were a dominant element.[16] On the basis of these arguments, I propose the hypothesis that the fact of the sixteenth-century miracle of the apparition of the Indian Virgin at Tepeyac and the creation of the colonial sanctuary at this place were closely connected to the extraordinary importance of the sanctuaries that were there previously, not only at Tepeyac but above all at Yoaltecatl and, in a wider sense, in the whole mountain range of Quauhtepec.

Tepeyac-Yoaltecatl formed the southeastern edge of the massif of the Sierra de Quauhtepec. Tepeyac means "tip, nose, promontory of the mountain"; that is, the name reflects exactly the geographical conditions, and undoubtedly Tepeyac was a major strategic point within the Valley. From there at least one big causeway, called the Calzada México-Tepeyac, led to the island of Tlatelolco-Tenochtitlan; it was one of the most important routes of communication that existed between the island and the mainland. According to Angel Palerm (1973:85), this causeway corresponded to the modern Calzada de Guadalupe; Palerm suggests that there might have existed in fact two causeways to Tepeyac, one leading to Tenochtitlan (corresponding to the modern Calzada de Guadalupe) and another leading to Tlatelolco that corresponded to the colonial Calzada de los Misterios. The latter *calzada* has exactly the same orientation as the colonial Basílica de Guadalupe according to Aveni's (1982a) measurements. Besides, at least one *albarradón,* or dike, ran out from the promontory of Tepeyac. Torquemada describes the "albarradón de Nezahualcoyotl" that divided the sweet waters of the Lake of Mexico from the salty waters of the Lake of Tetzcoco (Palerm 1973: 85; González Aparicio 1973:31–34). However, it has not been clarified completely whether this major pre-Hispanic construction in fact existed at all; it is mentioned by only some of the sources. According to González Aparicio this dike began at Atzacualco, a settlement situated at the foot of the southeastern edge of Yoaltecatl, where possibly there was a floodgate of the dike of Nezahual-

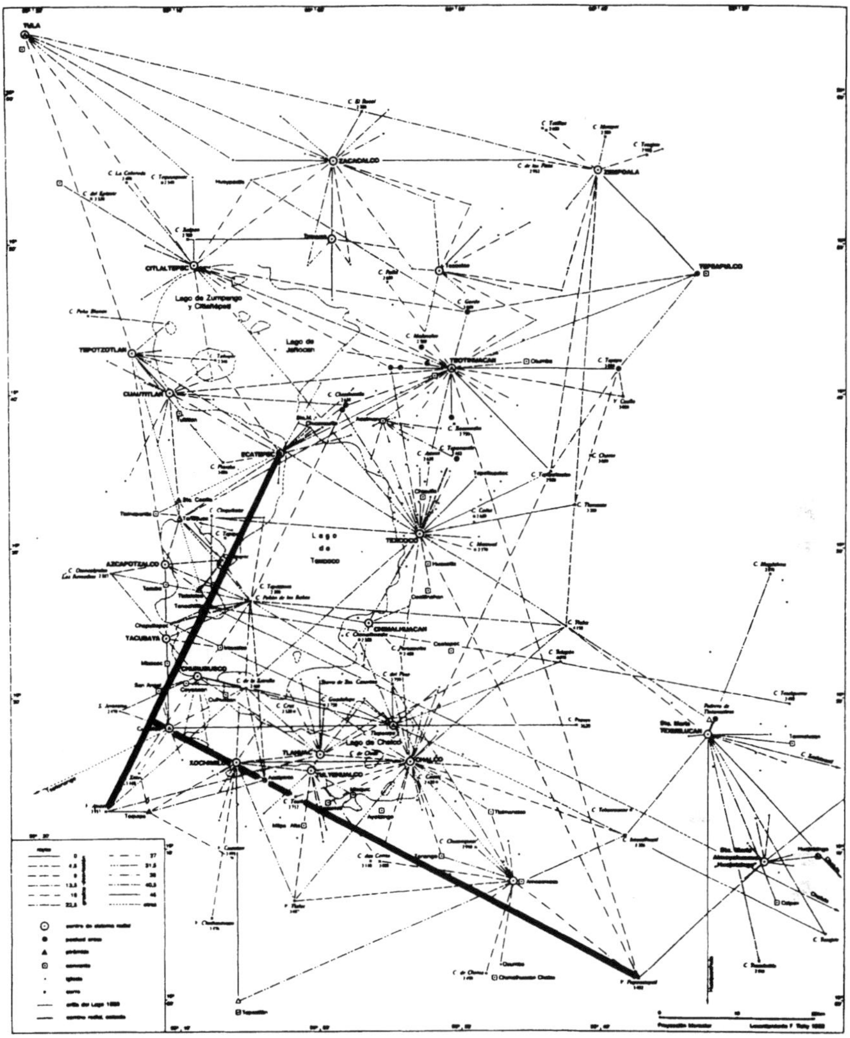

Figure 7.6. Alignments of Ajusco–Templo Mayor–Tepeyac, Yoaltecatl-Ecatepec, and Zacatepetl-Cuicuilco-Xochimilco-Acalpixca–C. Teutli–Popocatepetl. Map adapted from Tichy (1983, Fig. 4).

coyotl. Atzacualco[17] apparently was a place of such importance that in the nineteenth century José María Velasco, who was closely acquainted with the area around "La Villa," called the two mountains, Los Gachupines/Yoaltecatl, the "Hill of Atzacualco" (see n. 14). Possibly, there was at one time another pre-Hispanic dike that was built by Ahuítzotl and led from

Table 7.2. Alignments (Azimuths) from Tepeyac to Certain Points within the Basin.

From	Toward	Azimuth
Tepeyac	Templo Mayor	195° 16′
	Mt. Tlaloc	101° 32′
	Popocatepetl	134° 56′
	Cerro de la Estrella	170° 51′
	Tlalpan	193° 26′
	Cuicuilco	198° 08′
	Zacatepetl	202° 52′
	Ajusco	205° 43′
Yoaltecatl	Templo Mayor	200° 52′
	Mt. Tlaloc	103° 05′
	Popocatepetl	136° 03′
	Tlalpan	195° 19′
	Zacatepetl	204° 20′
	Ajusco	206° 35′

Note: Map measurements by Iván Sprajc. In no way do these data represent a final analysis. Some alignments have been explored previously by Tichy (1984 and in press), Ponce de León (1983), and Aveni (1988a, 1989a).

Tepeyac to San Lázaro, on the island of Tenochtitlan-Tlatelolco. It was erected to protect the town from inundations, just as the albarradón de Nezahualcoyotl was (Palerm 1973:78; González Aparicio 1973:34).

However, the causeways and dikes were not the only constructions that make Tepeyac-Yoaltecatl interesting in terms of its orientation. Several alignments are worth noting (see Table 7.2) and need to be studied more carefully in the future. At this point, I want to comment mainly on one aspect of the alignment between Tepeyac-Yoaltecatl and Mt. Tlaloc, which is 101° 32′ and corresponds exactly to the orientation of the pathway that gives access to the sanctuary at the summit of Mt. Tlaloc.[18] This causeway is skewed by eight degrees relative to the axis of the ground plan of the sanctuary.[19] This coincidence, certainly, is significant, because it implies a planned coordination between these two sites; that is, the Mt. Tlaloc causeway may have been constructed purposefully to point toward Tepeyac-Yoaltecatl.

The West: Yiauhqueme. The west was represented in the child sacrifices of Atlcahualo by Yiauhqueme, a mountain near Atlacuihuaya; that is, Tacubaya (Sahagún, 1956, vol. 1:140). The god Yiauhqueme was one of the pulque gods intimately related to the Tlaloque who were sacrificed during the month of XIII Tepeilhuitl (Broda 1971:310–11). Yiauhqueme means "the garment of *yauhtli*" (Sahagún 1958:131); yauhtli being a medicinal yellow flower (sweet-scented marigold [*Tagetes lucida*]) that grows wild in the mountains and fields and is still of great importance in Central Mexico and Guerrero. As he was one of the Tlaloque (i.e., mountain as well as pulque gods), the worship of Yiauhqueme is of great interest. Pedro Carrasco (1950:149, 159) suggested that he was probably of Tepanec origin. The location of this mountain in the western sierra is particularly intriguing since few archaeological sites and mountain sanctuaries are known from this area.[20] I have been unable to locate Yiauhqueme with precision. The slopes of the western sierra, with its innumerable *barrancas,* have been heavily urbanized in the last decades, and the mountain range of La Sierra de las Cruces belongs to the least explored areas of the Basin. It was only partly included in the Basin of Mexico survey of Sanders, Parsons, and Santley (1979).

The historical and cultural interest of this region lies in the fact that it was ancient Tepanec and Otomían domain and had connections both to the Valley of Toluca and to the ancient centers of Ocuillan, Chalma, and Malinalco; some of these cultural links perdure even today.[21] With respect to la Sierra de las Cruces, Pedro Carrasco (1950:31) comments that "Durán repeatedly speaks of an Otomí province, the *Quauhtlalpan,* for which it is not possible to elucidate an exact localization from his data, although it is clear that it comprised the area of Chiapan. Probably Quauhtlalpan was the entire wooded region of *sierras* that separated the Valleys of Mexico and Toluca." Although composite names with *quauh-* often are translated as "wood-" or "tree-" (*quahuitl*), their derivation from *quauhtli* (eagle) nevertheless seems much more probable and symbolically significant.[22]

The South: Cocotl. The southeast was represented by Cerro Cocotl, belonging to the domain of Chalco Atenco (Sahagún 1956, bk. II, vol. 1:140). It is a small but prominent mountain situated to the southeast of the modern town of Chalco and has Aztec ruins on it (see Figures 7.1, 7.2, and 7.4). Although in terms of its alignments it is not clear why this site was so important for the Aztecs,[23] nevertheless it is remarkable how frequently it is mentioned in the historical sources. According to Barlow (1949), Cocotitlan was the same place as Cocotlan and figures in the tribute lists of the Códice Mendocino as a direct tributary to the Petlacalco of Tenochtitlan (the very first tributary province of the empire)(Cooper Clark 1938, Plate 20). When it was conquered by the Mexica, extensions of land were granted to Tenochca warriors in this place (Parsons et al. 1982:86, Map 10), which indicates a particularly strong link with Tenochtitlan. However, another remarkable circumstance is that Cocotitlan was situated near the Preclassic site of Temamatla,[24] which apparently was an important ceremonial site and a settlement with Olmec influence related to Chalcatzingo. It is interesting to observe Cocotitlan's location next to an important Preclassic site, just as Zacatepetl is situated in front of Cuicuilco. While this does not necessarily imply a direct historical continuity from Preclassic to Postclassic times, nonetheless, it is worth noting that there might have been in some cases a continuing tradition of the quality of "sacred places." Cuicuilco means "the place of paintings or hieroglyphs" (see González Aparicio 1973: map). I believe that this name is not merely a coincidence, just as it is not merely random that Teotihuacan means "the abode of the gods."

Finally, in the region of Chalco-Amecameca there are a series of Preclassic sites situated on the piedmont of the volcanoes that seem to have been important ceremonial centers (M.-C. Serra Puche, personal communication). It is an intriguing possibility that they also had to do with mountain worship combined with solar observation, just as Preclassic Chalcatzingo did.

2. Huey Tozoztli: Child Sacrifices at Mt. Tlaloc and Pantitlan

I Atlcahualo was not the only month in which child sacrifices were made to propitiate the rains. As I have shown elsewhere (Broda 1971: 268–82, Table 1), these sacrifices probably started in XIII Tepeilhuitl (corresponding to October) and continued through XIV Atemoztli–XVIII Izcalli–I Atlcahualo–II Tlacaxipehualiztli–III Tozoztontli and IV Huey tozoztli (from December to the end of April). Sacrifices of a female and a male child at Pantitlan are specifically mentioned for XVI Atemoztli, I Atlcahualo and IV Huey tozoztli.

Table 7.3. IV Huey tozoztli: Child Sacrifices and Mountain Cult Sowing Festival and Petition for Rain

Cardinal Direction	Place-Name	Sacrifice
E	Mt. Tlaloc	male child
C	Pantitlan	female child

IV Huey tozoztli was an extremely important festival in this cycle. It was attended by the rulers of Tenochtitlan, Tetzcoco, and Tlacopan with all their nobility, who made sumptuous offerings at the sanctuary situated at the summit of Mt. Tlaloc; these offerings culminated in the sacrifice of one or more male children. Nobles from the "enemy towns" of Tlaxcala and Huexotzinco also participated in these rites (Broda 1971:277–79). Durán (1967, vol.1:82–93) is the only source that provides a detailed description. Since other authors and I have dealt in previous publications with this festival, I refer to it only briefly here. It corresponded to the end of April, preceding the onset of the rainy season, and coincided with the pre-Hispanic sowing festival. These rites have maintained a surprising continuity and were syncretized in the modern festival of the Holy Cross (May 3) that is important in all Indian regions of Mesoamerica, particularly among the Nahuas of northeastern Guerrero. I have dealt elsewhere, in detail, with these interesting rites (in press; n.d[b]). The importance of Mt. Tlaloc has been studied by Rickards (1929); Wicke and Horcasitas (1957); Townsend (1982); Tichy (1983); Iwaniszewski (1986a,b); Iwaniszewski and Sprajc (1987); Aveni, Hartung, and Calnek (1988); and Broda (1971, 1982, 1987a,b, and in press).

Another fundamental element of IV Huey tozoztli was its twofold, complementary nature — consisting of a mountain as well as a lake festival. While on Mt. Tlaloc a male child was sacrificed, the lake festival culminated at Pantitlan with the sacrifice of a girl dressed all in blue to represent the lake (Broda 1971:280). Pantitlan, the dangerous drain in the middle of the lake, probably was considered an entrance "into" the subterranean waters that connected the lakes of the Basin with the sea, as well as being linked to the annual cycle of rains.

Table 7.4. VI Etzalcualiztli: Sacrifice of Tlaloc and Chalchiuhtlicue (Goddess of the Lake and of Canoe-builders)
Cult of the Lake, Onset of the Rainy Season

Cardinal Direction	Place-Name
N	Citlaltepec (northernmost point of the Lake of Zumpango)
C (E)	Pantitlan
C (E)	Tecamazolco (southeastern shore of the island, facing Tepetzintli)
Unidentified places	Temilco Totecco (lakeshore; place of Xipe?)

4.1 The Onset of the Rainy Season and the Cult of the Lake: VI Etzalcualiztli

The reciprocity with nature that was implemented in the child sacrifices in order to procure water, rain, maize, and fertility in general was continued during the rites of VI Etzalcualiztli that took place at the beginning of June. This was the festival of Tlaloc and of Chalchiuhtlicue as the specific advocate of the lake and patroness of canoe-builders (Broda 1971:282–98, Table II; 1979). Adult victims representing Tlaloc and his wife Chalchiuhtlicue were sacrificed. These rites embodied the cult of the lake and the onset of the rainy season. In the course of this festival Sahagún mentions several sacred places. Besides the Pantitlan, action took place at two places on the lakeshore — Totecco and Tecamazolco. I have not so far identified Totecco, but Tecamazolco, according to González Aparicio, was the *embarcadero* on the eastern side of the island of Tenochtitlan right in front of Tepetzintli. From there the priests took canoes to go to Tepetzinco and Pantitlan. (Another place mentioned is Temilco, which I cannot identify). Further, it is remarkable that at the beginning of Etzalcualiztli the priests went as far as Citlaltepec, a town (and possibly a sacred mountain) situated at the northernmost point of the Lake of Zumpango in order to fetch a special kind of white reed that was used in the ceremonies. According to Tichy (1983: fig. 4), Citlaltepec was an important local center in terms of its alignments with other places. The name

Citlaltepec also makes one suspect a possible Venusian implication, a suspicion that is reinforced by the fact that the Aztecs believed the north was the direction of Mixcoatl (who had Venusian aspects). On the other hand, the reign of Xaltocan, of ancient Otomían roots (P. Carrasco 1950:34, 157), located next to Zumpango, was an important seat of the worship of the moon. During the offerings of Etzalcualiztli at Pantitlan, the human hearts were kept in the *mixcomitl*[25] and then hurled into the whirlpool (Broda 1971:294–95). The symbolism of rattle sticks was also of first importance at this festival; the sounding of the *chicahuaztli* was supposed to invoke the vigorous onset of the rains.

During Etzalcualiztli, the common people, the priests, and the king collaborated in the cult of Tlaloc and Chalchiuhtlicue (Broda 1971:296). The king had a fundamental role in these rites: He made a great fast called "Ayuno de Tlaloc" and offered incense before the image of Chalchiuhtlicue (Sahagún 1950–1982, bk. I:22). Thus, he worked for the good progress of the seasonal and agricultural cycle and for securing fertility in general.

4.2 The Cult of the Salty Water, the Lake, and the Sea: VII Tecuilhuitontli

In the context of the cult of water, we must mention VII Tecuilhuitontli. Sahagún (1950–1982, bk. II:86–90) describes the festival of Huixtocihuatl, the goddess of salt (and salty water, and, by extension, of the sea). According to an Aztec myth, Huixtocihuatl was the elder sister of the Tlaloque but she was banished (from the central highlands?) to the coast, where she invented the manufacture of salt (in fact, salt was and is still manufactured at both Pacific and Atlantic coasts, as well as from the salty waters of the Lake of Tetzcoco). This interpretation is reinforced by the circumstance that Huixtocihuatl was sacrificed by means of the snout of a swordfish, in such a way "that her blood gushed out as in a fountain" (Sahagún 1950–1982, bk. II:86).

However, in a certain way Huixtocihuatl also seems to have been the personification of the salty waters of the Lake of Tetzcoco, in contrast to the sweet waters of the other parts of the lake that were personified by Chalchiuhtlicue (Broda 1971:262–63; Seler 1960–1961, vol. 2:480). Both goddesses were sacrificed in consecutive months, on the tenth day of VI Etzalcualiztli and VII Tecuilhuitontli respectively. While Chalchiuhtlicue was the patroness of the canoe-makers, Huixtocihuatl looked after the guild of salt-makers, who apparently were predominantly women (Broda 1971, 1979). While Chalchiuhtlicue's color was blue, Huixtocihuatl's was yellow. The possible derivation of her name, meaning "woman of the Uixtotin," from the ethnic group Uixtotin is remarkable and enigmatic. The Olmeca-Uixtotin lived at the Gulf Coast around Cuetlaxtlan. On the other hand, her name was also related to the *ilhuicatl* Uixtotlan, the first of the nine layers of the sky according to the Codex Vaticanus A (Seler 1960–1961, vol. 2:480). In both cases a relation to the sea is implied.

5.1 The Cult of Maize, the Sun, and the Underworld and the Rituals of Cosmic Harmony Enacted by the King: VIII Huey Tecuilhuitl

The symbolism of VIII Huey tecuilhuitl revolved around the cult of maize, the sun and the underworld. July was the time of the year when the young maize germinated, the time when the sun in its aspect of the "night sun" sojourned in the underworld: that is, when the rainy season came to its peak (Broda 1987b:74–76). These aspects can be interpreted from the characteristics and the performance of the deities that intervened in the rites of VII Tecuilhuitontli VIII Huey tecuilhuitl. These gods were Xilonen-Cinteotl-Xochipilli-Piltzintecuhtli and Cihuacoatl. I have analyzed the symbolism of these rites elsewhere (Broda n.d.[a]) and will not go into detail here. However, in relation to the role of the goddess of tender maize, Xilonen, I must mention a highly significant rite linked to the symbolism of the cardinal directions and the four classes of calendrical years (*tlalpilli*). The more explicit meaning of this rite, however, remains obscure. It was called *xallaquia* (to enter the sand). I will quote literally from the Códice Florentino (Sahagún 1950–1982, bk. II:97):

> *Nauhcampa yn aquja anoço xalaquja.* In the four directions she entered, or went down into, the sand.... She [Xilonen] began the feast day when she entered Tetamaçolco. The second place where we went to arrive, we reached [to accomplish the ceremony], and it was a place named Necoquixecan. The third place in which she entered [the sand] was Atenchicalcan, and for this reason was it called Atenchicalcan — that here gushed forth the water, and also here faded away the wind. And the

> fourth place which she entered was over there at Xolloco. [And] there she stopped. [For] these were a part of, and carried together, the four year-bearers — Reed, Flint, House, and Rabbit. Thus do the year-bearers go describing circles, whirling around [as a measure of time].

Of the four places mentioned in this text, only Tetamazolco (apparently the same as Tecamaçolco) has been identified. Being located on the eastern shore of Tenochtitlan, it directly faced Tepetzinco; it was also visited during VI Etzalcualiztli on the way to Pantitlan (Broda 1971:295). According to A. M.Garibay (Sahagún 1950–1982, bk. II:92, n. 7), this rite was literally enacted, and the four places where Xilonen entered the sand may be identified in modern Mexico City and were associated with "water and sand." Note the reference to the spring at Atenchicalcan with its literal meaning of "where the wind faded away."

5.2 Social and Political Aspects of Huey Tecuilhuitl: The Ritual Banquets

As I pointed out earlier, with respect to VIII Huey tecuilhuitl we will touch quite different aspects of the ceremonial landscape of the Valley of Mexico. Tecuilhuitontli/Huey tecuilhuitl was the "Small and Big Festival of the Lords" and its multiple ritual banquets constituted the salient feature of its forty days (see my lengthy reconstruction of these ceremonies, Broda 1978, n.d.[a]). The supreme ruler played an important role at Huey tecuilhuitl; according to the indigenous sources, "he was the one who sponsored it." He dispensed food and drink to the poor of Tenochtitlan, to all the macehualtin, to the entire population. It was the time when there was a shortage of maize (before the new *jilotes* ripened) and the people suffered from famine. Through these distributions of food, the tlatoani showed his vassals that he protected and sustained them.

However, not only the poor of Tenochtitlan received these distributions of food, but it was dispensed to the subject population of the whole Valley, who on this occasion congregated at Tenochtitlan. The manuscript *Costumbres de Nueva España* informs us that

> this day there were grand dances and Moctezuma ordered everyone from all around Mexico and the lake to come to them and they arrived from Tetzcoco, Amecameca, Chalco, Tlalmanalco, Chimalhuacoatzinco,

Table 7.5. VII Tecuilhuitontli / VIII Huey Tecuilhuitl

10th Day of VII Tecuilhuitontli:	Sacrifice of Huixtocihuatl, Patroness of Salty Water and the Sea
Place:	Templo Mayor
10th Day of VIII Huey tecuilhuitl:	Sacrifice of Xilonen, Goddess of the Tender Maize
Rite: xallaquia	Xilonen offers incense at four places that represent the quarters of the universe or the four classes of calendrical years
Places:	Tetamazolco (the same as Tecamaçolco? See VI Etzalcualiztli) Necoquixecan Atenchicalcan Xolloco

> Mizquic, Cuitlahuac, Mexicaltzinco, Iztapalapa, Coyoacan, Xochimilco, Huitzilopochco, Culhuacan and from all the rest of the surrounding towns — and the Indians came and they gave to each woman a daily ration of twenty *tamales* and one *jícara de atole*, and to the men they gave the same [Gómez de Orozco 1945:45].

I have concluded previously (Broda 1978:241) that these circumstances expressed a political relation of domination and dependency between the *huey tlatoani* Mexica and the population of the southern and western parts of the Valley that formed the nucleus of the Mexica empire. In this sense, the references to concrete towns are an extremely interesting indication of a ceremonial landscape that reflected relations of political subordination.

On the other hand, ritual exchange and banquets also took place between the king and his warrior nobles, who were granted insignia and luxurious food. They, in return, reciprocated with banquets that they organized among each other. They also imitated the performance of the king by sponsoring banquets for the common people.

Even the subject towns and barrios were obliged to give ceremonial banquets to the warriors and lords. In this way the banquets expressed an economic reciprocity between the subject towns and the ruler as well as within the different strata of Aztec society; on occasion, even the independent, enemy city-states outside the Mexica empire were included in this network of reciprocities (Broda 1987:244–47).

As I have argued above, these ritualized political relations must be understood as reciprocal interactions within the structure of a highly stratified society, and they were by no means an exchange between equals. Ideological elements were extremely important in these transactions because they evoked a relation of cosmic harmony between the different strata of society and, on the territorial level, between the conquered towns and the imperial capital. In this context it is relevant that during Huey tecuilhuitl, the tlatoani also enacted his role as supreme judge as well as supreme receiver of tribute. But above all, the fact that he dispensed abundant quantities of food was crucial for his ideological role of enacting cosmic harmony within the great drama of the calendar festivals. The fact that during the festivals of Tecuilhuitontli/Huey tecuilhuitl the cult of maize, the sun, and the underworld was symbolically enacted in the ceremonies coherently substantiates this interpretation (Broda 1978, n.d.[a]).

Linking the rain cult to the cult of maize, the sun, and the underworld, I propose the following interpretation: The festivals dedicated to the rain gods centered on "the debt paid" to the mountain gods. Through the most valuable stake of child sacrifices, the Aztecs sought to obtain the "precious liquid"; that is, the rain. (Blood as well as water was considered, "precious liquid," which is an important and intriguing equivalency in Aztec cosmovision.) By these means they sought to oblige nature into a reciprocal relationship. On the other hand, during Tecuilhuitontli/Huey tecuilhuitl, such an ideal relationship of reciprocity was expressed in social and political terms between different towns and ethnic groups, and within the vertical strata of society (king, nobles, commoners, and conquered towns divided into their respective nobility and macehualtin). On other occasions as well, the Aztecs symbolized the ideal of cosmic harmony through the metaphor of maize as the basic foodstuff and the foundation of political legitimacy (see the myth of Quetzalxoch and her sacrifice at Pantitlan, [Broda 1971:256–60]).

6. Hunting Rituals at the Beginning of Time and the Origins of Cosmic Warfare: XIV Quecholli

The diversity of ceremonial landscapes and "performance as place" that can be found in Aztec ritual, and their mythical implications, are particularly well documented for the month of XIV Quecholli (corresponding to November), yet they have never been explored from the perspective of the geography of the Valley. In a way this example is the most intriguing and fascinating one.[26]

Zacatepetl, the sacred hill to the south that I was able to study during the spring of 1989,[27] is situated on the southwestern fringe of the Valley of Mexico, next to the Preclassic site of Cuicuilco, where the Valley bends toward the southeast in the direction of the lakes of Xochimilco and Chalco. Zacatepetl is located on the piedmont below the volcanoes Xitle and Ajusco, the latter being the highest peak of the western range of mountains, 3,937 meters in elevation. Zacatepetl reaches only to 2,360 meters; it is a small promontory surrounded by the Pedregal lava flow, the same that destroyed the great Mesoamerican ceremonial and urban site of nearby Cuicuilco. Zacatepetl has miraculously escaped destruction by the rapidly expanding modern city and preserves remarkable remains of an Aztec sanctuary, comparable in importance only to those on Mt. Tlaloc (see Figure 7.2). The sanctuary consisted of two rather large temples (Mounds II and JJ; the remains still stand some six and four meters high, respectively) connected by a long, linear causeway (about 105 m long) formed by two parallel stone walls (these have collapsed and now stand about 0.5 m tall, lying 8 m apart) (See Figure 7.5). This probably was a ceremonial causeway, running south from Mound II toward JJ, facing the peak of Ajusco, overhead. The orientation from the main structures of Zacatepetl toward Ajusco is 210° 46′. On the other hand, Mound II faced toward the northwest, a level area of some 25 by 140 meters that seems to have been a large ceremonial plaza. This plaza offers a magnificent view of the whole Valley, as well as of the nearby western mountain range (Ajusco, Sierra de las Cruces, Cerro del Judío). At the northwestern end of this former plaza there is another large mound (KK), which, however, is badly damaged and today is only some 1.5 meters high.[28] This site was included in the Valley of Mexico survey carried out by Parsons and others in 1972.[29] (see Figure 7.5). The only (and partial) excavation was undertaken by E. Noguera and the Dirección de Monumentos Prehispánicos at the end of the 1930s (Noguera 1940); the first report on Zacatepetl was published in 1934 by P. Martínez del Río.

A half-century ago, Zacatepetl lay a far way off from Mexico City and was covered by cactus and *pirules* (Martínez del Río 1934:298). Today it has more recently planted eucalyptus trees and the oaks that belong to its original habitat. One of the interesting aspects about Zacatepetl is that it is still possible to visualize to a certain degree the vegetation that once covered the rough lava zone that surrounded it. This inhospitable terrain formerly extended as far as the lakeshore around Coyoacan. In fact, this whole area belonged in pre-Hispanic times to the political domain of the Tepanec town of Coyoacan. Naturally, Mexico City has now encroached upon it, but the territory belonging to the Ciudad Universitaria with large, construction-free extensions right at the foot of Zacatepetl permits one to visualize its original setting, at least to some extent. This extremely rough and broken soil was covered by small brush, cactus, and oaks. Zacatepetl itself stuck out from this volcanic flow[30] and was also covered by oaks, brush, and *zacate del monte*, or mountain grass (A. Robles, personal communication). Apparently, this type of vegetation symbolized to the Aztecs Chichimec territory; that is, the rustic, inhospitable lands inhabited by Chichimec hunters and warriors.

1. The Ceremonies

With Quecholli we are dealing with an aspect of Aztec calendar festivals that is different from the water and fertility cult of I Atlcahualo–IV Huey tozoztli–VI Etzalcualiztli–VII Tecuilhuitontli, and differs also from the rituals of cosmic harmony enacted by the king during VII Tecuilhuitoni/VIII Huey tecuilhuitl. The rites of XIV Quecholli involve not only a relation toward nature and within Aztec society, but they deal above all with the Aztecs' own interpretation of history: referring to the Chichimec past; to the mythical time of peregrinations; and to the origins of cosmic warfare. Within the annual calendrical cycle, this month coincided with the harvest period and the time when military campaigns were initiated.[31]

The sixteenth-century chronicles clearly establish a link between the celebration of the monthly festival of Quecholli and the sacred mountain called Zacatepetl situated on ancient Tepanec territory of Coyoacan.[32] There was a sanctuary of the Chichimec god Mixcoatl here. Sahagún

(1950–1982, bk. II:126) informs that Mixcoatl also was "the God of the Otomi."

At the beginning of the month, the youths and seasoned warriors of Tenochtitlan and Tlatelolco[33] fabricated arrows for the ceremonial hunt shortly to take place and offered them in bundles of twenty at the Templo Mayor.[34] They also made offerings of miniature arrows to the dead. The next day, zacate was spread in the courtyard of the Templo Mayor; it was "grass from under the pine trees" (*ocozacate*), and on it (zacapan), the old women (*ilamatque*) received small children from their mothers to perform a dance with them (Sahagún 1950–1982, bk. II:124–26).

On the tenth day of the month, a ritual hunt in honor of Mixcoatl took place at "Zacatepec, there by Ixillan tonan (i.e., 'the navel of our mother')" (Sahagún 1950–1982, bk. II:126). A ceremonial path strewn with zacate was prepared that led from the town to the sanctuary on which the hunters went in procession arrayed as Mixcoatl (Durán 1967, vol. 1:281).[35] Among them went Motecuhzoma dressed equally as the god Mixcoatl (Gómez de Orozco 1945:50). The Tenochca as well as the Tlatelolca participated in this ritual hunt. Sahagún (1956, bk. II:126, 204) further adds that they were joined by the towns of Quauhtitlan, Quauhnahuac and Coyoacan.

On the plain facing Zacatepetl, they spent the night in grass shelters, lighting bonfires. Next morning they made a communal hunt encircling and seizing great numbers of deer, coyotes, rabbits, and hares. They killed them right on Zacatepetl and took only the severed heads, dripping with blood, back to Tenochtitlan. These heads were kept as trophies by the hunters who received awards and insignia from the king (Sahagún 1950–1982, bk. II:126–27). According to Durán (1967, vol. 1: 282), the successful hunters received the titles *amiztlatoque* and *amiztequihuaque* in analogy to warrior ranks.

The feast of Quecholli concluded on the twentieth day of the month with human sacrifices at the Templo Mayor. The gods Tlamatzincatl and Izquitecatl, with their wives, both called Coatlicue, as well as Mixcoatl and his consort Yeuatlicue were sacrificed at dawn after having performed the day before the rite of xallaquia or "entering the sand." Before the gods were killed, four captives were sacrificed who were bound and slain as if they were deer (Sahagún 1950–1982, bk. II:127–29).

According to Durán, this festival was dedicated to Camaxtli, god of Huexotzinco and Tlaxcala. He was the patron of hunting "and the first lord that the Chichimecs and hunters had." His insignia were the instruments for making new fire, "and those were the insignia with which he guided the Chichimecs and led them to the places where they are now, teaching them with those instruments to seek their livelihood from the mountains, when he moved and guided them to this land" (Durán 1967, vol. 1:71, 73). Thus, the fire cult was intimately related to the Chichimecs (see Durán 1967, vol. 1:76, 79). In more general terms, one might say that during Quecholli cult was given to nature in contrast to urban life: "[They made a] great celebration in the mountains of all the land, . . . invoking the clouds, the winds, the earth, the water, the sky, the sun, the moon, the stars, the trees, plants, and bushes; the hillsides and gullies, mountains and plains; snakes, lizards, tigers and lions, and all manner of beasts" (Durán 1967, vol. 1:282).

Apparently, the Chichimec element was of primordial importance in these rites, related to hunting, warfare, the cult of fire and the dead, as well as to the natural environment as opposed to civilized urban life. The god worshipped was Mixcoatl-Camaxtli, god of the Chichimecs and the Otomíes, diety of hunting and warfare.

According to Graulich,[36] Mixcoatl was intimately related to Venus, the planet that was a shooter of arrows. Mixcoatl was the prototype of the hunter and warrior, the initiator of the sacred war to nourish the sun and the earth. However, he was also the prototype of the first warrior who died in warfare, the victim that sustains the universe; in this sense he was assimilated to the deer. Graulich (1979–1980, vol. 2:480) proposes that the sacred hunt symbolized warfare. During Quecholli, the hunters stood for warriors, and the captured animals symbolized the victims. Durán (1967, vol. 1:281) is very outspoken in this respect when he states that "they did not on this day sacrifice men, but only animals, and thus the game served as victims to the gods."

A number of obscure myths relate Mixcoatl to the deer as well as to the ancient Chichimec earth and fire goddess Itzpapalotl who received animal sacrifices (Historia de los Mexicanos 1941:217). According to the Anales de Quauhtitlan, the Chichimecs of that town dressed during Quecholli in Mixcoatl's array and commemorated what Itzpapalotl had told them. Mixcoatl was also the ancestor of peoples, the warrior chief of the primordial time of peregrinations; according to different versions, he was either the husband of Ilancueitl, the ancient earth goddess[37] or of Chimalma, a warlike chthonic deity who became the wife of Mixcoatl and mother of Quetzalcoatl, dying in childbirth. Quetzalcoatl, was then reared by Cihuacoatl-Quilaztli. Chimalma, in a way, represented the sedentary autochthonous peoples of the south in contrast to the wandering Chichimecs who supposedly proceeded from the north (Graulich 1979–1980, vol. 1:197). These chthonic goddesses are variants of Coatlicue (see the myth of the birth of Huitzilopochtli) or of Cihuacoatl-Quilaztli-Chantico-Quaxolotl; the latter was the patroness of the towns of Culhuacan, Xochimilco, Cuitlahuac, and Chalman. She was also called Quauhcihuatl (eagle woman) or Yaocihuatl (warrior woman) and had a special relation with deer, fire, and warfare (Seler 1960–1961, vol. 4:77, 1053). In the rites of Quecholli, the consort of Mixcoatl that was sacrificed at the Templo Mayor was called Yeuatlicue, "the one with the skirt of [animal] skin," which further stresses her Chichimec links. Another name of this goddess in the origin myths was Cuetlachcihuatl, "the bear [or wolf] woman" (Graulich 1979–1980, vol. 2:483), while according to Durán (1967, vol. 1:77) the consort of Mixcoatl that died at Quecholli was called Yoztlamiyahual and was sacrificed by crushing her body against a large boulder (*teocomitl*); afterward she was decapitated and her blood was spilled over the rock; her head was carried around in a procession and a ritual dance was performed with it.

Was there a conceptual association between these goddesses and the deer slain at Quecholli? In both cases the victims were decapitated, an abundance of blood was shed, and the severed heads were exhibited in a procession. The Chichimec hunting and war rituals were symbolically linked to the cult of the ancient mother and earth goddess who, in a way, was assimilated to the captured deer. However, there also remains the possibility that the chthonic cult was the most ancient ritual component and was related to caves that were conceived of as the womb of the earth. It was also a lunar cult, just as Mixcoatl's cult was of stellar nature, particularly related to Venus, and both were opposed to the solar cult of Huitzilopochtli.

The above-mentioned elements of the cult of the ancient earth goddess seem to have been present in the rites of Quecholli that took place at the sacred hill of Zacatepetl. The name of the sanctuary was Ixillan tonan, "the navel of our mother." In the Spanish text, Sahagún (1956, bk. II, vol. 1:126) explains that "they say that this mountain is their mother." Several other toponyms around Zacatepetl are worthwhile noting since they might also point to the cult of the earth and mother goddess in this area: the nearby settlement of what today is San Angel was called Tenanitla in Aztec times, while Tenantongo is the name of a huge Preclassic structure belonging to the Cuicuilco period situated in what is today the southeastern limit of the park of El Bosque del Pedregal. I tentatively suggest a derivation of these names from *tenantzin,* "mother of people" (Molina), instead of *tenamitl,* "wall," as is usually done. Another striking element of Zacatepetl was the rough Chichimec environment it projected (apparently reminiscent of the dry steppe of the north). It symbolized the cosmological location of Chichimec territory and the cult of the mother and earth goddess in the southern section of the Valley, while Tepeyac-Yoaltecatl represented the same elements located to the north of Tenochtitlan-Tlatelolco.

2. Zacatepetl: Alignments in the Sacred Landscape

The interdisciplinary approach that I explained at the beginning of this chapter consists of combining the study of ethnohistorical sources with the surface reconnaissance of archaeological sites and the study of alignments. At Zacatepetl this method proves to be particularly successful, since the abundant historical data is enhanced by the excellent state of preservation; the site has remained relatively intact due to its location surrounded by the inhospitable terrain of the pedregal lava flow that was penetrated by modern urbanization only in the last decades.[38]

From the remains of the ceremonial plaza of Zacatepetl, oriented northwest-southeast (approximately 311°), one is confronted to the west by the domineering Ajusco and the range of the Sierra de las Cruces, an impressive view. Looking from the main structure of Zacatepetl (Structure II) to the southeast one can see, according to Ponce de León, the sun rise at the winter solstice behind Popocatepetl.[39] In fact, one of the intact parts of the eastern walls of Structure II yielded an azimuth of 26° 37′ (transit measurement I. Sprajc, May 29, 1989). The line perpendicular to this wall measures 116° 37′ or exactly the same orientation as the pyramid of Cuicuilco, pointing to sunrise at the winter solstice behind Popocatepetl.

In general terms, the view of the two imposing volcanoes, Popocatepetl and Iztac Cihuatl, as seen from Zacatepetl must have been awe-inspiring in ancient times.[40] Looking from Zacatepetl toward the east one could see the equinoctial sunrise over Cerro Papayo (Ponce de León, personal communication; see also Tichy, fig. 4). The latter is a prominent single peak on the eastern horizon that might have been used since the time of

Cuicuilco for calendrical observations. Mt. Tlaloc was also there on the eastern horizon, while to the forefront the Cerro de la Estrella caught the eye. Toward the north one overlooked the Lake of Mexico (with Tenochtitlan in the central perspective) and in the background, the range of Yoaltecatl-Tepeyac-Sierra de Quauhtepec formed the northern horizon. To the northeast the view passed over the small but conspicuous island of Tepetzintli (visible from this far distance) and led into the Lake of Tetzcoco with the mountains of Teotihuacan in the background.

While analyzing these observations, I was struck by the fact that Zacatepetl apparently forms a rough north-south axis with Tepeyac-Yoaltecatl.[41] The orientation from Tepeyac to Zacatepetl is 202° 52′ or 22° 52′ W of S; this alignment continues beyond Zacatepetl toward the south to the volcano Xitle, while the Ajusco is aligned by 205° 43′ as seen from Tepeyac, and by 206° 35′ as seen from Yoaltecatl (see Tables 7.4, 7.6). Sunrises and sunsets occur perpendicularly to this line. In fact, the sun rises on this perpendicular line, as seen from Zacatepetl and Cuicuilco, precisely on the day of the winter solstice, which seems to have been the main orientation of Structure II on Zacatepetl as well as the basic orientation of the pyramid of Cuicuilco some 1,700 years ago. These circumstances certainly deserve further pondering. Another remarkable fact catches the eye: This visual line from Cuicuilco to Popocatepetl further passes through Xochimilco, the Aztec petroglyphs of Acalpixca and Cerro Teutli; the latter is an important holy mountain up to the present and is perfectly visible from Cuicuilco, forming the base, like an altar, from which surges Popocatepetl in the distance. In Figure 7.6 I have adapted Tichy's map of alignments (see Figure 7.4) to mark on it the proposed N-S axis of Tepeyac, Yoaltecatl-Tenochtitlan-Zacatepetl-Ajusco, and the E-W axis of Popocatepetl–Cerro Teutli–Acalpixca-Xochimilco-Cuicuilco-Zacatepetl.

On the basis of these observations I propose the hypothesis that the alignments of 22° 52′-26° 35′ between Tepeyac-Yoaltecatl and Zacatepetl-Xitle-Ajusco had a special significance: They mark a rough north-south axis that passed over the island of Tenochtitlan-Tlatelolco and connected the high mountain range of Quauhtepec with the Serranía del Ajusco.[42] Had this axis not been skewed, it would not have passed over the island of Tenochtitlan. Tepeyac and Zacatepetl were two small promontories at the edge of these high mountain ranges that, because of their conspicuous shape and ecological context, were singled out by the Aztecs for ritual purposes.

The investigation — combining the study of alignments, geography, climate, and of historical data referring to toponyms as well as ceremonies — has brought to light a number of factors that seem to establish a dialectical symmetry between the northern and southern parts of the Valley as seen from Tenochtitlan as the center. North was supposedly the region whence the rains came; yet, in the climatic conditions of the Basin it happens to be the least humid part and was characterized by a dry scrub vegetation of zacate and *huizache*. This vegetation was for the Aztecs a synonym for Chichimec lands. Actually, as Noguez points out, the legend of the Virgin of Guadalupe is also full of references to Chichimecs, and the Sierra de Quauhtepec (the eagle mountain) was considered Chichimec territory right into colonial times. In this area there was a shrine to the mother and earth goddess Tonantzin who was the patroness of midwives and curing, called "our Mother Yoalticitl." This goddess was worshipped by young mothers with their small children, a tradition that was still alive in the nineteenth century and was represented by the famous Mexican painter José María Velasco in his painting *View from the Foot of Cerro Atzacualco* in 1873.

The south, on the other hand, was the most humid region of the Basin where there was almost twice as much precipitation as in the northern parts (Sanders, Parsons & Santley 1979: Map 2). The Serranía del Ajusco is probably the moistest region of the whole Valley, together with the area around the great volcanoes. At the foot of Ajusco, we find the counterpart of Tepeyac-Yoaltecatl: Cerro Zacatepetl (the mountain of zacate, or "grass mountain"), which constituted an ecological niche with a dry and hot microclimate situated within the extensive area of the pedregal lava flow (Robert Bye, personal communication). In the case of this low but striking hill, we have a unique source of information on the month of XIV Quecholli provided by the chroniclers Sahagún and Durán. The rites that the Tenochca and Tlatelolca performed there were a commemoration of Chichimec hunting rites. As we have seen above, mothers with their small children had a special relation to this festival. The female victims sacrificed at Zacatepetl all represented variations of the mother and earth goddess Coatlicue-Cihuacoatl-Tonantzin, and the hill itself was considered the navel or womb of the earth goddess. On the basis of these data I hypothesize the existence of a dialectical juxtaposition between Tepeyac-Yoaltecatl to the north and Zacatepetl to the south: both sacred mountains with shrines in which the Aztecs worshipped the mother and earth goddess. One form of this ancient goddess was the deer, one of her names being "the deer of Mixcoatl." The deer was but another symbol for Chichimec culture.

It is further significant that the sanctuaries of Yoaltecatl and Tepeyac both faced the south. The colonial Basílica de Guadalupe also faces south (in the direction of Tenochtitlan-Tlatelolco) with an azimuth of 200° 54′ or nearly 21° W of S, just as the Calzada de los Misterios looks southward by 199° 58′ (Aveni 1988a). It is interesting to note that south-oriented shrines seems to be typical of the cult of mother and earth goddesses not only in Mesoamerica but also in other parts of the Americas (see Broda n.d.[c]). An important part of the contours of the hill of Zacatepetl, as well as of its constructions and pathways, is oriented toward the south, facing Xitle and Ajusco. This orientation was also noticed by the surveyors of the Parsons report (Parsons et al. 1982:237 and 238, fig. 39).

Thus, we might conclude that on both ends of this north-south axis formed by Tepeyac-Yoaltecatl and Zacatepetl-Xitle-Ajusco we find shrines of the mother and earth goddess, a deity who (with the natural environment of these mountains) was related to the Chichimecs. The vegetation pointed to the Chichimec lands of the north, the realm of the god Mixcoatl and the cloud serpents (*mimixcoa*). The toponyms of both areas are full of references to zacate (Zacatepetl in the south and, in the north, around Tepeyac: Zacahuitzco, Zacatenco, Zacacalco, and others [see Map of Santa Isabel Tula of 1795 in *Maravilla Americana* . . . 1989:125]. Mixcoatl, god of the north, and Chimalma, the southern earth goddess, representing maybe the subdued ancient inhabitants of the land, were worshipped in the south of the Valley during the festival of Quecholli, in Chichimec commemoration rites. It is also worth noting that this dialectical juxtaposition between the north and south had its correspondence in toponyms referring to *quauhtli* (the eagle), a highly symbolical animal that was linked to Chichimec lineages of conquerors, to warfare, and to the solar cult. However, eagle feathers were also one of the main elements forming part of the array of the earth goddess. It has to be kept in mind that the Aztecs integrated the cult of the ancient earth mother into a warlike universe obsessed by the spilling of blood. Cihuacoatl became Yaocihuatl, "the warrior woman," and Quauhcihuatl, "the eagle woman." An important polity to the north of the Valley was the Chichimec *señorío* of Quauhtitlan; however, we also find Quauhnahuac to the south, beyond the limits of the Basin. While the northern sierra was Quauhtepec (eagle mountain), the main peak of the Serranía del Ajusco is called until today "the eagle's peak" (El Pico de Aguila). Ajusco and Zacatepetl formed part of the western mountain range of the Valley, an ancient Otomían and Chichimec territory that probably was known to the Aztecs as Quauhtlalpan — "the eagle's land."

7. Final Remarks

The historical study of Aztec society and religion is the point of departure for the present research; to be combined with the disciplines of geography, ecology, the study of cultural landscapes and of astronomical alignments. Investigating the material basis of the ideological phenomena of calendrical orientations and religious cult makes us discover a spatial dimension in the grand drama of Aztec ritual and enables us to reconstruct the ceremonial landscape of the pre-Hispanic Valley of Mexico. Finally, we have noted that there are certain continuities in the syncretism of Catholic Mexican religion in colonial and throughout modern times, embodied in the national cult of the Virgin of Guadalupe.

The southern counterpart to Tepeyac — Zacatepetl — was not selected in the sixteenth century to become an important place of syncretistic worship. The Aztec shrine of Zacatepetl nonetheless stood at a place where some two thousand years ago the inhabitants of the Valley had erected the first great pyramid in worship of their gods. This pyramid occupied a privileged location within the Valley, controlling the view over the Lake of Mexico to the north as well as toward the southern lakes of Xochimilco and Chalco, and it was also an ideal spot from which to view the sun's annual movement on the eastern horizon, along which lie Mt. Tlaloc, Telapon, Papayo, and, above all, Iztac Cihuatl and Popocatepetl. One of the main axes of the Cuicuilco pyramid faces the sunrise at the winter solstice, behind Popocatepetl. The same orientation was reproduced, two thousand years later, by the Aztec temple on top of Zacatepetl.

Thereby we discover one of the many ways in which the Aztecs became the heirs of the civilizations that had preceded them in the old cultural land of the Basin of Mexico. It makes us realize that there operated in pre-Hispanic times a historical consciousness and tradition with respect to "holy places" that became manifest in the existence of certain important sanctuaries. These were closely linked to astronomical observations, and thus, "visual lines" of particularly significant alignments are found to connect them. We are beginning to discover a structured whole of calendrical observations and of the creation of a cultural landscape, based on alignments and geometrical proportions, that seems to have originated in Preclassic times, although, naturally, it continued to evolve during the nearly two millennia that succeeded Cuicuilco as the first major center in the Basin of Mexico. Increasingly, more data accumulate indicating that the Mexica purposefully inserted themselves into this ancient landscape of the Valley and established the island of Tenochtitlan, with Templo Mayor at its center, as the principal pivot of this realm.

Notes

The discussion here is closely connected to (*a*) my previous studies on Aztec ritual, cosmovision, and archaeoastronomy, but adds a different perspective for looking at those subjects that I have been concerned about for many years; (*b*) this new angle from which to view Aztec ritual and society at the capital of Tenochtitlan has been greatly stimulated by my participation in the Mesoamerican Archive meetings, which have established a fruitful interdisciplinary collaboration over the past years. Aztec studies are enriched by analytical concepts derived from the history of religions that David Carrasco has introduced as guiding themes in these meetings, including such categories as "Center and Periphery," "Performance as Place," "The Aztec Vision of Place," "Ceremonial or Ritual Landscape," or the "Respiration of Sacred Space."

I would like to acknowledge the collaboration of the following colleagues at different stages of the research for this chapter: A. Aveni, F. Tichy, D. Carrasco, P. Arnold, A. Robles, and I. Sprajc with respect to the archaeoastronomy and cultural geography of the Basin of Mexico. To X. Noguez I owe the discussion of pre-Hispanic historical data derived from codices and colonial sources, and to him I am indebted for sharing with me his thoughts on the history of the cult of the Virgin of Guadalupe at Tepeyac and on the symbolic connotations of place-names in that area.

1. For an extensive bibliography on mountain worship in Mesoamerica, including historical, archaeological, and ethnographic data, see Broda (in press).

2. See Tichy 1976, 1981, 1983, 1988. Tichy (in press) provides a synthesis of his research of more than fifteen years in a major book that brings together his varied and rich studies of these subjects. From the point of view of the present investigation, I consider of particular interest the approach of human or historical geography, and the study of cultural landscapes — specialized fields of research that have a strong tradition in Germany and are particularly apt to be combined with the study of pre-Hispanic worldviews, or cosmovision, as Tichy's work shows.

3. See, to mention only some of his major publications, Aveni 1980, 1981, 1988a, 1989a; and the edited works 1975, 1977, 1988b, 1989b. See also Aveni and Urton 1982, and Aveni, Calnek, and Hartung 1988.

4. Parsons 1971; Parsons et al. 1982, 1983; Sanders, Parsons, and Santley 1979; Blanton 1972; see also Wolf (ed.) 1976.

5. The roman numerals refer to the sequence of the months within the yearly cycle as indicated by Bernardino de Sahagún. According to this chronicler, the first month of the year was I Atlcahualo. This terminology is used here for the purpose of better orientation concerning the place of a month in the sequence of the eighteen periods, but it does not imply any judgment concerning

the beginning of the year, which still constitutes an unresolved problem within the investigation on the pre-Hispanic calendar.

6. These expressions are used by Sahagún (1950–1982, bk. II:126) in the context of the feast of Quecholli.

7. In the time span between its two zenith passages, the sun travels to the north, events that coincide with the beginning and climax of the rainy season. E. Thompson (1970:249) pointed out that in some Mayan languages "the north is described as 'from here [proceeds] the water.' " The north was also associated with the planet Venus and with maize (Sprajc 1989:47). This coincidence between solar and Venusian phenomena, both being visible toward the north at the full onset of the rainy season, reinforced this meaning and established a link with the agricultural cycle of maize. Sahagún's informants describe the north as "the land of the mimixcoa, or cloud serpents" (Garibay 1961:49, 103, quoted by Sprajc 1989:47). Yet, from another angle, the north, "the land of the mimixcoa," was also the land of the Chichimecs, whose god was Mixcoatl.

8. The variations of the names of the different peaks of this sierra according to different sources are striking. The modern name of the whole range is Sierra de Guadalupe. I am assuming that the generic name for the sierra in pre-Hispanic times was Quauhtepec since there subsist several settlements on the foot of the southern and northern slopes that preserve the same name: Cuautepec El Alto; Cuautepec de Madero; San Mateo Cuautepec; and Santa María Cuautepec. The highest peak of the range is El Picacho (3,050 m) which is extremely steep and inaccessible. Today, the most frequented summit is Pico Tres Padres (3,020 m), which has an easy path of access. According to González Aparicio (1973, map) its former name was Cerro Tontepec. I am here identifying Pico Tres Padres with Cerro Quauhtepetl to which the Aztecs ascended during I Atlcahualo because of the ruins of the sanctuary found there.

9. X. Noguez called my attention to the fact that Quetzalxoch is the reverse of Xochiquetzal. As I have shown elsewhere (1971, 1979, 1987b), the goddess Xochiquetzal was intimately related to Chalchiuhtlicue, the goddess of the sweet waters of the lake and wife of Tlaloc, as well as to the earth goddess Cihuacoatl-Toci.

10. See also Gónzalez Aparicio (1973:43–49) who was the first to call attention to the strategic position of Tepetzinco within the Valley and with respect to the urban planning of Tenochtitlan-Tlatelolco.

11. In the case of Tepeyac, these rock carvings, obliterated today, represented Aztec female fertility deities (Noguez, personal communication; Pasztory 1983:132).

12. The city is rapidly expanding to cover this hilltop, and it will soon no longer be possible to study this site. According to the guards of the Secretaría de Desarrollo Urbano y Ecología, which administers this reserve, cultivation on the hilltop began some twenty-five years ago; naturally, the damage done to the archaeological remains is irreparable.

13. These sherds are Aztec or Tetzcocan late Postclassic and include Fine Orange and *guinda* with white decoration. They come from ceremonial vessels and braziers including sophisticated incense ladles similar to those found in the excavation of the Templo Mayor.

14. I was struck by the fact that the famous nineteenth-century Mexican painter José María Velasco depicted exactly this view in one of his most important early paintings, *View from the Mountain of Atzacualco* (1873). In the foreground a group of Indian women performs a traditional rite of worship addressed to an image of the Virgin of Guadalupe; this rite takes place at sunset at "Atzacualco"; i.e., certain boulders at the foot of the hill of Los Gachupines just in front of Yoaltecatl (Cf. Altamirano, n.d.). (I want to thank María Elena Altamirano for calling my attention to this yet unpublished painting by Velasco, hung in a private collection, Mexico City and for discussing the work of the painter with me.) According to my interpretation, this rite — as well as the view that leads beyond the Tepeyac and the basilica toward the towns of México-Tlatelolco and the Serranía del Ajusco in the background — may very well reflect a traditional viewing perspective of pre-Hispanic roots. It is worthwhile to investigate further how far this famous painter of the landscape of the Basin of Mexico was influenced by such traditional viewing perspectives that singled out certain historical landmarks of the Valley.

15. This orientation follows exactly the contour lines down from Yoaltecatl toward the south and along the foot of the eastern slope of Cerro Los Gachupines, toward the southeastern edge of Tepeyac, which is, precisely, the point of its oldest constructions near El Pozo, a spring of curative waters. The orientation of the causeway is 213° or 33° W of S (compass measurements, J. B. June 20, 1989). The guard on duty also told me that this used to be the footpath taken by local people down to the basilica.
16. This is documented in two paintings: the work by Velasco (see n. 14 above) and a famous anonymous painting dated 1653 that depicts the inauguration of the shrine of the Virgin of Guadalupe (Noguez 1989). Rites involving mothers with small children also took place during the month of XIV Quecholli that were related to Cerro Zacatepetl (see last section of this chapter).
17. "Donde se tapa el agua" (where the water is obstructed; González Aparicio 1973: map) or "donde grita el agua" (where the water yells; X. Noguez, personal communication).
18. I. Sprajc and A. Ponce de León called my attention to this fact; calculations by I. Sprajc based on his own transit measurements of the ruins on Mt. Tlaloc (Iwaniszewski & Sprajc 1987).
19. According to Aveni (Aveni, Calnek & Hartung 1988: 301), this 125-meter-long, walled pathway has an alignment of 281° 30′ or 11° 30′ N of W; the axis of the ground plan faces 273° 30′ and is thus directly on line with the Templo Mayor.
20. E. Noguera mentioned, in 1940 (p. 38), a sanctuary to Tlaloc at the archaeological site of "Cerro de las Palomas o de la Campana, cerca de Salazar, en el camino a Toluca," which I have not been able to locate.
21. To Andrés Medina and Beatriz Albores I owe many stimulating comments on the presence of Otomían cultural elements in the Basin of Mexico.
22. I will return to this point in the last section of this chapter.
23. Yet, it is worthwhile noting that from Cerro Cocotl a solstitial line (26° W of N) leads to the Cerro de la Estrella (Tichy, in press).
24. Temamatla is currently being excavated by Mari-Carmen Serra Puche and Noel Morelos in an archaeological project of the Instituto de Investigaciones Antropológicas, Universidad Nacional Autónoma de México (see Serra Puche 1988).
25. A "cloud vessel" instead of the customary "eagle vessel" (*cuauhxicalli*) was used on this occasion.
26. Although I have only recently initiated this investigation, I felt compelled to include it in this presentation since my discoveries related to Zacatepetl (Quecholli) and Cerro Yoaltecatl-Tepeyac, in a way, motivated and stimulated this whole lengthy chapter with its many varied elements.
27. A. Ponce de León, I. Sprajc, A. Robles, and C. Good also participated in some of the visits to Zacatepetl. I want to thank I. Sprajc for the transit measurements and calculations that he kindly made for me and that are cited in this chapter.
28. From Mound KK toward Cerro del Judío the azimuth is 283° 46′ (transit measurement I. Sprajc). Cerro del Judío is a conspicuous peak to the northwest, with unexplored archaeological remains, that must have been very important in pre-Hispanic times. Its ancient name apparently was Mazatepetl, or deer mountain (A. Medina, personal communication).
29. For more details on the archaeological site, see J. Parsons et al. (1982:237 and 238, fig. 39 [Site Xo-Az-91]) and Parsons (n.d.). I want to thank Phil Arnold for having provided me with Parsons's notes on Zacatepetl.
30. A magnificent example of these natural lava formations can be seen in the modern artistic project of El Espacio Escultórico, on the terrain of El Centro Cultural, Ciudad Universitaria.
31. Since I cannot remit myself in this case to a previous publication on the festival, my account has to be somewhat more detailed than in the other examples I have cited in this chapter. There exists an excellent analysis of the mythical themes of Quecholli by M. Graulich (1979–1980, vol. 2:468–86) that forms part of his global study of the mythical structure of Aztec calendar festivals.

Graulich's interpretation proved very useful for the present analysis. The main sources for Quecholli are Sahagún, Durán, and some anonymous texts and Indian annals. Eduard Seler (1960–1961, vol. 2:1018ff.), at the beginning of the century, also made some lucid comments on Quecholli and the cult of Mixcoat.

32. Zacatepetl, "un cerro que está en los montes de Cuyuacan . . . tres leguas de México" (Gómez de Orozco 1945:50); "Esta montaña o ladera donde iban a cazar llamaban Zacatepec" and was situated in "aquella sierra que estaba encima de Atlacuihuayan" (Sahagún 1956, bk. II, vol. 1:204).

33. This is one of the rare festivals for which participation of the Tlatelolca is specifically mentioned, in contrast to the Tenochca (Sahagún 1950–1982, bk. II:124).

34. The arrow bundles remind one of the offerings of ritually bundled objects (zacate, pine needles, or reed) that are documented from recent ethnographic accounts on the Tlapanecs and Mixtecs of Guerrero recorded by Schultze-Jena (1938), Nowotny (1961:272), and Loo (1987); there, these offerings form part of hunting rites belonging to the mountain cult.

35. They were painted black around eyes and mouth, were adorned by eagle feathers, and their legs were painted with white stripes.

36. Graulich 1979–1980, vol. 2:470–71; see also Seler 1960–1961, vol. 2:1018ff.

37. Graulich 1979–1980, vol. 2:472, 485; Motolonía 1967:9; Mendieta 1945, vol. 1:159–60.

38. Due to the fortunate circumstance that Zacatepetl belongs today to the wealthy residential area of El Pedregal de San Angel, it has managed to escape from total urbanization so far. There is some encroachment on its eastern side; however, to the west, north, and south, the hill is free of modern construction. Zacatepetl, today, gives the impression of a private natural reserve. The several streets on its eastern side are blocked to the traffic and watched over by private guards. The view to the east, being situated in front of the biggest modern shopping center of Latin America, called Perisur, is overwhelming when one considers that the Aztec ruins on the summit still give testimony of the existence of the important pre-Hispanic sanctuary. On the llano (plain), where according to the chroniclers the Tenochca and Tlatelolca spent the night before their ritual hunt, there lie today Perisur and the elegant villas that extend as far as the ecological reserve of El Bosque del Pedregal. This park includes a range of small mountains, probably with archaeological remains, that may once have formed part of Zacatepetl, but today the connection between this range of hills and Zacatepetl is interrupted by the passage of the urban highway of El Periférico. At the southern limits of El Bosque del Pedregal there are the remains of the huge Preclassic structure of Tenantongo that belonged to the Cuicuilco settlement but was not covered by the lava flow of the eruption of Xitle. Therefore Tenantongo must have been known to the Aztecs, and I propose the hypothesis that it may have formed part of the sanctuary on sixteenth-century Zacatepetl.

39. More precisely speaking, the sun appears to rise behind the Postclassic site of Collado de Nexpayantla on the northern slope of Popocatepetl (Ponce de León, personal communication; see also Ponce de León 1983:90–91, where he gives the alignments for Cuicuilco [these are equally valid for Zacatepetl]).

40. Today they are hardly ever visible due to the smog that is particularly heavy in this part of the Basin.

41. The actual N-S line connected Tepeyac with the ancient Toltec town of Culhuacan (see Figure 7.2). This circumstance is in itself remarkable; however, it is not relevant for the present argument.

42. It needs to be further investigated to what extent this alignment coincided with the one of 27° noted by Tichy (1983, fig. 4) that led from Ajusco to Templo Mayor and may be prolonged as far as Ecatepec (fig. 6). That would mean that the proposed N-S axis passed, almost exactly, through the "very Center," or Templo Mayor of Tenochtitlan. It is not necessary to point out the interest of this argument.

References

Altamirano Piolle, María Elena
n.d. *José María Velasco* (book in preparation).

Arnold, Philip P.
1986 The Aztec ceremonial landscape in the Valley of Mexico: Implications of examining religion and environment. M.A. diss., Institute of Archaeology, University of London.

1989 Eating landscape: human sacrifice and sustenance in Aztec Mexico. Paper presented at the History of Religions Colloquium, University of Chicago, spring.

Aveni, Anthony F.
1980 *Skywatchers of ancient Mexico.* Austin: University of Texas Press.

1981 Archaeoastronomy. In *Advances in Archaeological Method and Theory,* vol. 4, New York: Academic Press.

1988a Preliminary report of fieldwork undertaken in Mexico, January 1988. Unpublished manuscript.

1989a Mapping the ritual landscape: The debt payment to Tlaloc during the month of Atlcahualo. Paper presented at the Mesoamerican Archive Symposium on Aztec Ceremonial Landscapes: Focusing on Specifics, Museo del Templo Mayor, Mexico City, June.

Aveni, Anthony F., ed.
1975 *Archaeoastronomy in pre-Columbian America.* Austin: University of Texas Press.

1977 *Native American astronomy.* Austin: University of Texas Press.

1988b *New directions in American archaeoastronomy.* BAR International Series, no. 454. Oxford.

1989b *World archaeoastronomy.* Cambridge: Cambridge University Press.

Aveni, Anthony F., Edward Calnek, and Horst Hartung
1988 Myth, environment and the orientation of the Templo Mayor of Tenochtitlan. *American Antiquity* 53, no. 2:287–309.

Aveni, Anthony F., and Gary Urton, eds.
1982 *Ethnoastronomy and archaeoastronomy in the American tropics.* Annals of the New York Academy of Sciences, no. 385. New York: New York Academy of Sciences.

Barlow, Robert
1949 *The extent of the empire of the Culhua-Mexica.* Ibero-Americana, no. 28. Berkeley: University of California Press.

Blanton, Richard R.
1972 Prehispanic settlement patterns of the Ixtapala Peninsula region. Occasional Papers in Anthropology, no. 6. University Park: Pennsylvania State University Department of Anthropology.

Boehm de Lameiras, Brigitte
1986 *Formación del estado en el México prehispánico.* Zamora: El Colegio de Michoacán.

Broda, Johanna
1971 Las fiestas aztecas de los dioses de la lluvia. *Revista Española de Antropología Americana* 6:245–327.

1978 Relaciones políticas ritualizadas: El ritual como expresión de una ideología. In *Economía política e ideología en el México prehispánico,* edited by Pedro Carrasco and Johanna Broda. Mexico City:CIESAS–Nueva Imagen.

1979 Estratificación social y ritual mexica. *Indiana* 5:45–82.

1982 El culto mexica de los cerros y del agua. *Multidisciplina* 3, no. 7:45–56. Escuela Nacional de Estudios Profesionales Acatlan, UNAM.

1987a The provenience of the offerings: Tribute and cosmovision. In *The Aztec Templo Mayor,* edited by Elizabeth H. Boone. Washington, DC: Dumbarton Oaks Library and Collection.

1987b Templo Mayor as ritual space. In *The great temple of Tenochtitlan: Center and periphery in the Aztec world.* Johanna Broda, Davíd Carrasco, and Eduardo Matos. Berkeley: University of California Press.

1989 Geography, climate and the observation of nature in pre-Hispanic Mesoamerica. In *The imagination of matter: Religion and ecology in Mesoamerican traditions,* edited by Davíd Carrasco BAR International Series, no. 515. Oxford.

In press Cosmovisión y observación de la naturaleza: El ejemplo del culto de los cerros. In *Arqueoastronomía y etnoastronomía en Mesoamérica,* edited by Johanna Broda, Stanislaw Iwaniszewski, and Lucrecia Maupomé. Mexico City: Universidad Nacional Autónoma de México, Instituto de Investigaciones Históricas.

n.d.(a) El culto del maíz, del sol y del inframundo en Tecuilhuitontli/Huey tecuilhuitl. Unpublished manuscript.

n.d.(b) Significant dates of the Mesoamerican agricultural calendar and archaeoastronomy. Unpublished manuscript.

n.d.(c) Malinalco: Santuario solar y calendárico de los aztecas. Unpublished manuscript.

Carrasco, Davíd

1982 *Quetzalcoatl and the Irony of Empire.* Chicago: University of Chicago Press.

Carrasco, Pedro

1950 *Los Otomíes.* Mexico City: Universidad Nacional Autónoma de México, Instituto de Historia.

Charnay, Desiré

1973 *The ancient cities of the New World, being voyages and explorations in Mexico and Central America from 1857–1882.* Antiquities of the New World, no. 10. Early Explorations in Archaeology. Cambridge, MA: 1887; AMS Press, Peabody Museum of Archaeology and Ethnology, Harvard University.

Cooper Clark, James, ed. and trans.

1938 *Codex Mendoza: The Mexican manuscript known as the Collection of Mendoza and preserved in the Bodleian Library, Oxford.* 3 vols. London: Waterlow and Sons.

Durán, Fray Diego

1967 *Historia de las indias de Nueva España,* 2 vols. edited by Angel María Garibay. Mexico City: Porrúa.

Garibay, Angel María

1961 *Vida económica de Tenochtitlan: Pochtecayotl.* Fuentes Indígenas de la Cultura Nahuatl: Informantes de Sahagún, no. 3. Mexico City: Universidad Nacional Autónoma de México, Instituto de Historia.

Gibson, Charles

1967 *Los aztecas bajo el dominio español, 1519–1810.* Mexico City: Siglo XXI.

Gómez de Orozco, F., ed.

1945 Costumbres, fiestas, enterramientos y diversas formas de proceder de los indios de Nueva España. *Tlalocan* 2, no. 1:37–63.

Gónzalez Aparicio, Luís

1973 *Plano reconstructivo de la región de Tenochtitlan.* Mexico City: Instituto Nacional de Antropología e Historia.

Graulich, Michél

1979–1980 Mythes et rites des Vingtaines du Mexique central prehispanique. 3 vols. Doctoral diss., Université Libre de Bruxelles, Belgium.

Historia de los Mexicanos (HMP)

1941 Historia de los mexicanos por sus pinturas. In *Colección de documentos para la historia de México.* Vol. 1, *Relaciones de Texcoco y de los señores de la Nueva España.* Juan Bautista Pomar and Alonso de Zurita. Mexico City: S. Chávez Hayhoe.

Iwaniszewski, Stanislaw

1986a De Nahualac al Cerro Ehécatl: Una tradición prehispánica más en Petlacala. In *Arqueología y etnohistoria del Estado de Guerrero.* Mexico City: Instituto Nacional de Antropología e Historia and Gobierno del Estado de Guerrero.

1986b La arqueología de alta montaña en México y su estado actual. *Estudios de Cultura Náhuatl* 18:249–73.

Iwaniszewski, Stanislaw, and Iván Sprajc

1987 Field reconnaissance and mapping of the archaeological site at Mt. Tlaloc, December. Unpublished manuscript and map.

Loo, Peter L. van der

1987 *Códices costumbres continuidad: Un estudio de la religión mesoamericana.* Indiaanse Studies, no. 2. Leiden: Archaeologisch Centrum R.U. Leiden.

Lorenzo, José Luís

1957 *Las zonas arqueológicas de los volcanes Iztaccíhuatl y Popocatepetl.* In Dirección de Prehistoria, no. 3. Mexico City: Instituto Nacional de Antropología e Historia.

Map of Sta. Isabel Tula of 1795

1989 In *Maravilla Americana: Variantes de la Iconografía Guadalupaua, siglos XVII–XIX.* Patrimonio Cultural del Occidente, A.C. Mexico.

Martínez del Río, Pablo

1934 Les Chasses "Chacu" au Mexique et les ruines du Zacatepec. *Journal de la Société des Américanistes* 26:293–300.

Mendieta, Fray Gerónimo de

1971 *Historia eclesiástica indiana.* Mexico City: Porrúa.

Molina, Fray Alonso de

1970 *Vocabulario en lengua castellana y mexicana y mexicana y castellan.* Facsimile ed. 1571; Mexico City: Porrúa.

Montero García, I. Arturo

1988 Iztaccíhuatl: Arqueología en alta montaña. Thesis, Escuela Nacional de Antropología e Historia, Mexico City.

Motolinía, Fray Toribio de

1967 *Memoriales,* edited by Luís García Pimentel. Facsimile ed. of 1903. Reprint. Guadalajara: Editorial E. Aviña Levy.

Noguera, Eduardo

1940 Los monumentos arqueológicos y la cerámica de Zacatepec. *Revista Mexicana de Estudios Antropológicos* 4, no. 1–2:16–43.

Noguez, Xavier

1989 An anonymous painting of 1653 from the collection of the Museum of the Basílica de Guadalupe. Lecture read at the Instituto de Investigaciones Estéticas, Universidad Nacional Autónoma de México, October.

n.d. *Cuáuhyotl* y *oceloyotl.* Un problema de status adscritos y adquiridos en la sociedad mexica prehispanica. In *Historia Mexicana.* Centro de Estudios Historicos, El Colegio de México (in press).

Nowotny, Karl Anton

1961 *Tlacuilolli.* Monumenta Americana, no. 3. Berlin: Verlag Gebr. Mann.

1971 Rituale in Mexiko und im Nordamerikanischen Südwesten. *Jahrbuch für Geschichte von Staat, Wirtschaft und Gesellschaft Lateinamerikas* 8:4–38. Cologne: Böhlau Verlag.

Palerm, Angel

1973 *Obras hidráulicas prehispánicas en el sistema lacustre del Valle de México.* Mexico City: Instituto Nacional de Antropología e Historia.

Parsons, Jeffrey R.

1971 *Prehistoric settlement patterns in the Texcoco region, Mexico.* Memoirs of the Museum of Anthropology, no. 3. Ann Arbor: University of Michigan.

n.d. Valley of Mexico survey. Unpublished field notes.

Parsons, Jeffrey R., et al.

1982 *Prehistoric settlement patterns in the southern Valley of Mexico, the Chalco-Xochimilco region.* Memoirs of the Museum of Anthropology, no. 14. Ann Arbor: University of Michigan.

1983 *Archaeological settlement pattern data from the Chalco, Xochimilco, Ixtapalapa, Texcoco and Zumpango Regions, Mexico.* Museum of Anthropology Technical Reports, no. 14. Research Reports in Archaeology, no. 9. Ann Arbor: University of Michigan.

Pasztory, Esther

1983 *Aztec art.* New York: H. N. Abrams.

Ponce de León, Arturo

1983 Fechamiento arqueoastronómico en el altiplano de México. In *Calendars in Mesoamerica and Peru: Native computations of time,* edited by Anthony F. Aveni and Gordon Brotherston. BAR International Series, no. 174. Oxford.

Rickards, Constantine G.

1929 The ruins of Tlaloc, State of Mexico. *Journal de la Société des Américanistes* 21:197–99.

Sahagún, Fray Bernardino de

1950–1982 *Florentine Codex: General history of the things of New Spain.* translated and edited by Arthur J. O. Anderson and Charles Dibble. 12 bks. in 13 pts. Santa Fe: School of American Research and the University of Utah.

1956 *Historia general de las cosas de Nueva España,* edited by Angel María Garibay. 4 vols. Mexico City: Porrúa.

1958 *Ritos, sacerdotes y atavíos de los dioses.* Translated by M. León-Portilla. Fuentes Indígenas de la Cultura Nahuatl: Informantes de Sahagún, no. 1. Mexico City: Universidad Nacional Autónoma de México, Instituto de Historia.

Sanders, William T., Jeffrey R. Parsons, and Robert S. Santley

1979 *The Basin of Mexico: Ecological processes in the evolution of a civilization.* New York: Academic Press.

Schultze-Jena, Leonhard

1938 *Bei den Azteken, Mixteken und Tlapaneken der Sierra Madre del Sur von Mexiko.* Indiana, vol. 3. Jena: G. Fischer-Verlag.

Seler, Eduard

1960–1961 *Gesammelte Abhandlungen zur amerikanischen Sprach- und Altertumskunde.* 5 vols. Facsimile ed. Graz: Akademische Druck- und Verlagsanstalt.

Serra Puche, Mari-Carmen

1988 *Los recursos lacustres de la Cuenca de México durante el Formativo.* Coordinación General de Estudios de Posgrado, A. Instituto de Investigaciones Antropológicas. Mexico City: Universidad Nacional Autónoma de México.

Sprajc, Iván

1989 Venus, lluvia y maíz: Simbolismo y astronomía en la cosmovsión mesoamericana. Diss., Escuela Nacional de Antropología e Historia, Mexico City.

Tezozómoc, Hernando Alvarado

1949 *Crónica Mexicayotl.* Translated by Adrián León. Mexico City: Universidad Nacional Autónoma de México, Instituto de Historia.

Thompson, J. Eric S.

1970 *Maya history and religion.* Norman: University of Oklahoma Press.

Tichy, Franz

1976 *Orientación de las pirámides e iglesias en el altiplano mexicano.* Suplemento Comunicaciones, no. 4. Puebla: Fundación Alemana para la Investigación Científica.

1981 Order and relationship of space and time in Mesoamerica: Myth or reality? In *Mesoamerican sites and world-views,* edited by Elizabeth P. Benson. Washington, DC: Dumbarton Oaks.

1983 El patrón de asentamientos con sistema radial en la meseta central de México: "Sistemas ceque" en Mesoamérica? *Jahrbuch für Geschichte von Staat, Wirtschaft und Gesellschaft Lateinamerikas* 20:61–84. Cologne: Böhlau Verlag.

1988 Measurement of angles in Mesoamerica: Necessity and possibility. In *New directions in American archaeoastronomy,* edited by Anthony F. Aveni. BAR International Series, no. 454. Oxford.

In press *Die geordnete Welt indianischer Völker: Ein Beispiel von Raumordnung und Zeitordnung im Vorkolumbischen Mexiko.* Wiesbaden: Franz Steiner-Verlag.

Townsend, Richard F.

1982 Pyramid and sacred mountain. In *Ethnoastronomy and archaeoastronomy in the American tropics,* edited by Anthony F. Aveni and Gary Urton. Annals of the New York Academy of Sciences, no. 385. New York: New York Academy of Sciences.

Wicke, Charles, and Fernando Horcasitas

1957 Archaeological investigations on Monte Tlaloc, México. *Mesoamerican Notes* 5:83–96.

Wolf, Eric R., ed.

1976 *The Valley of Mexico: Studies in pre-Hispanic ecology and society.* School of American Research Book. Albuquerque: University of New Mexico Press.

8

Migration Histories as Ritual Performance

Elizabeth Hill Boone

In working with the pictorial codices that present the history of the Aztec migration from Aztlan to Tenochtitlan, I am struck by the very humanness of the migration story. It is not that the narrative is particularly personal in itself; in fact, the opposite is the case: Named individuals are only occasionally distinguished. Rather, the migration is a period of impersonal tribal movement and activity guided by the deity Huitzilopochtli. It is the story of a people rather than of persons.

The Aztec pictorial manuscripts, however, present the migration story in decidedly human terms. In order to record the movement of the Mexica through time and space, they depict the movement of human figures, who appear and reappear at irregular intervals along the journey. The whole conception, and particularly the way the drama of the migration is presented on a human level, recalls a play. In fact, the migration pictorials have the peculiar visual quality of a stage set, as if they are rendering scenes in a play. The human figures drawn in the codices are the actors, whose actions bring the story line to life. The different episodes of the migration are like the individual dramatic scenes that convey both time and location, so that a change in scene signals a change in time, in location, or both. The journey itself is the foundation of the narrative or the story line, with individual scenes or episodes defined and separated as they would be in a play. The pictorial codices narrate the migration story by showing the actors in their specific roles as the narration moves from scene to scene.

What the narrative strategy of the pictorial manuscripts suggests is that the Aztec migration from Aztlan to Tenochtitlan is a drama. More than being a series of events that happened in the past, it has the qualities of a performance. It can be thought of as a historical or narrative play, but it is too ideologically and culturally important to be merely a secular play. It has all the trappings and stylizations of a ceremony, and I think it most similar to a ritual performance — in particular a ritual performance of great social and ideological significance for the Mexica and for all of the later Aztec world.

Thus, I argue that the migration can effectively and revealingly be analyzed as a ritual, with the migration histories recording its performance. In this sense, the migration ritual is not altogether different from some of the monthly feast ceremonies at which the celebration carries the participants from place to place. In the migration, the Mexica move from location to location; they do things or things happen to them at some of these locations, and these ideologically significant events transform them. I will argue at the end that they return to their point of origin, for I believe that Tenochtitlan is a re-creation in the Valley of Mexico of Aztlan.[1] Thus, like some of the monthly feast ceremonies, the Mexica travel in a vague circuit along a ritual path and are transformed in the process.

The kind of ritual being enacted is a rite of passage, by which the Mexicas undergo a profound change in social and ideological status, from a small nomadic band to a people appropriate as rulers of Mesoamerica. The whole manner in which the migration is presented shows it to have great importance in validating Mexica rule.

Sources for the Migration History

The Aztec or Mexica migration is recorded pictorially and textually in a score of documents preserved from the sixteenth century. All of them, like all existing Aztec manuscripts, were created after the conquest, but many are direct reflections of pre-Columbian codices or oral recitations. The fullest of the records are those that fall within the specific genre of migration histories, and these migration histories themselves fall into two general categories.

First there are the pictorial codices that, although they were painted after the conquest, are largely native in their conception and presentation; at a minimum they preserve parts of the native tradition of manuscript painting. There are basically ten painted codices that pertain to the Mexican migration. The Codex Boturini, the Codex Azcatitlan, the Codex Mexicanus, the Codex Aubin, and the Mapa Sigüenza are the most important, detailed, and complete, but the cognate codices Telleriano-

Remensis and Vaticanus A/Ríos, the Tira de Tepechpan, and Fonds Mexicain numbers 40 and 85 also recount the migration in varying degrees of detail. The Codex Mendoza pictures the founding of Tenochtitlan but not the events preceding it.

To these pictorial accounts can be added a dozen or so textual sources for the migration. Some, like the Historia de los Mexicanos por sus Pinturas (of c. 1533) and the Historia de Tlatelolco (of 1528) are first-generation copies or readings from pictorial histories.[2] Others are later derivations that have been recast along the conventions of European narrative presentation; the migration histories of Diego Durán, Juan de Tovar, José de Acosta, Fernando de Alvarado Tezozómoc, and the other manuscripts of the Crónica X group fall into this category, as do the works of Bernardino de Sahagún, Juan de Torquemada, and Cristóbal del Castillo.[3] These textual sources are fundamentally useful for understanding the events of the migration story, for they chronicle it with a richness possible in a verbal record. But because they are written transcriptions or translations of oral accounts and earlier pictorial documents, they are further from the indigenous presentation and thus are of less use in understanding the original structure of the migration story and the manner in which it was cast and recorded by the Aztecs themselves before the conquest. For this, one must rely more heavily on the existing pictorial codices.

Of the major migration codices, the Mapa Sigüenza is the only one structured as a cartographic history, wherein events are presented sequentially on a geographic foundation in the form of a map (see Figure 8.1). In many cases such a map presents a conceptualized geography that corresponds in a general sense to the arrangement of sites and geographic features on the ground; it may be cartographically accurate in some areas, and in other areas be a conventional landscape without direct links to actual distances or directions. The cartographic form of presenting history is an efficient way of recording a people's journey from location to location, and it is a particularly useful form for the migration, in which movement through space is the principal message.

In the upper-right quadrant of the Mapa Sigüenza, the Aztecs leave their island homeland of Aztlan, here rendered as a green hill in the center of a watery square. The leaders of the tribe, shown standing in two files, are identified by name-glyphs above their heads. From Aztlan, the migration proceeds visually by a path marked by footprints, from site to site,

Figure 8.1. Mapa Sigüenza. Photograph reprinted from Zertuche Muñoz and Molina Tapia, eds., *El territorio mexicano* (Mexico City, 1982), by permission of the publisher.

each site identified glyphically. The path leads around the upper-right quadrant in a roughly counterclockwise direction to the lower right, then to the far upper left, and then to Chapultepec, the "hill of the grasshopper" situated prominently in the left side of the sheet. With Chapultepec, the Aztecs have entered the lakeside, and the presentation becomes inverted. Once the map is turned upside down, the visual narrative follows the Aztecs through several other relocations until they are finally forced into the middle of the swamp to settle at Tenochtitlan, depicted as a nopal cactus on a rock (below and to the right of Chapultepec in Figure 8.1). In this cartographic presentation of the migration, all the locations are recorded, and the action is indicated by footprints along the migratory path. The protagonists of the story, the Aztecs, are identified at the beginning and again at the end where the secular tribal leader, Tenoch, and some of his captains are named glyphically. The passage of time is both implied by the journey and stated by the blue discs painted beside each place-glyph that record the number of years the Aztecs lingered in each location. No concrete dates are given.

Figure 8.2. Codex Boturini, p. 1. The Mexica leave Aztlan. Photographs of Codex Boturini panels are reprinted from Corona Núñez, ed., *Antigüedades de México* (Mexico City, 1964), by permission of the publisher.

Whereas the Mapa Sigüenza uses the map form as the armature of the story and subsumes the actions and dates, the migration histories of the codices Aubin, Azcatitlan, and Boturini construct the narrative around the year-dates and the events. In these manuscripts the Aztec painters have combined the continuous year-count annal with an event-oriented history;[4] all the years are given, but the count of the years halts for each event.

The Codex Boturini, for example, is a screenfold manuscript, to be read as a long strip left to right. On page 1 (see Figure 8.2) the Aztecs leave the island of Aztlan, canoeing across the lake to a place identified as a bent hill (Culhuacan), where they erect a rude temple to their titulary deity Huitzilopochtli, identified by the hummingbird-helmeted face. The year they left Aztlan, 1 Flint, is prominently displayed. Eight groups, each identified by a house and a seated leader and distinguished one from another by their name-signs, leave together (see Figure 8.3). Four tribal leaders (identified by their name-glyphs) carry the image and insignia of Huitzilopochtli in bundles on their backs. They travel to a place where a

Figure 8.3. Codex Boturini, p. 2. The eight tribes are seen on the left and four god-bearers on the right.

tree miraculously breaks, after which one of the eight groups (the Acolhua) separates out and leaves the others. From there the journey continues until they reach an unnamed place where they perform ritual sacrifices. The migration proceeds to Chocayan (place of tears) and then immediately to Coatepec (hill of the serpent), where they settle for twenty-eight years (see Figures 8.4–8.5). All of these years at Coatepec are named, clustered in a boustrophedon fashion, reading from the lower left (2 House) to the right (3 Flint). In the year 2 Reed, toward the end of their stay, they celebrated a New Fire ceremony to mark the beginning of a new fifty-two–year cycle; this is signaled by a reed drill creating smoke from a fire board. The migration is largely uneventful, but where significant events occurred, the artist has depicted some of them graphically.

The journey continues in this manner from place-glyph to place-glyph until they reach Chapultepec along the shores of Lake Texcoco in the valley (see Figure 8.6). After this the Codex Boturini details some of the deprivations that befall the Aztecs (see Figure 8.7) and, regrettably, breaks off

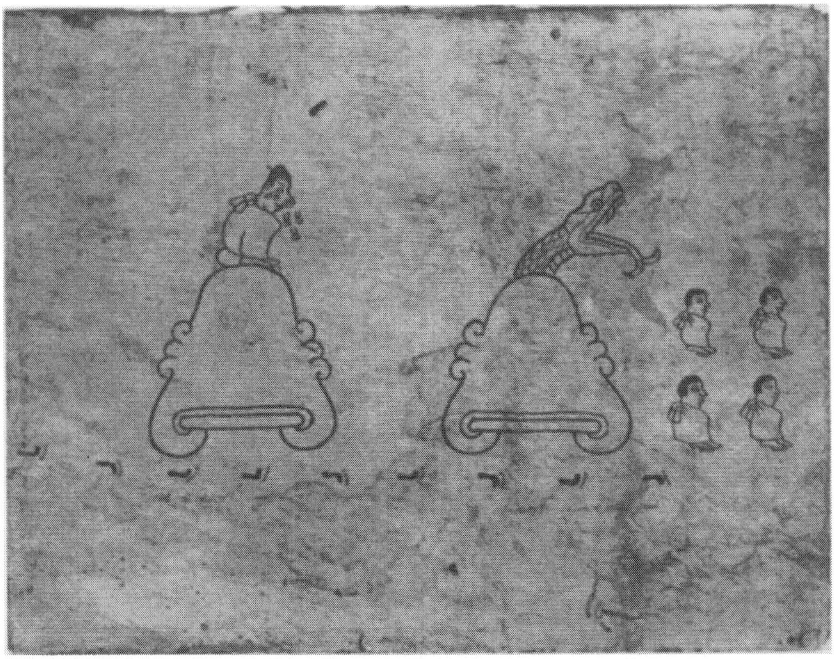

Figure 8.4. Codex Boturini, p. 5. The Mexica arrive at Coatepec.

before they finally settle and found their city of Tenochtitlan. The Codex Boturini is fragmentary, but it is important because it fixes the various components of the migration firmly in time and details some of the significant events in the story in a way that is impossible in a cartographically based presentation. Its format, which presents all the sequent years but stops time to present individual actions and events, allows it to be temporally specific and to provide the details of the action.

The Codex Aubin has a similar structure, except that it is more static and conventionalized, it moves less fluidly from scene to scene, and the human quality of its story is reduced because its actors appear less frequently. Painted on European paper bound as a book, the Codex Aubin has lost the transitional and directional footprints, and the narrative is thus presented as a series of individual, still shots rather than as movement from scene to scene, but the Aubin is nearly identical to the Boturini in its content. The migration begins with Aztlan as an island city, from which the same eight groups leave (see Figure 8.8); the groups are named in the

Figure 8.5. Codex Boturini, p. 6. The count of the years at Coatepec.

Nahuatl text but not indicated glyphically. Then the narrative proceeds with the god-bearers to the scene with the tree and continues on to Coatepec (see Figures 8.9–8.10). At Coatepec a New Fire is celebrated as it was recorded in the Codex Boturini. The years of the stay at Coatepec are depicted first, whereas in the Codex Boturini they are depicted after the place-sign. The migration continues onward past Tollan and to Chapultepec (see Figure 8.11). As in the Codex Boturini, the migration story is presented in more detail from Chapultepec onward, until the founding of Tenochtitlan (see Figure 8.12).

The Codex Azcatitlan is fairly detailed throughout its presentation. Painted on European paper that is bound as a book, the Azcatitlan manuscript is considerably acculturated. For example, the style of the drawing is Europeanized, with figures conceived as plastic forms appearing in three dimensions and moving through space. There is landscape, and, especially in contrast to other migration histories, the pages are crowded with figures and activity. Yet beneath these European contrivances, the

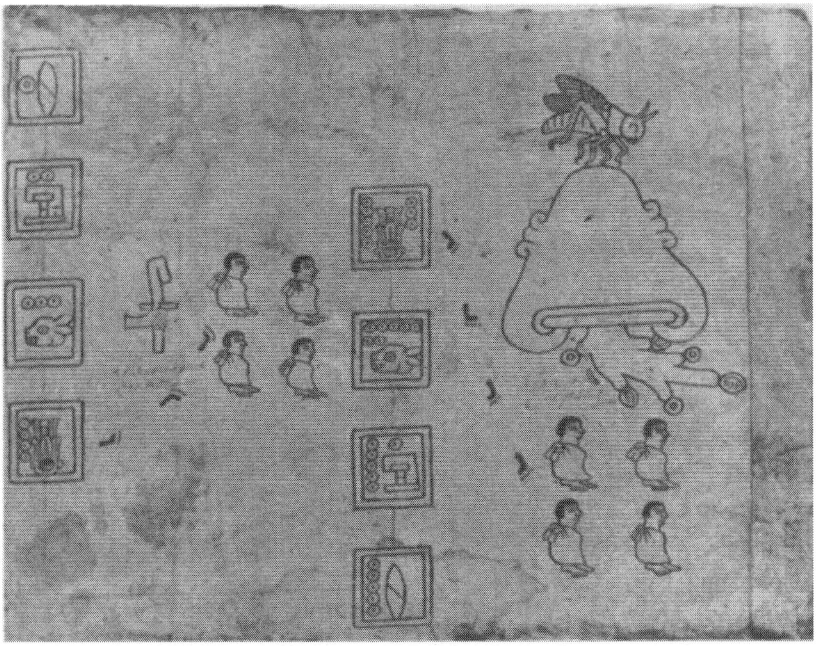

Figure 8.6. Codex Boturini, p. 18. The Mexica arrive at Chapultepec.

indigenous structure remains, and it is the structure of an interrupted year-count annal, where the sequent years are given but the count stops to allow for the depiction of the events. The Codex Azcatitlan begins with Aztlan, presented as is expected as an island city (see Figure 8.13); here the hill of Aztlan proper is conical, rendered bumpy by the graphic vestiges of the convention for hill. The island is sharply rectangular, but it is surrounded by swirling water, across which an Aztec rows in a canoe, as in the Boturini. From there the narrative follows the same path as does the Boturini to arrive at Culhuacan (the curved hill) in the year 1 Flint (shown beside the top of the hill; see Figure 8.14). There the Aztecs build a shrine to Huitzilopochtli, the shrine looking much like a cave and containing the god's bird or hummingbird manifestation. As in the Boturini and Aubin, the eight groups are presented, here identified by houses and distinguished from each other by their name-signs. The god-bearers are present, too, only here they have multiplied.

The Azcatitlan migration seems both more leisurely and more perilous

Figure 8.7. Codex Boturini, p. 19. Chapultepec.

because of the pictorial elaboration given to the terrain, as well as to the flora and fauna along the way (see Figure 8.15). The personal quality seen somewhat in the Boturini is even more pronounced here, too. Footprints mark the journey at the beginning, but they are replaced later in the manuscript by a simple line of flow. The migration proceeds linearly from place to place, in almost the same fashion that it does in the cartographically structured Mapa Sigüenza, except that here the movement is more consistently from left to right and the years of each stay are specified by blocks of year-signs.

Although structurally some of these pictorials are more annalistic, others more event-oriented, and others more spatially arranged, they all share compositional and conventional features. Equally important, they are all telling essentially the same story. Some may emphasize certain features over others, and some provide greater elaboration while others condense, but they all follow a single basic outline for the migration narrative. Where they agree on a detail or an episode, one can feel confident that the detail or episode has been intellectually and graphically

Figure 8.8. Codex Aubin, folio 3r. The eight tribes leave Aztlan. Photographs of Codex Aubin folios are reprinted from Lehmann, Kutscher, and Vollmer, eds., *Geschichte der Azteken* (Berlin, 1981), by permission of the publisher.

Figure 8.9. Codex Aubin, folio 4r. The god-bearers.

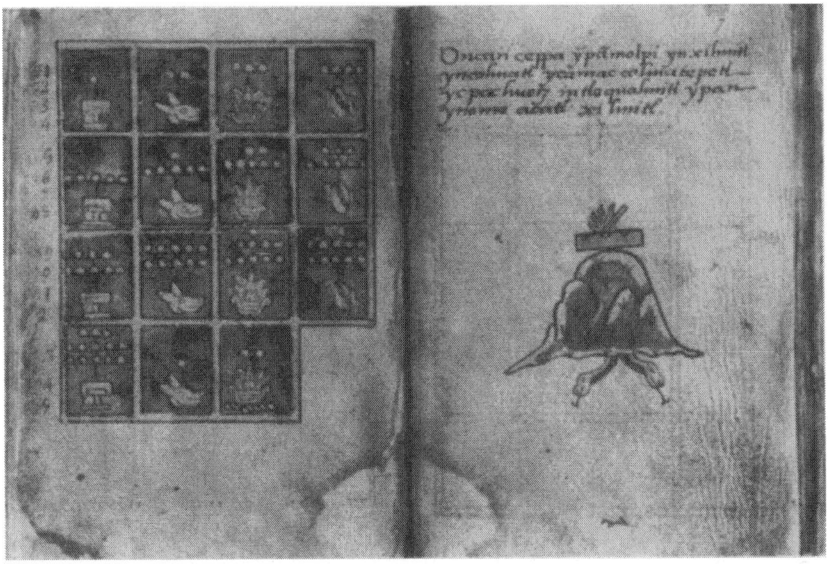

Figure 8.10. Codex Aubin, folios 6v–7r. Coatepec.

codified. Together, and assisted by explanations from the textual sources, the pictorials preserve the main indigenous story of the migration.

THE MIGRATION

The migration itself begins with Aztlan, proceeds along a set course through a series of locations at which events occur, and ends with the founding of Tenochtitlan. The first important event is the leaving of Aztlan, which is always an island city in the middle of a lake. The lake has a hill or stepped pyramid in the middle of it, and the island is generally dotted with house-glyphs (see Figures 8.1, 8.2, 8.8, 8.13). In the Mapa Sigüenza a bird speaks or sings from the top of a tree growing out of the hill in the lake; in the Codex Azcatitlan the bird is Huitzilopochtli in his hummingbird costume. The narration proceeds immediately in the year 1 Flint to the Place of the Bent Hill, Culhuacan or Teoculhuacan (the deified Culhuacan), where a shrine to Huitzilopochtli is built and from which he gives instructions to the Aztecs (see Figures 8.2, 8.8, 8.14). At this time the eight separate groups are identified by name. They are the Matlatzinca (the hunting net), the Tepaneca (stone), the Chichimeca or

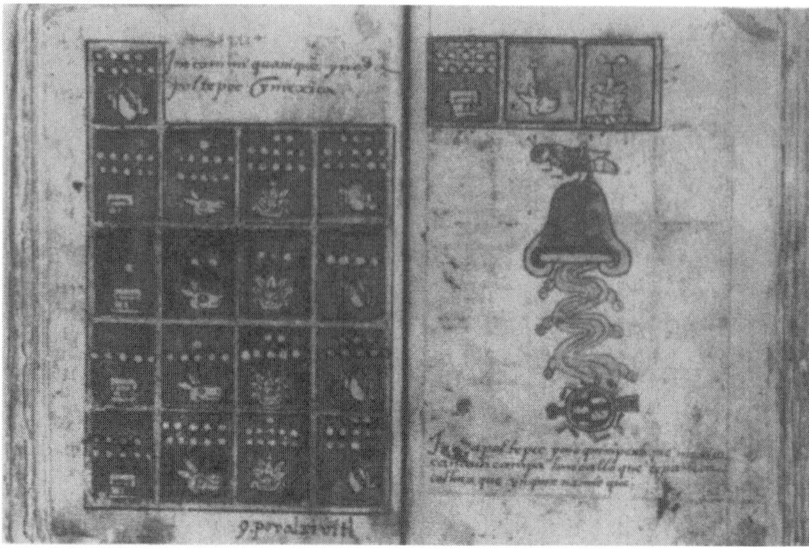

Figure 8.11. Codex Aubin, folios 18v–19r. Chapultepec.

Tlahuica (bow and arrow), the Malinalca (malinalli grass), the Culhuaca (bent water), the Xochimilca (flower and field), the Chalca (turquoise), and the Huexotzinca (tree and rump). In the Boturini, Aubin, and Azcatitlan they are presented in the same order;[5] in the Mapa Sigüenza (see Figure 8.1) they are represented by their named rulers, who also appear in the Azcatitlan.

The next scene of fundamental importance is the stay in Coatepec. There the Mexica reside for several decades and celebrate a New Fire ceremony (according to the Boturini and Aubin) and there (according to the Azcatitlan and the written sources) their god Huitzilopochtli was born (see Figure 8.16).[6] Since, in theory, Huitzilopochtli already existed at least as early as Aztlan whence he directed the Aztecs to migrate, it is clear that his birth at Coatepec is not historical but metaphoric. His teotl or sacrality guided the Mexica from Aztlan, but his corporeality or ixiptla was manifest at Coatepec.[7] There at Coatepec, Huitzilopochtli burst forth fully grown and armed from the womb of his mother Coatlicue, to slay his sister Coyolxauhqui and his four hundred, or innumerable, brothers the Centzonhuitznahua, the episode functioning as a metaphor for Mexica dominance over enemy peoples.

Figure 8.12. Codex Aubin, folio 25v. The founding of Tenochtitlan.

Figure 8.13. Codex Azcatitlan, pp. 2–3. The Mexica leave Aztlan. Photographs of Codex Azcatitlan pages are reprinted from *Journal de la Société des Américanistes*, n.s. 37 (1949), by permission of the publisher.

Figure 8.14. Codex Azcatitlan, pp. 4–5. The eight tribes at Culhuacan; note the shrine of Huitzilopochtli on the left.

Figure 8.15. Codex Azcatitlan, p. 9. The migration as shown here covers rough country, well filled with a variety of plants and animals.

The next important stop is Tula, the ancient Tollan. Although the Tollan stay is not differentiated in any way in the pictorial manuscripts, in which it is simply presented as another pause on the journey, in the textual sources it assumes importance. According to Durán (1967, vol. 2:32–33), there the Aztecs dammed a river to create a lake around the hill on which they settled. It was said to be a model of their future home, where they learned to foster and harvest the lacustrine resources. At the same time, Tollan was also a copy of their original home of Aztlan, and there the Mexica wished to stay, until Huitzilopochtli drove them forward again.

Chapultepec is the next crucial point in the migration story; it is the pivot at which the narrative changes from reviewing long journeys of migration to detailing the trials of the Mexica after they arrived along the shores of Lake Texcoco (see Figures 8.6, 8.7, 8.11). At Chapultepec, the Mexica are physically close to their eventual destination, but they are not yet socially close. While they were staying at Chapultepec, a warrior named Copil — whose sorceress mother Malinalxochitl had been abandoned by

Figure 8.16. Codex Azcatitlan, p. 11. Coatepec; note Huitzilopochtli, armed, atop the pyramid.

the Mexicas earlier in the migration—came to destroy them. Along the way he inflamed hatred for the Mexicas among the settled peoples around the lake. The Mexica captured and killed Copil; tearing out his heart, they threw it in the middle of the lake. From this spot grew the nopal cactus that later marked the site of Tenochtitlan. Although Copil was dead, the enmity against the Mexica continued and the other peoples attacked them. The Mexica escaped by fleeing Chapultepec, but their ruler Huitzilhuitl (hummingbird) and his wife or sister Chimalaxochitl (shield water flower) were captured, led off to the lord of Culhuacan, and killed.

The next episode, the Culhuacan episode, begins when the Aztecs begged the Culhuan ruler for a place to stay. He allowed them a home at Tizapan, where they feasted on the vipers and lizards there and thrived. It was at this time that they asked for and were granted the Culhuan ruler's daughter to be the wife of their god Huitzilopochtli. The Mexica then slew the daughter, dressed a priest in her flayed skin, and invited the Culhuacan ruler to come worship her. Once the ruler realized the fate of his daughter,

Figure 8.17. Codex Azcatitlan, p. 23. The founding of Tenochtitlan.

he drove the Mexica once again from his land. From there they wandered in misery around the lake.

Finally, the Mexica came to the island in the lake where a great nopal cactus grew from a stone, in the spot where the heart of Copil had landed years before (see Figure 8.17). There an eagle nested and was spotted perched on one of the nopal branches; in the Codex Aubin (see Figure 8.12) and in Durán's historical treatise (1967, vol. 2: Plate 6), and as pictured much later in the Mexican national flag, he devours a serpent; elsewhere in Durán (1967, vol. 2: Plate 63) he eats a bird, and in the Codex Mendoza he is simply perched (see Figure 8.18). With the founding, the migration story ends.

A question that must be addressed at this point is how much of the migration story is history and how much is myth. On one pole, Pedro Carrasco (1950, 1971) has accepted most of the episodes as being historically accurate; on the extreme other side, Barbara Price (1980), contending that the Aztecs were native to the Basin of Mexico, has questioned the

Figure 8.18. Codex Mendoza, folio 2r. The founding of Tenochtitlan. Photograph reprinted from Echeagaray, ed., *Códice Mendocino* (Mexico City, 1979), by permission of the publisher.

very existence of migrations. A middle ground, taken by Paul Kirchhoff (1948), H. B. Nicholson (1978), Nigel Davies (1980), Michael Smith (1984, wherein he reviews the others' positions), and probably most Mesoamericanists, "accept[s] the existence of a number of waves of immigrants and attempt[s] to relate these events to the sociopolitical dynamics of Postclassic Central Mexico, without necessarily accepting as historical fact all of the details of the accounts" (Smith 1984:155). Within this middle ground, however, some may lean more toward history and others more toward myth. Nicholson (1971:66) has declared himself skeptical of the historicity of the migration accounts, seeing them as belonging to a stage before genuinely historical accounts begin. On the other hand, Smith (1984:179–80) more recently has looked at the sequence given in the migration sources for the arrival of the various groups into the Basin of Mexico and has found remarkable agreement, which he corroborates with data from local histories, historical linguistics, settlement patterns, and the appearance of ceramic styles. This, then, supports the notion that the migration histories contain more-accurate historical information than many of us had previously thought.

This problem with the historicity of the migration story has arisen because we see the migration accounts as histories, and we want histories to be accurate, or at least specific, in chronology and event; we ask histories to give us the who, what, where, and when of a story. We value them for their historical information. When vaguenesses, internal inconsistencies, and disagreements between sources bring their historical validity into question, it undercuts in our minds their very usefulness as cultural records.

I feel we must move away from this narrow position if we are to increase our understanding of the migration accounts. If we can cease seeing the migration story as history, other opportunities for understanding the documents and Aztec culture in a larger sense become open. If, for example, we can view the migration story not as a historical occurrence but instead metaphorically as a ceremony or ritual, our perspective changes considerably. We do not ask ceremonies or rituals to be factually accurate; we expect them, like myths, to convey deeper truths, and they convey them through the stylized and sometimes repetitious actions of the participants. The essential message being conveyed by the migration story is not the journey of a people from one physical place to another; rather, the message is the transition of the Mexica from a small and relatively insignificant band to the people destined to rule the world as it was then known. If we analyze the migration narrative as we would a ritual or ceremony, this basic function becomes readily apparent, and we can see how the migration story achieves this goal so effectively.

Davies (1980:85–86) has discussed the Aztec celebration of their humble past, saying: "The claim to rustic — or 'Chichimec' — ancestors lent color to tales of tribal origins and satisfied a Mesoamerican yearning for a pedigree that spelled progress from rags to riches . . . the 'rags to riches' legend almost amounted to a status symbol." Much more is involved in the migration story than a "rags to riches" progression, however; it is not merely a question of a people gaining wealth and material power. The migration story actually functions to transform the Mexica as a tribal group, by endowing them with spiritual power. It does this by stripping them to their purest strain and putting them through hazards, by testing their faith in Huitzilopochtli, and by developing Huitzilopochtli's own strength. It thus makes them fit to assume the imperial role.

Migration as Ceremony

In what way can the Mexican migration be considered in terms of a ceremony, a ritual, or a performance? Certainly, it satisfies Sally Moore and Barbara Myerhoff's (1977:22) definition of a ritual as "a set of formal acts which deal with or refer to postulated matters about society or ideology (or matters those mounting the ritual *want* to be unquestioned)." As Moore and Myerhoff note, "ritual is a good form for conveying a message as if it were unquestionable." Collective ritual is a "traditionalizing instrument," which not only can "mirror existing social arrangements and existing modes of thought" but can also function to "reorganize them or even help to create them" (Moore & Myerhoff 1977:5–6). Ritual can both propagate cultural ideas and shape them (Geertz 1966:36, 41; Turner 1969). The ideas being perpetuated by the Mexica migration story are, clearly, the supremacy of the deity Huitzilopochtli over other deities; the loyalty, perseverance, and strength of character of the Mexica people; the rightness of Tenochtitlan as their capital; and ultimately their suitability to rule. This message is conveyed by the story, and it is formed by the migration itself.

As does a ritual, the migration has a set program, a sense of purpose, and a sense on the part of the Mexica that their actions are special. In this, it fulfils what Lawrence Sullivan (1986:5, citing Stanley Tambiah) has noted as being the common claims about the nature of performance, that "all performances contain 'a commonly acknowledged procedure' that orders their actions; a 'sense of collective or communal enactment that is purposive'; and a communal 'awareness' that the performed acts 'are different from "ordinary" everyday events.' " The fundamental program for the migration was established in advance by Huitzilopochtli — who could even be considered the director of the drama — as a journey from Aztlan to Tenochtitlan. A sense of communality among the Mexica is stressed throughout the story, as the people must wander and must often stand alone against enemies surrounding them. Throughout the story, the Mexica are reminded of their special mission and of the distinctive nature of their journey. Their actions and condition are set apart from what Hannah Arendt has called the "brute behavior" of everyday life (Sullivan 1986:5, 9).

Milton Singer has described performances as having "a definitely limited time span, a beginning and end, an organized program of activity, a set of performers, an audience, and a place and occasion of performance" (cited in Sullivan 1986:2). The migration has its duration, its beginning and end, its program, and its actors, all of which I have mentioned before. It may be more of a challenge to define the audience for the drama, but it surely is composed of the Mexica themselves as well as the other ethnic and cultural groups they later conquered. Metaphorically, the audience of the original migration performance would have been the Mexica and the Nahuatl-speakers of the future. The place of performance is the Basin of Mexico, and the occasion can be recognized as directly preceding the Mexica rise to power.

Like a performance the migration is circular, highly structured, and ritualized to a great degree. I say it is circular because the action begins and ends at the island city of Aztlan/Tenochtitlan. Aztlan and Tenochtitlan are similar in bracketing all the action. Technically, one begins the story and the other ends it, but they are the same place. The Mexica leave Aztlan, are transformed, and return to their point of origin. The symmetry or identity of Aztlan/Tenochtitlan exists within the story, too. After the Mexica leave Aztlan, they arrive immediately in Teoculhuacan (the deified place of the curved hill), which parallels the Culhuacan that is the last major stop before arriving at Tenochtitlan. Coatepec, the location of Huitzilopochtli's birth, then parallels and corresponds to Chapultepec, where Copil was killed and sacrificed. The correspondences between Coatepec and Chapultepec are noteworthy because both are mirrored at the Templo Mayor. Coatepec is the serpent mountain, of which the Templo Mayor is a metaphor, place of the birth and first victory of Huitzilopochtli. Chapultepec, or more precisely the Chapultepec episode in the migration story, demonstrates how the heart of the enemy, Copil, provides the identity for Tenochtitlan. Copil's heart, once it is thrown into the lake, establishes the location of the capital; from his heart grows the nopal cactus, and on this spot the Templo Mayor is later built to mirror the hill of Coatepec. The migratory stay at Tollan is the centermost episode in the migration; it is preceded by Aztlan, Teoculhuacan, and Coatepec, and it is succeeded by Chapultepec, Culhuacan, and Tenochtitlan. It is also where the Mexica create a model of Tenochtitlan and, by extension, a model of Aztlan. Thus, the location in the center is a conscious reflection of the points of beginning and ending.

Like several of the monthly festivals, the migration proceeds along a ritual circuit. There are stops along the way, and at five of these stops the Mexica perform activities or are affected by events — they do things, have things done to them, or both — that alter or shape them and the rest of the program.

Migration as Rite of Passage

Richard Schechner (1981:91) has differentiated two kinds of performances, which he calls "transformations" and "transportations." He calls "performances where performers are changed 'transformations' and those where performers are returned to their starting places 'transportations'. 'Transportation' because during the performance the performers are 'taken somewhere' but at the end, often assisted by others, they are 'cooled down' and reenter ordinary life just about where they went in." The Mexica migration is fundamentally a transformation, because it alters them and prepares them to accept rule. They are taken from Aztlan to Tenochtitlan (which is a quasi Aztlan), but they are changed in the process, so that they cannot in fact ever return to the Aztlan condition they left. As Schechner (1981:92) notes: "Transformation performances are clearly evidenced in initiation rites, whose very purpose it is to transform people from one status or social identity to another. An initiation not only marks a change but is itself the means by which persons achieve their new selves: no performance, no change." With this in mind, I think it is clear that the migration can most effectively be seen in terms of an initiation rite, which transforms the Mexicas from one social identity or state of being to another.

The classic study of initiation rites remains that of the Belgian ethnographer Arnold van Gennep, who published his analysis of rites of passage in 1906. Gennep's work has since been expanded and developed much further, but not rendered obsolete, by Victor Turner's focus on the state of liminality. Gennep (1960:2) saw the life of an individual in any society as "a series of passages from one age to another and from one occupation to another," or as a series of "transitions from group to group and from one social situation to another. . . . For every one of these events," he said, "there are ceremonies whose essential purpose is to enable the individual to pass from one defined position to another which is equally well defined; . . . the individual involved has been modified by passing through several stages and traversing several boundaries." Looking to discover the structure, and thus the essential significance, of these rites of passage within a ceremonial whole, he demonstrated that the underlying pattern or arrangement of transitional rituals was always the same. Rites of passage, according to Gennep, have three distinguishable phases; these are separation, margin or limen, and incorporation or reaggregation (Gennep 1960:vii, ix, 10–11; Turner 1975:196, 1977:36). The first stage separates the individual from his or her former situation, and the third stage attaches the individual to his or her new situation, or as Turner (1977:36) has phrased it, "they detach ritual subjects from their old places in society and return them, inwardly transformed and outwardly changed, to new places." The second or middle stage was the "neutral zone," a "symbolic and spatial area of transition" through which one passed to move from one territory to another (Gennep 1960:18). Gennep (1960:191) further made the point that the liminal or transitional periods sometimes acquire a certain autonomy, a point Turner has developed. Finally, Gennep "paid particular attention to the correlation between status movement and change of *spatial* position" (Turner 1975:196). He noted that "the spatial separation of distinct groups is an aspect of social organization," and that "a change of social categories involves a change of residence"; "the passage from one social position to another is identified with a territorial passage" (Gennep 1960:191–92).

These structural components and features of rites of passage are clearly reflected in the Mexica migration. Aztlan and Tenochtitlan are the separation and attachment points; the long migration is the liminal or transitional corridor. The change in location marks the completed change in status.

Between the separation and attachment, the liminal phase functions principally to effect the change; rather than a vacant period, it seems to work as the agent of transformation. As Turner (1977:36–37) has described it:

> A *limen* is a threshold, but at least in the case of protracted initiation rites or major seasonal festivals, it is a very long threshold, a corridor almost, or a tunnel which may, indeed, become a pilgrim's road. . . . Those undergoing it — call them 'liminaries' — are betwixt-and-between established states of politico-jural structure. They evade ordinary cognitive classification, too, for they are neither-this-nor-that, here-nor-there, one-thing-not-the-other. . . . But the most characteristic mid-liminal symbolism is that of paradox, of being *both* this *and* that. Usually there are words and phrases which indicate that they are 'being grown' into a new postliminal state of being. . . . They may be said to be in a process of being ground down to a sort of homogeneous social matter, in which possibilities of differentiation may still be glimpsed, then later positively refashioned into specific shapes compatible with their new postliminal duties and rites and incumbents of a new status and state. This grinding down process is accomplished by ordeals; . . . hazing, endurance of heat and cold, impossible physical tasks.

Turner (1969:167) also notes that the liminality characterizing rituals of status elevation wherein "the ritual subject or novice is being conveyed irreversibly from a lower to a higher position, . . . usually involves a putting down or humbling of the novice." "Their behavior is normally passive and/or humble; they must obey their instructors implicitly, and accept arbitrary punishment without complaint" (Turner 1969:95). "Humbling and submission to ordeals, whether inflicted by self or others, goes with preparation for elitehood — whether in this world or the next" (Turner 1977:39).

Thus, we have the Mexica situation. During the migration, which is directed by Huitzilopochtli — who here acts as the instructor to the initiates — the people undergo real hardship. They wander in poverty and alone and are humbled both by Huitzilopochtli and by their settled neighbors in the Basin of Mexico. Throughout, the Mexica are passive before Huitzilopochtli, although not passive before their enemy neighbors, whose battles become other ordeals. As with initiates, the Mexica are in the process "fashioned anew and endowed with additional powers to enable them to cope with their new situation in life" (Turner 1969:95). All this must be endured before they can emerge in their elite position. Once they arrive at Tenochtitlan, they have acquired a social equality within the group that is characteristic of initiates, who experience what Turner (1975:202) calls "communitas," a relationship of equals that has been formed during the liminal passage. This relationship of equals is presented graphically in the foundation scene of the Codex Mendoza (see Figure 8.18), where Tenoch and the other named warriors are shown seated and having essentially the same status. It is only later, after fifty-one years, that the Mexican monarchy begins with Acamapichtli.

Previously, I viewed the Aztec migration as a way for the Aztecs to celebrate and distinguish their humble past from the perspective of their then-present greatness. This was in accord with the idea that Itzcoatl, following his conquest of Azcapotzalco, had all the painted books burned and had the histories rewritten.[8] I saw the Aztecs developing this story of their humble beginning purposely in order to set up a sharp contrast to their later imperial success and power.

The migration story does convey this message, but it is more than an account or even a fable of humble beginnings and present greatness. It is more than Davies's "rags to riches" idea. It is even more than a morality play in which fundamental truths are revealed through the actions — although it is this, also. The migration functions as a rite of passage. Not only does it recount and symbolize the elevation of the Mexica to elite status, it functions actively to effect this transition and elevation. The features of the migration story separate the Mexica from their earlier condition, endow them with the spiritual and mental fitness for rule, and then return them thus altered to the world at Tenochtitlan. The migration is itself the performance that transforms the Mexica from an unremarkable "Chichimec" tribe to the people who are specially destined to control Mesoamerica.

Notes

1. Paralleling this, Eduard Seler (1961:44) mentioned the possibility that Aztlan was fashioned in the image of Tenochtitlan as a mythical hypostatizing of the later capital.
2. The Historia de Tlatelolco is described by Glass and Robertson (1975:173–74) and Gibson and Glass (1975:351) under the heading "Unos annales históricos de la nación mexicana," document 5.
3. For a synopsis of the Crónica X group see Glass and Robertson 1975:236–37.
4. See Boone 1991 for the distinction between year-count annals and event-oriented or res gestae histories.
5. The only difference is that the sequence in the Codex Azcatitlan is exactly reversed.
6. See, for example, Durán (1967, vol. 2:218) and Sahagún (1950–1982, bk. 3:1–5).
7. See Hvidfeldt (1958) for a discussion of teotl and ixiptla.
8. This thought is reported only by Sahagún (1950–1982, bk. 10:191).

References

Acosta, José de

1979 *Historia natural y moral de las Indias.* Edited by Edmundo O'Gorman. Mexico City: Fondo de Cultura Económica.

Alvarado Tezozómoc, Fernando de

1878 *Crónica mexicana, . . . precedida del Códice Ramírez.* Edited by Manuel Orozco y Berra. Mexico City: Porrúa.

Boone, Elizabeth Hill

1991 The Aztec pictorial history of the Codex Mendoza. In *The Codex Mendoza,* edited by Frances F. Berdan and Patricia R. Anawalt. Los Angeles: University of California Press.

Carrasco, Pedro

1950 *Los Otomíes: Cultura e historia prehispánica de los pueblos mesoamericanos de habla Otomiana.* Mexico City: Universidad Nacional Autónoma de México.

1971 The people of Central Mexico and their historical traditions. In *Handbook of Middle American Indians,* edited by Robert Wauchope, Gordon F. Ekholm, and Ignacio Bernal. Vol. 11. Austin: University of Texas Press.

Castillo, Cristóbal del

1908 *Fragmentos de la obra general sobre historia de los Mexicanos escrita en lengua Nauatl por Cristóbal del Castillo,* edited by Francisco del Paso y Troncoso. *Biblioteca Nauatl* 5, no. 2:41–107.

Codex Aubin

1981 Geschichte der Azteken, 1168–1607 (Codex Aubin). In *Geschichte der Azteken: Codex Aubin und verwandte Dokumente,* edited by Walter Lehmann, Gerdt Kutscher, and Günter Vollmer. Berlin: Gebr. Mann Verlag.

Codex Azcatitlan

1949 El Códice Azcatitlán. Facsimile edition with a commentary by Robert Barlow. *Journal de la Société des Américanistes,* n.s. 37:101–35, Atlas.

Codex Boturini

1964 Códice Boturini. In *Antigüedades de México, basadas en la recopilación de Lord Kingsborough,* edited by José Corona Núñez. Vol. 2, pt. 1. Mexico City: Secretaría de Hacienda y Crédito Público.

Codex Mendoza
1979 *Códice Mendocino o Colección de Mendoza que se conserva en la Biblioteca Bodleiana de Oxford*, edited by José Ignacio Echeagaray. Mexico City: San Angel.

Codex Mexicanus
1952 Codex Mexicanus, Bibliothèque Nationale de Paris, nos. 23–24. Facsimile edition with a commentary by Ernst Mengin. *Journal de la Société des Américanistes*, n.s. 41:387–498, Atlas.

Codex Telleriano-Remensis
1899 *Codex Telleriano-Remensis, manuscrit mexicain du cabinet de Ch. M. Le Tellier, Archevêque de Reims, à la Bibliothèque Nationale*. Lithographic facsimile with a commentary by Ernst T. Hamy. Paris: Duc de Loubat.

Codex Vaticanus A/Ríos
1900 *Il manoscritto messicano Vaticano 3738 detto il Codice Rios*. Color lithographic facsimile with a commentary by Franz Ehrle. Rome: Duc de Loubat.

Davies, Nigel
1980 *The Toltec heritage: From the fall of Tula to the rise of Tenochtitlan*. Norman: University of Oklahoma Press.

Durán, Diego
1967 *Historia de las Indias de Nueva España e islas de la tierra firme*. Translated and edited by Angel María Garibay K. 2 vols. Mexico City: Porrúa.

Fonds Mexicain 40
1981 Geschichte der Azteken, 1168–1573 (Ms. 40). In *Geschichte der Azteken: Codex Aubin und verwandte Dokumente*, edited by Walter Lehmann, Gerdt Kutscher, and Günter Vollmer. Berlin: Gebr. Mann Verlag.

Fonds Mexicain 85
1981 Geschichte der Azteken, 1196–1405 (Ms. 85). In *Geschichte der Azteken: Codex Aubin und verwandte Dokumente*, edited by Walter Lehmann, Gerdt Kutscher, and Günter Vollmer. Berlin: Gebr. Mann Verlag.

Geertz, Clifford
1966 Religion as a cultural symbol. In *Anthropological approaches to the study of religion*, edited by M. Blanton. A.S.A. Monograph, no. 3. London: Tavistock.

Gennep, Arnold van
1960 *The rites of passage*. Translation of the 1908 French ed. Chicago: University of Chicago Press.

Gibson, Charles, and John B. Glass
1975 A census of Middle American prose manuscripts in the native historical tradition. In *Handbook of Middle American Indians*, edited by Robert Wauchope and Howard F. Cline. Vol. 3. Austin: University of Texas Press.

Glass, John B., in collaboration with Donald Robertson
1975 A census of Middle American pictorial manuscripts. In *Handbook of Middle American Indians*, edited by Robert Wauchope and Howard F. Cline. Vol. 14. Austin: University of Texas Press.

Historia de los mexicanos por sus pinturas
1941 Historia de los mexicanos. In *Nueva colección de documentos para la historia de México*, edited by Joaquín García Icazbalceta. Vol. 3. Mexico City: Chávez Hayhoe.

Historia de Tlatelolco
1948 La historia de Tlatelolco desde los tiempos mas remotas. In *Anales de Tlatelolco: Unos annales históricos de la nación mexicana y Códice de Tlatelolco*, edited by Robert H. Barlow with notes by Heinrich Berlin. Mexico City: Antigua Librería Robredo, José Porrúa e Hijos.

Hvidfeldt, Arild
1958 *Teotl and ixiptlatli: Some central concepts in ancient Mexican religion*. Copenhagen: Munskgaard.

Kirchhoff, Paul
1948 Civilizing the Chichimecs: A chapter in the culture history of ancient Mexico. *Latin American Studies* 5:80–85.

Mapa Sigüenza
1982 Mapa Sigüenza. In *El territorio mexicano*, edited by Fernando Zertuche Muñoz and Lenin Molina Tapia. Mexico City: Instituto Mexicano de Seguro Social.

Moore, Sally F., and Barbara G. Myerhoff,
1977 *Secular ritual*. Assen, Netherlands: Van Gorcum.

Nicholson, H. B.
1971 Pre-hispanic Central Mexican historiography. In *Investigaciones contemporáneos sobre historia de México: Memorias de la tercera reunión de historiadores mexicanos y norteamericanos (1969)*. Austin: University of Texas Press.

1978 Western Mesoamerica: A.D. 900–1520. In *Chronologies in New World archaeology*, edited by R. E. Taylor and Clement W. Meighan. New York: Academic Press.

Noguez, Xavier, ed.
1978 *Tira de Tepechpan*. 2 vols. Mexico City. Biblioteca Enciclopédica del Estado de México.

Price, Barbara
1980 The truth is not in accounts but in account books: On the epistemological status of history. In *Beyond the myths of culture: Essays in cultural materialism*, edited by Eric B. Ross. New York: Academic Press.

Sahagún, Bernardino de
1950–1982 *Florentine Codex: General history of the things of New Spain*. Translated and edited by Arthur J. O. Anderson and Charles E. Dibble. 3 pts. Santa Fe: School of American Research and the University of Utah.

Schechner, Richard
1981 Performers and spectators transported and transformed. *Kenyon Review* 3, no. 4:83–113.

Seler, Eduard
1961 Wo lag Aztlan, die Heimath der Azteken? In E. Seler, *Gesammelte Abhandlungen zur amerikanischen Sprach- und Altertumskunde*. Vol. 2. Reprint of the 1902 Berlin edition. Graz: Akademische Druck- und Verlagsanstalt.

Smith, Michael E.
1984 The Aztlan migrations of the Nahuatl chronicles: Myth or history? *Ethnohistory* 31, no. 3:153–86.

Sullivan, Lawrence E.
1986 Sound and senses: Toward a hermeneutics of performance. *History of Religions* 26, no. 1:1–33.

Torquemada, Juan de
1975–1979 *Monarquía indiana. De los veinte y un libros rituales y monarquía indiana, con el origen y guerras de los indios occidentales, de sus poblazones, descubrimiento, conquista, conversión y otras cosas maravillosas de la mesma tierra*. Edited by Miguel León-Portilla. 5 vols. Mexico City: Universidad Nacional Autónoma de México.

Tovar, Juan de
1972 *Manuscrit Tovar, origines et croyances des indiens du Mexique*. Translated and edited by Jacques Lafaye. Graz: Akademische Druck- und Verlagsanstalt.

Turner, Victor
1969 *The ritual process: Structure and anti-structure*. Chicago: Aldine.

1975 *Dramas, fields, and metaphors: Symbolic action in human society*. Ithaca, NY: Cornell University Press.

1977 Variations on a theme of liminality. In *Secular ritual*, edited by Sally F. Moore and Barbara G. Myerhoff. Assen, Netherlands: Van Gorcum.

9

The Myth of the Half-Man Who Descended from the Sky

Alfredo López Austin
Translated by Ralph Kite

Mesoamericanists encounter notably persistent historio-graphic problems. One of them, and it is one of the most serious, is the interpretation of historical myth: Narratives in which the actions of gods and men are mixed together in the playing out of the miracle tale are frequent. The basis for Mesoamerican historical tales consists of a creation myth. The peoples had come to life through the intervention of the gods, emerging from the earth's interior or from the mount of the seven wombs, or falling from the heavens like seeds in a divine projectile. So, it appears that the lack of a miracle story would have taken away human legitimacy. Each people presented itself to the rest as the result of a birth through which it had established ties with the patron god, and marvelous life accompanied it to its definitive settling place, where the story is completed by the foundation myth.

This is the outline of the first stage of the history of the Mesoamerican peoples. Nevertheless, it is difficult to understand the meaning of the various episodes of the originating migrations. How, for example, can the supernatural deeds in the migration of the Mexicas be explained? Does the myth of Coyolxauhqui, Coatlicue, and Huitzilopochtli have its origin in an actual event? Was Huitzilopochtli a man of flesh and blood who, through his feats, achieved the status of a god?

Some historians explain the mythical overtones by referring to the primitive forms of tradition. From this point of view there existed a distortion caused by immature historical recall: Human events were full of wonders that made the narration more interesting to an audience accustomed to marvelous deeds, and important men became heroes, then gods, through a transforming process of the oral tradition. This is an interpretation of the old euhemerist type that many scholars still prefer. For other historians, however, the explanation rests in the predominance of the archetype over the narration and, going a bit further, in the presence of myth as a model for human activity.

Mesoamericanists are still far from agreement on the methods and foundations of the interpretation of the marvelous stories. The solution will be made easier to the extent that we increase the number of analyses of tales of this type and distinguish more clearly the differences among the mythical tale, the openly historical tale, and the tale of the marvelous initial stage, so common in Mesoamerican historiography.

Here, I put forth a case that may be enlightening. It is an interesting and well-known tale: the myth of the origin of a people as it was told in one of the most important cities in the lacustrine Basin of Mexico — Tetzcoco. This city, like many others of the Mesoamerican Postclassic period, had a mixed population, separated into neighborhoods that maintained their own customs and traditions. A large part of the population of Tetzcoco was Chichimecan, that is, of recent barbarian origin. The Chichimecas of Tetzcoco had arrived in the lacustrine Basin of Mexico, led by their chief, Xolotl, in the thirteenth century, taking advantage of the fact that the peoples of the Basin found themselves in political chaos. Another segment of the population consisted of the Aculhuas, a sedentary people with an ancient history in Mesoamerica who had made the most of the invasion of the Chichimecas and established an alliance with them, providing them with the basic means of becoming sedentary.

The myth has two versions: that of the Tetzcocan Aculhuas and that of the people of Chichimecan origin. The first narrative shows the typical form of the myth. In the second, one can recognize one of the ways in which history has influenced the myth and transformed it. The version we can consider primary is recorded in the *Historia Eclesiástica Indiana* by Fray Gerónimo de Mendieta (1945, vol. 1:87–88):

> Those from Tezcuco offered . . . in their paintings another version of the creation of the first man . . . relating that their ancestors had come from that land where the gods fell . . . and from that cave of Chicomóztoc. And what they showed afterward in painting and declared to the above-mentioned Fray Andrés de Olmos, was that the first man

> from whom they descended had been born in the land of Aculma, which is two leagues from Tezcuco and five from Mexico, or a little more, coming this direction. They say that with the sun at nine o'clock, it shot an arrow in said area and made a hole, from which emerged the first man, whose body consisted only of the part above the armpits, and afterward emerged a complete woman; and upon being asked how that man procreated without a complete body, they uttered something nonsensical and dirty that is not fit to be repeated here, and that man was called Acúlmaitl, and it is from here that the pueblo that calls itself Aculma took its name, because *aculli* means shoulders and arms; that is, that he was almost all shoulders and arms because (as has been said) that first man's body only went from the armpits up, according to this fiction and lie.

The primary character of this version of the myth is easily located in a very common similarity among Mesoamerican traditions. There is an eponymy that relates the name of the personage, Acúlmaitl, to the place of origin, Aculma, and to the physical characteristics of the original man, "who was almost all shoulders and arms"; that is, almost all aculli. One need only add the obvious: that the Tetzcocans to whom the myth of Acúlmaitl in Aculma refers are the Aculhuas.

There are, nevertheless, other Tetzcocans who repeat this creation narrative. They appropriate the myth of others and the version varies insofar as they are not Aculhuas, but Chichimecas. Indeed, in the version of the myth that appears in the document known as the *Histoire du Mechique* it is said that the descendants of the half-man were Otomíes. Why Otomíes? The Chichimecas of Tetzcoco were Otomíans and the same source affirms that the Chichimecan governing class were Otomíes (Rosales Munguía 1965:98–100). The differences in the second version of the myth are adaptive:

> Tezcuco is a main city, situated eight leagues from that of Mexico, either by water or by land, of which the present occupiers affirm that they and their ancestors were the founders, in the following way:
>
> One day at dawn an arrow was shot from the sky and it hit a place called Tezcalco, which is now a town.
>
> From the hole formed by the arrow a man and a woman emerged: his name was Tzontecómatl, that is, "head," and also Tlohtli, "hawk"; her name was Tzompachtli, "hair of a certain grass."

At the time said man had no body, except from the armpits up, nor did the woman, and they mated by his putting his tongue in the woman's mouth.

They walked by hopping along like magpies or swallows.

The man then made a bow and arrow with which he shot at flying birds, and if by chance he did not hit the bird he shot at, the arrow fell on some rabbit or some other animal, which they ate raw, since they did not have the use of fire, and they dressed in hides.

In this condition they had six boys and a girl who went to the place that is now Tezcuco, which then was only a dense wilderness, full of all kinds of beasts, in whose hides they dressed, and neither the males nor the females cut their hair.

They offered to the earth a precious herb so that the earth would give them food.

They lived this way in great peace and friendship since they would not have dared to do or say anything offensive to one another.

Similarly, if someone found some dead beast wounded by another, even though the other had not come to get it, the finder did not take it away, but rather told the others so that the one who had killed it could go and get it. Thus were they lacking in malice.

Nor did they worry about time, nor did they know how to count months nor years, until the Mexicans took them a calendar with some characters designed on it.

The aforementioned Tlohtli, then, and his woman were the first lords of Tezcuco, but their children left and went through the country to see new lands, and they remained wherever they wanted to, so they populated many places; but they did not remain in any fixed place, but rather lived in caves that they made or they built some branch huts that they covered with grass.

The product of the hunt was taken to their master, who was their father.

They showed such continence with the women that at the time of a man's death he had known no other woman but his own, for doing so was considered a great infamy.

The first to find idols was one of the sons of Tlohtli, who, having stayed away from Tezcuco for a long time, returned to his father and brought an idol called Tezcatlipoca and built an altar in Tezcuco.

From this time on they began to sow corn and beans, which are some grains they have, in Chalco, which is six leagues from Tezcuco, and from there they carried the seed to Tezcuco where they planted it.

> Tlohtli was still alive then, but he died around that time, and left his son as his successor. He immediately married a daughter of the lord of Culhuacan, which is near Mexico.
>
> And thus they multiplied, they married each other and this nation began to be called Otomí, and they began to build houses [Rosales Munguía 1965:91–93].

In this narrative the place of creation changes: It says it was Tezcalco. The life of the first men was that of the Chichimecas, long-haired bow and arrow users who ate raw meat, did not know fire, wandered from one place to another, lived in caves or straw huts, and dressed in hides. Their life was that of hunters, peaceful men without malice who respected the laws of the hunt and paid part of their catch in tribute to their master. Their morality was that of the Chichimecas, characterized by seriousness and rigidity. Their religion was simple. They did not know the mysteries of the calendar until these were revealed to them by the sedentary peoples.

There exists here an interesting genre switch: Despite the sparse record of Fray Gerónimo de Mendieta, the first narrative has the characteristics of myth. The second, on the other hand, opens up at the end to the point of acquiring the characteristics of a historical story of the creation of the Tetzcocan people. In the switch the historical adjustment also causes confusion in what is told in the myth: Chichimecas are nomadic, and the Chichimecan version requires that they be the founders of Tetzcoco. The solution is to explain the wandering of the hunter sons of Tzontecómatl and Tzompachtli as a thirst for adventure. In this way the founders of a city could have gained the tradition of nomads.

But the change that constitutes the key to the grafting of history onto the myth is the shift in the names of the characters: Acúlmaitl, who was almost all shoulders and arms, is now called Tzontecómatl because it can also be affirmed that he is mostly just a head. Tzontecómatl was the name of the Aculhua chief who allied himself with Xólotl; but if the name is mentioned here it is because of its strongly descriptive nature. The second name of the original man, on the other hand, is not descriptive: Its character is totally historical — it is Tlohtli, the name of the third Chichimecan governor, son of Nopaltzin and grandson of Xólotl.

The name of his wife is more interesting. The myth calls her Tzompachtli, or, *pastle* hair.[1] Even though in the documentary sources the wife of Tlohtli receives a different name, Pachxochitzin or "pastle flower," there is a sufficient basis to affirm that Pachxochitzin and Tzompachtli are the names of the same woman. The basis is in the pictographic document that carries the name of the third Chichimecan governor: the Mapa Tlotzin.[2] The name of the character appears in the ancient form with a glyph that alludes to the meaning. In the various scenes in which the wife appears in that document, her name is represented, not by a flower, but rather with a disheveled female head. It is the only case of a Chichimecan lady whose head is shown disheveled. Her hair is as mussed up as is the plant known as pastle or woodland hay.

There are interesting political points in the Chichimecan version: The appropriation of a myth belonging to others, belonging to a culturally prestigious community, is a fact that illuminates the relationship between two ethnic groups who form part of the same political entity. Not only is the creation of a people reported, but one of its governors is included as a creating personage and, as such, a legitimizer of his descendants, the governors of Tetzcoco.

With regard to the historiographical aspect, I believe that the case mentioned, besides exemplifying one type of intrusion by historical tradition into the mythical tale, has as an advantage its being a document in which was captured the transition of a mythical text into a historical text.

NOTES

The main ideas expressed here about this myth are taken from Alfredo López Austin's *Los mitos del Tlacuache: Caminos de la mitología mesoamericana* (Mexico City: Alianza Editorial Mexicana), p. 542, and Chapter 25, "La historia en el tiempo del mito."

1. Pastle is the woodland hay, *Tillantsia usneoides* L.
2. Tlotzin, or, better, Tlohtzin, is the respectful form of Tlohtli.

REFERENCES

López Austin, Alfredo
1990 *Los mitos del tlacuache: Caminos de la mitología mesoamericana.* Mexico City, Alianza Editorial Mexicana.

Mapa Tlotzin
1886 Mapa Tlotzin: Historia de los reyes y de los estados soberanos de Acolhuacan. Fragment of the work of M. Aubin titled *Memoire sur la peinture didactique et l'escriture figurative des anciens mexicaines. Anales del Museo Nacional de México* 3:304–20 and foldout.

Mendieta, Fray Gerónimo de
1945 *Historia eclesiástica indiana,* with comments by Fray Juan de Domayguia. 4 vols. Mexico City: Salvador Chávez Hayhoe.

Rosales Munguía, Ramón, trans.
1965 Historia de México [Histoire du Mechique]. In *Teogonía e historia de los mexicanos: Tres opúsculos del siglo XVI,* edited by Angel María Garibay K. Mexico City: Porrúa.

10

The Octli Cult in Late Pre-Hispanic Central Mexico

Henry B. Nicholson

Introduction

The complex religious/ritual system of late pre-Hispanic Central Mexico featured numerous cults involving the propitiation of various deities believed to control different aspects of the natural and human universe. One of the most interesting and colorful of these focused on the maguey or "century plant" (*Agave salmiana* Otto, *Agave otrovirens* Kawr, etc.) and its saccharine exudate, *aguamiel* (Gonçalves de Lima 1956:13–23; Museo Nacional de Culturas Populares 1988). The aguamiel was fermented, with the addition of certain roots to strengthen its effects, to produce the standard alcoholic tipple of western Mesoamerica. It was called octli in Nahuatl — and, since the early colonial period, pulque, a term of uncertain origin (Hough 1908; Museo Nacional de Culturas Populares 1988:61–79). The additive roots were called ocpahtli, "octli medicine." In my classification of the deities of late pre-Hispanic Central Mexico (Nicholson 1971), I distinguished an "Ometochtli Complex," assigned to the major pantheonic theme, Rain/Moisture/Agricultural Fertility, and comprising the numerous deities that were propitiated within the ideological and ritual framework of the octli cult. This paper is devoted to a concise summary of the ethnohistorical and archaeological information available concerning these deities and the major ceremonies performed in their honor.

Sources

The most important primary ethnohistorical sources for knowledge of this cult and the deities that expressed it are the *Primeros Memoriales* and *Historia General (Universal) de las Cosas de Nueva España* of Fray Bernardino de Sahagún (1905, 1950–1982, 1958, 1970, 1979, 1981, 1988), the *Historia de las Indias de Nueva España y Islas de Tierra Firme* of Fray Diego Durán (1967), and the two pairs of partially cognate, annotated native-tradition colonial pictorials: Codex Magliabechiano (1970, 1983) and Códice Tudela (1980); and Codex Telleriano-Remensis (1899) and Codex Vaticanus A (1979). A few additional and relevant items are found in other primary textual and pictorial sources, but those named contain the great bulk of the available data. There are also numerous archaeological pieces that display the characteristic iconographic devices and symbols of the cult, including images of the gods themselves — plus one fairly well preserved temple dedicated to one of the principal members of the octli pantheon.

Octli Origins

Before entering into a discussion of the cult itself, some accounts of the origin of the maguey plant and of octli in various Central Mexican cosmogonies and legendary histories should be mentioned. In the *Histoyre du Mechique* (1906:27–28), seemingly derived from the writings of Fray Andrés de Olmos, an important Franciscan predecessor of Sahagún in compiling a major ethnography of indigenous Central Mexico, the first maguey (Nahuatl: *metl*) grew from the bones of a virgin goddess, Mayahuel, rescued, after a series of mythic adventures, by the god Ehecatl-Quetzalcoatl. A somewhat similar transformation myth is found in the Codex Vaticanus A (1979: fol. 24v). In the Italian annotation to the illustration of Mayahuel, patroness of the eighth trecena of the tonalpohualli commencing 1 Malinalli (Twisted Grass), it is stated that she was a woman with four hundred (i.e., "innumerable") breasts who, for this exceptional fecundity, was transformed by the gods into the maguey whose juice was fermented to produce the native "wine." In the *Historia de los Mexicanos por sus Pinturas* (1891:237), another important early account of Mexica cosmogony and history apparently also derived from materials collected by Olmos, the "invention" of octli, ten years after the creation of the Fifth Sun, is credited to the stellar-hunting god Mixcoatl-

Camaxtli. Eight years earlier he had created the Chichimeca, described as the rustic original inhabitants of Central Mexico, who, having become incessantly intoxicated on the new beverage, were slaughtered, to provide hearts and blood to sustain the sun, by other beings previously created by the god.

The best-known account of octli origins is contained in Chapter 29 of Book 10 of the Florentine Codex version of Sahagún's *Historia General* (1950–1982, pt. 11:193–94), which is devoted to descriptions of the various ethnic groups of Central Mexico. In the last section that is concerned with the Mexica, we are told how the early settlers of the land, who had migrated from the Panuco region of the Gulf Coast, discovered, while residing at Tamoanchan, how to bore the maguey and to ferment, with the aid of certain roots, its juice to produce octli. The discovery of the first process is credited to a woman named Mayahuel, and that of the second to Pahtecatl, while those who prepared the drink are named Tepoztecatl, Cuatlapanqui, Tlilhua, Papaztac, and Tzocaca. This occurred at Mount Chichinauhia, and, because the octli foamed up, they named it Pozonaltepetl (Foam Mountain). A feast was then prepared, to which the leaders and elders were invited. All drank just four cups of octli except the leader of the Cuexteca, the Huastecs. He drank five (i.e., the number signifying excess), became drunk, and while in this state removed his loincloth. Thus shamed, he fled with his people, the Huastecs, who gained the reputation of being great drunkards, back to the land from whence they had come, Pantlan (= Panuco).

The role of Pahtecatl as the discoverer of the hallucinogenic roots employed in the octli fermentation process is confirmed by the annotators of the Codex Telleriano-Remensis (1899: fol. 15v) and Codex Vaticanus A (1979: fol. 24v). They also describe him as the husband of Mayahuel. However, in another passage, Sahagún (1970 bk. 1:74) credits the invention of octli to Tezcatzoncatl.

Although not explicitly concerned with the origin of octli per se, the 1579 *relación geográfica* of Meztitlan (Chávez 1986), a rustic Nahua-speaking polity on the borders of the Huasteca, recounts a relevant myth involving Ome Tochtli, "dios del vino." Tezcatlipoca, the supreme deity, "killed the god of the wine, with his consent and acquiescence, saying that in this way he became eternal and that, if he had not died, all those who drank wine would die. But that the death of Ome Tochtli was as the dream of a drunkard, which, when he returns from it, leaves him healthy and well" (Chávez 1986:62).

A more "historical" account of the discovery of "la miel prieta de maguey" is found in the Toltec history of Fernando de Alva Ixtlilxochitl (1975, vol. 1:274–76), the mestizo descendant of Tetzcocan royalty. This accomplishment is ascribed to a Toltec noble, Papantzin, during the reign of the next-to-last Toltec ruler, Tecpancaltzin (Iztaccaltzin). Papantzin's daughter, Xochitl (Quetzalxochitzin), presented the new delicacy to Tecpancaltzin, who instantly became enamored of the beautiful maiden. He arranged to have her established as his mistress in a secret palace. After a time Xochitl gave birth to a son, Meconetzin (son of the maguey), also known as Topiltzin, who eventually ascended the throne as the last Toltec ruler and whose reign was beset with disastrous calamities resulting in the destruction of the Toltec imperium.

According to some accounts — Codex Boturini (1964:13, 14); Codex Aubin of 1576 (1963:27) — the migrating Azteca/Mexica, well before they founded Mexico Tenochtitlan, acquired the cultivation of maguey and the technique of octli production from the province of Chalco. This occurred while they were residing at Coatitlan, in the northwest Basin of Mexico (1 Tecpatl, 1220-7 Acatl, 1239, in the chronology of these two pictorial histories).

Octli Cult Ritual

Octli played a ubiquitous role in numerous ceremonies, particularly as an offering to the deity of fire, Xiuhtecuhtli-Huehueteotl, poured as a libation into the hearth fire (see, e.g., Durán 1967, vol. 1:203). The imbibing of octli was normally strictly controlled by law, but special license was given to ritual celebrants to consume it in considerable quantities during certain ceremonies. One of the most important of these was that celebrated on 2 Tochtli (Rabbit), the day, recurring every 260 days, that was especially dedicated to the cult. Before the image of Izquitecatl — called in one passage of Sahagún (1950–1982, pts. 5, 6:17) the principal octli deity, in another (Sahagún 1981, bk. 2:36), the second—a stone basin, called *ometochtecomatl*, the "two rabbit vessel," carved in the shape of a rabbit, was set up and filled to the brim with octli. Dipping their cane sucking-tubes into the liquid, those permitted to

Figure 10.1. Ceremony Performed on Day 2 Tochtli. Two men, with sucking-reeds, imbibe octli from a large vessel, called ometochtecomatl, in the form of a rabbit. Reprinted from Sahagún, *Florentine Codex: General History of the Things of New Spain* plate 12, pt. 5 (Santa Fe, 1979) after Paso y Troncoso edition, by permission of the publisher.

Figure 10.2. Ceremony to Propitiate an Octli God. The god is imbibing the drink with a reed sucking-tube from a vessel adorned with a ritual paper (*tetehuitl*) decorated with the lunar nose ornament, or yacameztli, of the octli deities. Reprinted from the *Codex Magliabechiano*, fol. 85r (Berkeley, 1983), by permission of the publisher.

imbibe, the old men and women and the warriors, drank their fill (Sahagún 1950–1982, pts. 5, 6:17; 1988, vol. 1:240–41). In addition to the relevant illustration in the Florentine Codex (see Figure 10.1), this or a similar ceremony is pictured in the Codices Magliabechiano (see Figure 10.2) and, with notable variants, Tudela (1980: fol. 70r).

A related ritual was performed by the octli priests, called Centzontotochtin, headed by one called Pahtecatl (Sahagún 1958:88–89; 1981, bk. 2:207). The latter placed 260 putative cane sucking-tubes, only one of which was actually hollow, in a vessel filled with octli. The priests jostled and vied with each other to locate this one viable tube, after which the lucky discoverer alone had the right to drink the contents of the vessel to the point of intoxication.

Although the octli deities were propitiated in various of the eighteen major *veintena* ceremonies that composed the 365-day year, the *xihuitl*, none seems to have been exclusively dedicated to their cult. However, they received particular attention in Tepeilhuitl (Mountain Feast), primarily celebrated in honor of the mountain/rain gods, the Tepeticton, who were merged with the Tlaloque, the rain deities par excellence (Sahagún

Figure 10.3. The Veintena of Huey Pachtli. The goddess Xochiquetzal stands at the left while a boy and girl drink octli during the ritual of Pillahuana (Drunkenness of Children). Reprinted from the *Codex Magliabechiano*, fol. 41r (Berkeley, 1983), by permission of the publisher.

1958:93–98, 105–108; 1981, bk. 2:209–11, 214–15). At this time victims arrayed with the insignia of various of the octli deities were sacrificed, along with other victims dedicated to the mountain/rain gods.

In the Codex Magliabechiano (1970: fol. 40v), the annotation to Huey Pachtli, another name for Tepeilhuitl, states that among the Tlalhuica of what is now the State of Morelos a ceremony called Pillahuana (Drunkenness of Children) was celebrated, during which boys and girls, aged nine and ten, danced, drank octli to intoxication, and committed sexual acts. The young goddess of flowers and feminine sensuality, Xochiquetzal, with her name sign, is pictured before a hill with a rattlesnake adorned with ritual papers, below which a boy and girl are drinking from bowls of octli (see Figure 10.3). The cognate scene in the Códice Tudela (1980: fol. 23r) is quite similar, including the imbibing children. However, the annotation varies considerably, stating that in this ceremony (fiesta de los cerros) dedicated to the maize goddess Chicomecoatl, only the lords danced and feasted and drank octli to intoxication, each invoking the octli deity of his choice.

Pantheon and Iconography of the Octli Deities

The octli gods in the aggregate were known as the Centzontotochtin (Four Hundred Rabbits) — or just Totochtin (The Rabbits) — which appellation was also applied to the drink itself, "because it has many and diverse ways of intoxicating one" (Sahagún 1988, vol. 1:239). The seven-

Figure 10.4. The Octli Deity Tepoztecatl. ***Codex Magliabechiano***, fol. 49r. Reprinted from Seler, ***Gesammelte Abhandlungen***, vol. 2 (Berlin, 1902–1923).

teenth Sahaguntine sacred chant is dedicated to these deities (Seler 1902–1923, vol. 2:1083–87; Garibay 1958:192–99), who could also be designated collectively by their calendric name, Ome Tochtli, 2 Rabbit. However, quite a number were known by individual names and propitiated under these names. Some of these were gentilitial, that is, connoted that the deity was of a particular community. Typical members of this group were Tepoztecatl (He of Tepoztlan [Place of the Copper Ax]) (see Figure 10.4), Tezcatzoncatl (He of Tezcatzonco [Place of Mirror-Hair])

Figure 10.5. Octli Deity Tezcatzoncatl. ***Florentine Codex: General History of the Things of New Spain*** plate 21, pt. 2 (Santa Fe, 1979) after Paso y Troncoso edition, by permission of the publisher.

Figure 10.6. The Octli Deity Totoltecatl as Depicted in Sahagún's *Primeros Memoriales*, fol. 265v. Reprinted from Seler, *Gesammelte Abhandlungen*, vol. 2 (Berlin, 1902–1923).

(see Figure 10.5), Toltecatl (He of Tollan [Place of Reeds]), Totoltecatl (He of Totollan [Place of Turkeys]) (see Figure 10.6), Yauhtecatl (He of Yauhtepec [Hill of Yauhtli, powdered sweet-scented marigold, *Tagetes lucida*]), Izquitecatl (He of Izquitlan [Place of Toasted Maize Grains]), Colhuatzintecatl (He of the Small Colhuacan), and Chimalpanecatl (He of Chimalpan [Place of the Shield]). Acolhua might also be included in this group, for this was a gentilitial term for the people of the province of Acolhuacan, whose capital in late pre-Hispanic times was Tetzcoco. Others bore proper names with various meanings; for example, Pahtecatl (He of the Medicine) (see Figures 10.7, 10.8), Papaztac (White Locks of Hair),

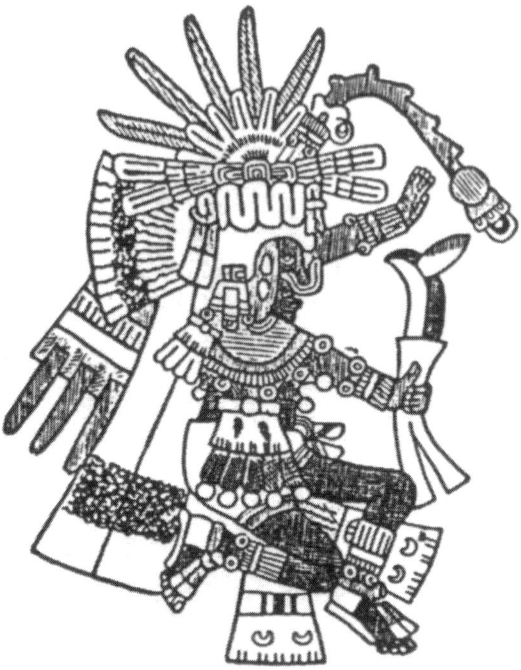

Figure 10.7. The Octli Deity Pahtecatl. Codex Borbonicus 11. Reprinted from Seler, *Comentarios al Códice Borgia*, vol. 2 (Mexico City, 1963), by permission of the publisher.

Cuatlapanqui (Head Breaker), Tlilhua (Possessor of Black), and Tlaltecayohua and Tzocaca (etymologies uncertain).

Sahagún, in his *Primeros Memoriales* (Sahagún 1958:142–43; Seler 1902–1923, vol. 2:488–90), illustrates and describes the costume and insignia of a god named Macuiltochtli (5 Rabbit) (see Figure 10.9), who holds the stone ax (*itztopilli*) that constituted a prominent item in the standard insignia of the octli gods. However, otherwise this deity's insignia identifies him as a member of the "Xochipilli/Centeotl Complex" (Nicholson 1971:416–19), specifically as one of the Macuiltonaleque, the gods headed by Macuilxochitl who contained the numeral 5 (= excess) in their names. These were deities — with solar connotations — of music, feasting, poetry, flowers, and sensuality in general. They overlapped conceptually with the octli gods, and Macuiltochtli expressed this syncretism with particular clarity (see Durán 1967, vol. 1:200–04); it is also highlighted

Figure 10.8. The Octli Deity Pahtecatl. Reprinted from the *Codex Magliabechiano*, fol. 53r (Berkeley, 1983), by permission of the publisher.

by the title *ometochtzin* borne by the "master of all the singers whom they had in charge of singing in the temples" (Sahagún 1988, vol. 1:194).

Sahagún (1958:94–97) also, in his listing of priestly titles in his *Primeros Memoriales*, includes some (e.g., *yauhqueme, tomiyauh, nappatecuhtli*) that obviously merge the octli gods with the rain/mountain deities, the Tepictoton and the Tlaloque. The fact, mentioned above, that

Figure 10.9. The Deity Macuiltochtli as Drawn in Sahagún's *Primeros Memoriales,* fol. 265v. Reprinted from Seler, *Gesammelte Abhandlungen,* vol. 2 (Berlin, 1902–1923).

the principal rituals propitiating the octli deities occurred in the veintena of Tepeilhuitl, dedicated primarily to the Tepictoton, clearly evidences this additional syncretism.

As mentioned, a goddess called Mayahuel (etymology uncertain, possible Mixtec language derivation?? Lehmann [1938:108] opted for *me-yahualli,* "hollowed-out agave"; Sullivan [1982:24] suggested "Powerful Flow") figures prominently in the myths concerning the origin of octli (Quiñones Keber 1989). Mayahuel was the feminine personification of the maguey and — judging from the iconography of her pictorial images — was conceptually merged with the whole intricate complex of maternal fertility goddesses of the "Teteoinnan Complex" (Nicholson 1971:420–22).

The gentilitial names of the octli gods imply that those who bore them were either the special patrons (*abogados,* in sixteenth-century Spanish parlance) of the communities or provinces from which they took their appellations or that their cults were of particular importance there. Certain primary sources state explicitly that some octli deities did function as the tutelary deities of their communities. Examples are Tepoztecatl–Ome Tochtli in Tepoztlan, Morelos (Códice Tudela 1980: fol. 31r; Gutiérrez de Liébiana 1985:189), and Ome Tochtli in Piaztlan, southern Puebla (Vera 1985:58).

The evident geographical distribution of the communities and provinces that appear in these gentilitial names extended from Tollan in the north to Piaztlan in the south, with a certain concentration in the southern zone of this fairly extensive Central Mexican region (Tepoztlan, Yauhtepec, Totollan, Piaztlan). Since, as just indicated, octli gods served as the particular patrons of at least two of these communities, this area south of the Basin of Mexico appears to been one of the principal centers of the octli cult. Tamoanchan, the semimythical "terrestrial paradise" where in Sahagún's account octli was invented, was almost certainly located, in the Contact period Central Mexican traditions, in what is now the State of Morelos and was probably identified with the ruin of Xochicalco (Jiménez Moreno 1942:132–36; Nicholson 1971:107). And, as Jiménez Moreno noted, Monte Chichinauhtzin, northwest of Tepoztlan, is probably to be identified with the eminence Chichinauhia-Pozonaltepetl of the Sahaguntine tradition concerning the origin of octli.

However, the overall distribution of the octli cult clearly extended well beyond the region that can be delimited by locating the communities indicated by the gentilitial appellations of some of the octli gods. The cult was important in Tlaxcala (Muñoz Camargo 1984:193); and the occurrence of versions of the octli deities in four members of the Codex Borgia group (Borgia, Vaticanus B, Fejérváry-Mayer, Laud), which appear to derive from various locations within the "Mixteca-Puebla heartland" (southern Puebla/western Oaxaca/central Gulf Coast; Nicholson 1966b; Sisson 1983), clearly indicates the presence of the octli cult in this region. And this is confirmed by page 25 of the Codex Vindobonensis, picturing a ceremony that Caso (1963; see also Furst 1978:201–03) interpreted, I think correctly, as the origin of octli in the Mixteca. In the other direction, in the northeast, the cult, as we have seen, extended at least as far as Meztitlan on the borders of the Huasteca. Although the specifics of the religious/ritual system in the Huasteca itself are poorly known (see Beyer 1934; Stresser-Péan 1971:596–601; Nicholson 1987:423–24), some version of the cult almost certainly flourished there. And off to the west, in Tarascan Michoacan, still another version of the cult appears to be indicated by the probable presence in the pantheon of a deity connected with pulque (see the discussion in Seler 1902–1923, vol. 3:146–47).

The imagery of the numerous deities that constitute the Ometochtli Complex is one of the most striking and standardized in the entire late pre-Hispanic Central Mexican iconographic system (Nicholson 1973). Nearly a century ago, Seler (1900–1901:87–88) systematically listed the principal diagnostic elements of the costume and insignia of the octli gods as portrayed in the Central Mexican pictorials (Codices Borbonicus, Magliabechiano/Tudela, Telleriano-Remensis/Vaticanus A, Tonalamatl Aubin, etc.), Sahagún and Durán, and various archaeological pieces:

1. A bicolored facial painting, *chictlapanqui,* the central field red, flanked by two fields of black or dark green (occasionally, vice versa), sometimes decorated with yellow lozenge-shaped elements; as Seler noted, this black-and-red bicolored facial format was so diagnostic that stylized versions of it alone were frequently employed to decorate various objects connected with the octli cult, such as mantles, vessels for octli battle standards.

2. A U-shaped nasal ornament, *yacameztli, yacahuicolli,* an insigne typical of the Huasteca and also worn by an earth/fertility goddess, Tlazolteotl-Ixcuina and her avatars, who derived from this region; this ornament has long been recognized as a lunar symbol, as was the rabbit, the creature seen in the moon, that was so closely connected with the octli cult — an association highlighted by the myth recorded in the *Leyenda de los Soles* (Lehmann 1938:345), wherein the octli god Papaztac, just subsequent to the creation of the Fifth Sun and Moon at Teotihuacan, smashed the face of the latter orb with a *tochtecomatl,* a "rabbit vessel," an octli pot.

3. A quadrangular bark-paper earplug, *amanacochtli;* this is shared by the octli gods with the rain and other fertility deities.

4. A long, loose neckpiece, *chayahuac cozcatl,* composed of grass tipped with yellow circles (identified by Seler, probably correctly, as *malinalli* (*Muhlenbergia emersleyi* Vasey and other subspecies), usually bound with a red leather strap and a bark-paper device; this often depends from a wide greenstone collar edged with gold bells or shells, from which hangs a

Figure 10.10. The Octli Deity Totochtin from Sahagún's *Primeros Memoriales*, fol. 261v. Reprinted from Seler, *Gesammelte Abhandlungen*, vol. 2 (Berlin, 1902–1923).

circular gold pectoral. Both this collar and grass neckpiece, as an ensemble, are frequently draped over the *xicolli,* the sleeveless cotton priestly jacket.

5. A headdress, *aztatzontli,* also typical of Tlaloc and related rain/fertility deities, largely composed of white heron feathers; green quetzal feathers, single or in a bunch, are often interspersed with or attached to the heron feathers — and, occasionally, the blue-tipped scarlet feathers, *cuezalin,* of the macaw. A fanlike ornament, worn at the nape of the neck or as a back device, called *cuezalhuitoncatl,* with red macaw feathers

Figure 10.11. The Octli Deity Tlilhua. Reprinted from the *Códice Tudela*, fol. 41r (Madrid, 1980), by permission of the publisher.

projecting from a fan of dark feathers, one of the standard insignia of the creator/wind deity, Ehecatl-Quetzalcoatl, was also ascribed to an octli god, Totochtin, in Sahagún's *Primeros Memoriales* (1958:118–19; Seler 1902–1923, vol. 2:438–42; see Figure 10.10). Pahtecatl, who was apparently particularly connected with Ehecatl-Quetzalcoatl and displays various insignia typical of this god, is also depicted in one instance with the cuezalhuitoncatl (see Figure 10.7).

6. The stone ax, itztopilli, *tecpatopilli,* typically carried by the octli gods in their right hands; there are some exceptions, such as Pahtecatl in the Codices Magliabechiano (see Figure 10.7) and Tudela (1980: fol. 35r) and the Tonalamatl Aubin (Seler 1900–1901:11), who holds instead the curved baton studded with small, white circles — the *ehecahuictli, chicoalli,* or *ehecaxonecuilli,* of Ehecatl-Quetzalcoatl. Also, Tlaltecayohua and Tlilhua (see Figure 10.11) in Magliabechiano (1970: fols. 55r, 59r) and Tudela (1980: fols. 37r, 41r) hold instead the *tlachieloni* or *itlachiaya*, the "seeing instrument" of Tezcatlipoca.

Other relatively standard elements in the iconography of the octli gods, not included by Seler in his classic list, are: the bark-paper neck fan, the *amacuexpalli* (always called by Seler, erroneously, the *tlaquechpanyotl),* typical of the fertility deities; a prominent, radiating-feather back device (see, e.g., Figures 10.4, 10.5, 10.11, 10.12); and shields carried by the gods on their left arms. The shields can be quadrangular (see Figures 10.2, 10.4, 10.6, 10.11) or round (see Figures 10.5, 10.8, 10.9, 10.10, 10.12), more often (especially in Codices Magliabechiano and Tudela) quadrangular. Called *ometochchimalli,* they are usually decorated with the black-and-red bicolored facial painting of the octli gods, plus the yacameztli.

Figure 10.12. An Octli Deity. The god depicted here was included among other deities (or deity impersonators) in the pictorialization of the veintena of Tititl. Reprinted from the *Codex Borbonicus* 36 (Graz, 1964), by permission of the publisher.

The axes held as weapons and the quadrangular shields perhaps point to an area particularly associated with the octli cult where these accoutrements were characteristic. Jiménez Moreno (1942:133) noted that the shields carried by the warrior figures on the Pyramid of the Feathered Serpent at Xochicalco (= Tamoanchan?) are quadrangular and that this type of shield is also occasionally depicted on paintings and sculptures in the Lowland Maya region. He also suggested a possible connection between the stone ax, itztopilli, carried by the octli gods and the similar stone ax, *mactepoztli,* mentioned by Sahagún (1950–1982, pt. 11:188) as a typical weapon of the Olmeca-Uixtotin-Mixteca of the Gulf Coast region.

Figure 10.13. Mayahuel. Codex Borbonicus 8. Reprinted from Seler, *Comentarios al Códice Borgia*, vol. 2 (Mexico City, 1963), by permission of the publisher.

Jiménez Moreno further noted that this weapon is frequently portrayed in the Mixteca pictorials from western Oaxaca. All this tends to confirm the view expressed above that the octli cult was particularly at home in, and associated by the Central Mexicans with, areas to the southeast of the Basin of Mexico — in addition to the Huasteca of the northern Gulf Coast region.

Mayahuel, the feminine member of the Ometochtli Complex, is normally represented as a goddess who shares various elements of costume and insignia with other members of the prominent complex of closely interrelated female fertility deities (Nicholson 1963), especially Chalchiuhtlicue, the water goddess, and Tlazolteotl-Teteoinnan, the earth mother (see Figures 10.13, 10.14; for a discussion of Mayahuel iconography, with relevant illustrations from the native-tradition pictorials, see

Seler 1963, vol. 1:191–92 and Thompson 1966). Mayahuel is most often portrayed within a maguey or with this plant as a backdrop, and the lower portion of her face is often painted blue.

Another designation for Mayahuel, or an avatar, was Tezcacoac-Ayopechtli (Mirror Snake/Tortoise Bench). She is pictured in Sahagún's *Primeros Memoriales* (see Figure 10.15) and in the Codices Magliabechiano (see Figure 10.16) and Tudela (1980: fol. 47r). In the *Memoriales Primeros*

Figure 10.14. Mayahuel. Depicted in the Codex Vaticanus A, fol. 21v. Reprinted from Seler, ***Comentarios al Códice Borgia,*** vol. 2 (Mexico City, 1963), by permission of the publisher.

the lower half of her face is appropriately painted blue. The twelfth of the Sahaguntine sacred chants (Seler 1902–1923, vol. 2:1045–47; Garibay 1958:128–33) is dedicated to her. The annotation in the Codex Magliabechiano designates her "Atlacoaya," a name otherwise unknown; however, the name-sign that accompanies her picture clearly connotes Tezcacoac (see Thompson 1966). Her portrayal here virtually duplicates that of the water goddess Chalchiuhtlicue.

Figure 10.15. Tezcacoac Ayopechtli from Sahagún's *Primeros Memoriales,* fol. 265v. Reprinted from Seler, *Gesammelte Abhandlungen,* vol. 2 (Berlin, 1902–1923).

Archaeological Data

Nearly all of the Central Mexican archaeological data relevant to the octli cult date to the Late Postclassic. However, the cliff paintings of Ixtapantongo, in the southern Basin of Toluca, which are in classic Toltec style, indicate that the cult was already well developed by Early Postclassic times. These paintings include images that can be identified as the Toltec version of Mayahuel, complete with her maguey plant, an adjacent figure that appears to wear the yacameztli as a nose ornament and may therefore represent an octli god, and scenes of imbibing from a large tub (Villagra 1954). The "Mural de los Bebedores," on an early stage of the Great Pyramid of Cholula (Marquina 1971; Gendrop 1971:41–45), although not including any figure that can be identified as an octli deity, appears to indicate that the ritual imbibing of the intoxicant goes back at least as early

Figure 10.16. "Atlacoaya" (=Tezcacoac). Reprinted from the *Codex Magliabechiano*, fol. 75r (Berkeley, 1983), by permission of the publisher.

as the Early Classic period. And this is ostensibly confirmed by the representation of a putative octli drinker near a maguey in the "Tlalocan" mural of the Tepantitla palace at Teotihuacan (Gendrop 1971:34). In any case, judging from the "Maguey Bloodletting Ritual" murals from the structure called Tlacuilapaxco in another area of Teotihuacan (Clara Millon, in Berrin 1988:195–205), maguey cultivation flourished in Central Mexico during the Classic era.

Late Postclassic archaeological pieces that relate to the octli cult are numerous and varied. They include stone images of octli gods bearing typical insignia (see Figure 10.17; Seler 1902–1923, vol. 3:542–44; Mena 1912; Hernández Pons 1982; Nicholson and Quiñones Keber 1983:90–91); ceramic and stone versions of the characteristic winged octli vessels *octecomatl*, and ometochtecomatl (see Figure 10.18; Bankmann 1984); and other types of stone vessels for containing octli, some in the form of rabbits (see, e.g., Bernal 1972:127; Museo Nacional 1902:Plate 143). The most spectacular of these stone vessels is the famous Bilimek cup in the Vienna Museum für Völkerkunde, intricately carved with images and

Figure 10.17. Stone Image of an Octli God. Courtesy of the Museum of Fine Arts, Houston, Texas.

Figure 10.18. Sculpted Frieze, North Side of the East Bench, Cella, "Casa del Tepozteco," Tepoztlan, Morelos. The second panel from the right shows an image of a winged octli pot, or ometochtecomatl. Reprinted from Seler, *Gesammelte Abhandlungen*, vol. 3 (Berlin, 1902–1923).

symbols that relate to the octli cult — and also connoting the punishment administered to the habitual toper (Seler 1902–1923, vol. 2:913–52; Nicholson and Quiñones Keber 1983: 62–63).

Temples to the octli gods must have been numerous in Central Mexico at the time of the Conquest, but the only one that has survived relatively intact and that has been investigated archaeologically is the "Casa del Tepozteco," on a towering cliff overlooking Tepoztlan, Morelos (Saville 1896; Rodríguez 1897; Seler 1902–1923, vol. 2:200–14, vol. 3:486–513). The temple is dedicated to Tepoztecatl, the patron deity of the community, and judging from certain carvings embedded in its substructure it may have commemorated the death of the eighth ruler of Mexico Tenochtitlan, Ahuitzotl, in 10 Tochtli, 1502. In form it is a typical, late pre-Hispanic pyramid temple (Nicholson, in press), featuring a two-stage substructure with principal stairway facing west and a shrine with a vestibule and an inner cella. A series of relief carvings on benches in both rooms display many symbols and images connected with the octli cult.

Significance of the Octli Cult

A few general observations concerning the octli cult and its broader significance are now in order. First, Eduard Seler's ideas (1900–1901:87–90; 1902–1923, vol. 2:209–13, 438–42, 920–29, 1083–87, vol. 3:488–92; 1963, vol 1:107–12, vol. 2:198–203), which have been so influential in the interpretation of the cult, will be concisely summarized. Citing the statement in the Codex Magliabechiano (1970: fol. 48v) that dancing and drinking revels, while the celebrants invoked the octli deities, took place following the maize harvests, he initially interpreted the Centzontotochtin as, fundamentally, "harvest gods," expressing the concept of fruitfulness in general. Later, he expanded his interpretation to include the concepts of the alternations of growth and decay, of dark and light, of life and death, of sleeping and awakening (citing the Tezcatlipoca/Ome Tochtli myth recounted in the *relación geográfica* of Meztitlan). In keeping with his increasingly "lunarized" iconographic and mythological interpretations after 1906 (see Nicholson 1966a), Seler strongly stressed the lunar associations of the cult and its deities. He also emphasized the partial blending and overlapping of the octli gods with the rain/mountain deities, Tlaloque and Tepictoton, and with the gods of sensual pleasures and entertainments featured in the Xochipill/Centeotl Complex — as well as Mayahuel's sycretistic merging with various other female fertility deities. Although I believe that with the greater knowledge gained in recent years by anthropologists and historians of religion concerning the religious aspect of culture in general, some deeper interpretations of the cult should now be possible, I — with some reservations concerning his emphases — regard most of these Selerian interpretations as still essentially valid.

Clearly, the major motivation of most of the intense activity that typified the ceremonial aspect of late pre-Hispanic Central Mexican religion was the promotion and maintenance of fertility. And the highly useful maguey and its intoxicating, fermented fluid exudate represented the very essence of the fruitfulness toward which this incessant ritualism was primarily directed. Aztec civilization has often been characterized as essentially Spartan and puritanical in its behavioral control mechanisms, with a grim, death-obsessed religion. Although there is certainly some truth in this view, the octli cult — along with that of Xochipilli-Macuilxochitl with which it overlapped — represented a more sensual, hedonistic, "Dionysian" facet of the culture, balancing to some degree its more characteristic restraining, inhibitory orientation. And, as Seler recognized, the cult's important sexual aspect was logically connected in the native view with the promotion of fertility that constituted the core of the whole ritual system. At the same time, an ambivalent dualism was embedded in the ideology of the cult, the severe punishments for excessive imbibing of octli contrasting with the tolerance for the pleasurable effects induced by its consumption.

Considering its importance, the late pre-Hispanic Central Mexican octli cult deserves more investigation and analysis than it has received. Its pictorial expression in the ritual/divinatory screenfolds of the pre-Hispanic Codex Borgia group, which could not be considered here because of space limitations, definitely warrants more study. The UCLA Aztec Archive includes most of the published archaeological pieces that relate to the octli cult, but this section of the archive will certainly be expanded with additional archaeological fieldwork in Central Mexico and further research in unpublished collections. And it would be quite interesting to compare the octli cult with similar cults that revolved around intoxicating beverages in other areas of the indigenous New World — and in the Old World as well, including the ancient Mediterranean cults of Dionysius and Bacchus. In the meantime, it is hoped that this summary of the available data concerning the octli cult will stimulate further research into one of the most fascinating subsystems of the overall religious/ritual system of late pre-Hispanic Central Mexico.

REFERENCES

Alva Ixtlilxóchitl, Fernando de

1975–1977 *Obras históricas.* Edited by Edmundo O'Gorman. 2 vols. Mexico City: Universidad Nacional Autónoma de México.

Bankmann, Ulf

1984 *Ometochtecomatl:* Ein altmexikanischen Pulquegefäss im Museum zu Basel. *Verhandlungen der Naturforschungs Gesellschaft Basel* 94:307–20.

Bernal, Ignacio

1972 *Museo Nacional de Antropología: Arqueología,* 3d ed. Mexico City: M. Aguilar.

Berrin, Kathleen, ed.

1988 *Feathered serpents and flowering trees: Reconstructing the murals of Teotihuacan.* San Francisco: Fine Arts Museums of San Francisco.

Beyer, Hermann

1934 Shell ornament sets from the Huasteca, Mexico. *Tulane University, Middle American Research Institute Publications* 5:155–216.

Caso, Alfonso

1963 Representaciones de hongos en los códices. *Estudios de Cultura Nahuatl* 4:26–36.

Chávez, Gabriel de

1986 Relación de la alcaldía mayor de Meztitlan y su jurisdicción. In *Relaciones geográficas del siglo XVI: México,* vol. 2, edited by René Acuña. Mexico City: Universidad Nacional Autónoma de México.

Codex Aubin of 1576

1963 *Historia de la nación mexicana.* Full-color reproduction of the Codex of 1576 (Códice Aubin). Edited with introduction notes, indexes, paleography, and translation from the Nahuatl by Charles E. Dibble. Colección Chimalistac de Libros y Documentos acerca de la Nueva España, no. 16. Madrid: José Porrúa Turanzas.

Codex Borbonicus

1964 *Codex Borbonicus: Bibliothèque de l'Assemblée Nationale, Paris (Y 120).* Complete facsimile edition of the codex in its original format, with commentary by Karl Anton Nowotny on the original content of the codex and a codicological description by Jacqueline de Durand-Forest. Codices Selecti: Phototypice Impressi, vol. 44. Graz: Akademische Druck- und Verlagsanstalt.

Codex Boturini

1964 Códice Boturini o Tira de la Peregrinación, with commentary and interpretation by José Corona Núñez. In *Antigüedades de México basadas en la recopilación de Lord Kingsborough,* vol. 2. Mexico City: Secretaría de Hacienda y Crédito Público.

Codex Magliabechiano

1970 *Codex Magliabechiano, CL. XIII 3 (B.R. 232), Biblioteca Nazionale Centrali di Firenze.* Introductory summary and resume by Ferdinand Anders. Codices Selecti: Phototypice Impressi, vol. 23. Graz: Akademische Druck- und Verlagsanstalt.

1983 *The book of life of the ancient Mexicans: The Codex Magliabechiano.* Book 1: *Introduction and facsimile,* Zelia Nuttall. Book 2: *The Codex Magliabechiano and the lost prototype of the Magliabechiano Group,* Elizabeth Hill Boone. Berkeley: University of California Press.

Codex Telleriano-Remensis

1899 *Codex Telleriano-Remensis: Manuscrit Mexicain du Cabinet de Ch.-M. Le Tellier, Archevêque de Reims à la Bibliothèque Nationale (Ms. Mexicain No. 385).* Chromophotographic reproduction, with an introduction and full transcription by E.-T. Hamy. Anger: Imp. Burdin, Section Orientale de l'Imp. Camis et Cie, Paris.

Códice Tudela

1980 *Códice Tudela.* With a prolog by Donald Robertson and epilog by Wigberto Jiménez Moreno. Authorized reproduction of tables by Ferdinand Anders and S. Jeffrey K. Wilkerson. Madrid: Ediciones Cultura Hispánica, Instituto de Cooperación Iberoamericana.

Codex Vaticanus A

1979 *Codex Vaticanus 3738 ("Cod. Vat. A," "Cod. Ríos").* Codices Selecti: Phototypice Impressi, vol. 65. Graz: Akademische Druck- und Verlagsanstalt.

Durán, Fray Diego

1967 *Historia de las indias de Nueva España e islas de la tierra firme.* Paleographic edition of the handwritten Madrid manuscript, with introductions, notes, and glossary of indigenous and archaic words. Edited by Angel María Garibay K. 2 vols. Mexico City: Porrúa.

Furst, Jill Leslie

1978 *Codex Vindobonensis Mexicanus I: A Commentary.* Institute for Mesoamerican Studies, State University of New York at Albany Publications, no. 4.

Garibay, Angel M.

1958 *Veinte himnos sacros de los nahuas. Los recogió de los nativos Fr. Bernardino de Sahagún, Franciscano,* with introduction, notes, and appendices of other sources. Fuentes Indígenas de la Cultura Náhuatl: Informantes de Sahagún, no. 2. Mexico City: Universidad Nacional Autónoma de México.

Gendrop, Paul

1971 Murales prehispánicos. *Artes de México* 18, no. 144.

Gonçalves de Lima, Oswaldo

1956 *El maguey y el pulque en los códices mexicanos.* Mexico City: Fondo de Cultura Económica.

Gutiérrez de Liébana, Juan

1985 Relación de las cuatro villas del Marquesado del Valle (Acapiztla, Huaxtepec, Tepoztlan, Yauhtepec). In *Relaciones geográficas del siglo XVI: México,* vol. 1, edited by René Acuña. Mexico City: Universidad Nacional Autónoma de México.

Hernández de Pons, Elsa C.

1982 Sobre un conjunto de esculturas asociadas a las escalinatas del Templo Mayor. In *El Templo Mayor: Excavaciones y estudios,* edited by Eduardo Matos Moctezuma, coordinator. Mexico City: Instituto Nacional de Antropología e Historia.

Historia de los mexicanos por sus pinturas

1891 In *Nueva colección de documentos para la historia de México,* vol. 3, edited by Joaquín García Icazbalceta. Mexico City.

Histoyre du Mechique

1906 Histoyre du Mechique, Manuscrit Français Inédit du XVIe Siècle, publié par M. Edouard de Jonghe. *Journal de la Société des Américanistes de Paris,* n.s. 2, no. 1:1–41.

Hough, Walter

1908 The pulque of Mexico. *Proceedings of the United States National Museum, Washington, D.C.* 38:577–92.

Jiménez Moreno, Wigberto

1942 El enigma de los olmecas. *Cuadernos Americanos* 1, no. 5:113–45.

Lehmann, Walter, trans. and ed.

1938 *Der Geschichte der Königreiche von Colhuacan und Mexico (Anales de Cuauhtitlan* and *Leyenda de los soles).* Quellenwerke zur alten Geschichte Amerikas aufgezeichnet in den Sprachen der Eingeborenen herausgegeben vom Ibero-Amerikanischen Institut, Berlin, no. 1.

Marquina, Ignacio

1971 La pintura en Cholula. *Artes de México* 18, no. 140:25–40.

Mena, Ramón

1912 Arqueología mexicana: Mixcoatl y El Quecholli. *Memorias de la Sociedad Científica "Antonio Alzate"* 32, no. 7–8:275–79.

Muñoz Camargo, Diego

1984 Descripción de la ciudad y provincia de Tlaxcala. In *Relaciones geográficas del siglo XVI: Tlaxcala,* vol. 1 edited by René Acuña. Mexico City: Universidad Nacional Autónoma de México.

Museo Nacional de Culturas Populares

1988 *El maguey: "Arbol de maravillas."* Mexico City: Museo Nacional de Culturas Populares/Gobierno del Estado de Hidalgo.

Museo Nacional de México

1902 *Album de antigüedades indígenas que se conservan en el Museo Nacional de México.* Mexico City: Imprenta del Museo Nacional.

Nicholson, H. B.

1963 An Aztec stone image of a fertility goddess. *Baessler Archiv* 11, no. 1:9–30.

1966a A note on "Comentarios al Códice Borgia." *Tlalocan* 5, no. 2:125–32.

1966b The problem of the provenience of the members of the "Codex Borgia Group": A summary. In *Summa antropológica en homenaje a Roberto J. Weitlaner.* Mexico City: Instituto Nacional de Antropología e Historia.

1971 Religion in pre-Hispanic Central Mexico. In *Handbook of Middle American Indians,* edited by Robert Wauchope. Vol. 10, *Archaeology of northern Mesoamerica,* edited by Gordon Ekholm and Ignacio Bernal. Austin: University of Texas Press.

1973 The late pre-Hispanic Central Mexican (Aztec) iconographic system. In *The iconography of Middle American sculpture.* New York: Metropolitan Museum of Art.

1987 Mesoamerican religions: Postclassic cultures. In *The encyclopedia of religion,* edited by Mircea Eliade. Vol. 9. New York: Macmillan.

In press Late pre-Hispanic Central Mexican ("Aztec") sacred architecture: The "Pyramid Temple." In *Circumpacifica: Festschrift für Thomas S. Barthel,* edited by Bruno Illius and M. Laubscher. Frankfurt and Bern: Peter Lang Verlag.

Nicholson, H. B., and Eloise Quiñones Keber

1983 *Art of Aztec Mexico: Treasures of Tenochtitlan.* Washington, DC: National Gallery of Art.

Quiñones Keber, Eloise

1989 Central Mexican pictorial manuscripts: Mayahuel and maguey: Sustenance and sacrifice in an Aztec myth. *Latin American Indian Literatures Journal* 5, no. 2:72–83.

Rodríguez, Francisco M.

1897 Descripción de la pirámide llamada "Casa del Tepozteco" perteneciente al pueblo de Tepoztlán, del Estado de Morelos . . . In Congreso Internacional de Americanistas, *Actas de la undécima reunión, 1895.* Mexico City: Congreso Internacional de Americanistas.

Sahagún, Fray Bernardino de

1905 *Primeros memoriales.* In *Historia general de las cosas de Nueva España por Fr. Bernardino de Sahagún,* edited by Francisco del Paso y Troncoso. Vol. 6. Madrid: Hauser y Menet,

1950–1982 *Florentine Codex: General History of the Things of New Spain.* Translated and edited by Arthur J. O. Anderson and Charles E. Dibble. Santa Fe: School of American Research and the University of Utah.

1958 *Ritos, sacerdotes y atavíos de los dioses,* edited with introduction, paleography, translation, and notes by Miguel León-Portilla. Mexico City: Universidad Nacional Autónoma de México.

1970 *General History of the Things of New Spain, Fray Bernardino de Sahagún.* Translated and edited by Arthur J.O. Anderson and Charles E. Dibble. Book 1 — *The Gods.* 2d ed., rev. *Monographs of the School of American Research, Santa Fe, New Mexico,* no. 14, part II.

1979 *Códice Florentino, Ms. 218–220 de la Colección Palatina de la Biblioteca Medicea Laurenziana.* Color photoreproduction. 3 vols. Florence: Giunti Barbera.

1981 *General History of the Things of New Spain, Fray Bernardino de Sahagún.* Translated and edited by Arthur J.). Anderson and Charles E. Dibble. Book 2 — *The Ceremonies.* 2d ed., rev. *Monographs of the School of American Research, Santa Fe, New Mexico,* no. 14, part III.

1988 *Fray Bernardino de Sahagún, historia general de las cosas de Nueva España: Primera versión íntegra del texto castellano del manuscrito conocido como Códice Florentino.* Introduction, paleography, glossary, and notes by Alfredo López Austin and Josefina García Quintana. 2 vols. Madrid: Alianza.

Saville, Marshall H.

1896 The Temple of Tepoztlan, Mexico. *Bulletin of the American Museum of Natural History* 8:221–26.

Seler, Eduard

1900–1901 *The tonalamatl of the Aubin Collection: An old Mexican picture manuscript in the Paris National Library (Manuscrits Mexicains No. 18–19).* English ed. by A. H. Keane. London and Aylesbury: Hazell, Watson & Viney.

1902–1903 *Gesammelte Abhandlungen zur amerikanischen Sprach- und Altertumskunde.* 5 vols. Berlin: Verlag A. Asher and Verlag Behrend.

1963 *Comentarios al Códice Borgia.* Translated by Mariana Frenk. 3 vols. Mexico City: Fondo de Cultura Económica.

Sisson, Edward B.

1983 Recent work on the Borgia group codices. *Current Anthropology: A World Journal of the Sciences of Man* 29, no. 5:653–56.

Stresser-Péan, Guy

1971 Ancient sources on the Huasteca. In *Handbook of Middle American Indians,* edited by Robert Wauchope. Vol. 11, *Archaeology of northern Mesoamerica,* edited by Gordon Ekholm and Ignacio Bernal. Austin: University of Texas Press.

Sullivan, Thelma D.

1982 Tlazolteotl-Ixcuina: The great spinner and weaver. In *The art and iconography of Late Post-Classic Central Mexico: A conference at Dumbarton Oaks, October 22nd and 23rd, 1977,* edited by Elizabeth Hill Boone. Washington, DC: Dumbarton Oaks, Trustees for Harvard University.

Thompson, J. Eric S.

1966 Ayopechtli, an aspect of the Nahua goddess of the maguey. In XXXVI Congreso Internacional de Americanistas, España, *Actas y Memorias (1964),* vol. 2. Seville.

Vera, Juan de

1985 Relación de Acatlan y su partido (Chila, Petlatzinco, Icxitlan, Piaztlan). In *Relaciones geográficas del siglo XVI: Tlaxcala,* vol. 2, edited by René Acuña. Mexico City: Universidad Nacional Autónoma de México.

Villagra, Agustín

1954 Pinturas rupestres "Mateo A. Saldaña," Ixtapantongo, Edo. de México. *Revista Goodrich Euzkadi "Caminos de México"* 9.

11

Dryness Before the Rains: Toxcatl and Tezcatlipoca

Doris Heyden

The god Tezcatlipoca and his fiesta Toxcatl had religious, political, and economic importance in relation to seasonality: periods of dryness in contrast to times of rain. For the association of human activity with this pattern in nature, I have been inspired by Pedro Carrasco's (1976) pioneering study in which he associated the months and fiestas of the Aztec year with the seasons and the world directions, by Johanna Broda's (1970) penetrating analyses of pre-Hispanic fiestas, and by Carmen Aguilera's (1982) article "Xolpan y Tonalco" in which she distinguishes the wet season (*xopan*: "wind of rains," time of greenness) from the dry (*tonalco*: "time of the sun's heat, dryness" [Simeón 1988:780]). In my own previous studies (Heyden 1988) I have touched briefly on the fiesta Toxcatl, which Durán translated as "dry thing" or "something dry," as the prelude to the rains.

Toxcatl, the fifth Aztec month, corresponding to our May, signifies, according to Francisco de las Navas (n.d.:133–34), *deslizadero* or *resbaladero,* meaning "that which is slippery" — that is, the dryness does not end with a bang but slips into the wet season at that time. This month celebrates many things. According to Sahagún (1950–1982, II:9), it was the most important of all the fiestas, honoring the god who was supreme among the deities. Huitzilopochtli, tutelary god of the Aztec-Mexicas, was also honored, as well as Cihuacoatl, and in every home the household gods were bathed in smoke from burning incense.

Tezcatlipoca and His Mirror

Tezcatlipoca, the Smoking Mirror (or smoke from the mirror), the "true god," the invisible one "whose abode was everywhere, in the land of the dead, on earth, and in heaven" (Sahagún 1950–1982, II:5), was a complex figure. He was positive and negative: He bestowed riches upon men but he took them away whenever he felt like it; he gave nobility, honor, and rulership to those who deserved them; he judged people's actions but he himself was capricious; he gave power to the tlatoani (the ruler); he took care that those who governed did so fairly, yet he distributed illness to anyone who went against him. He brought discord to people; he mocked them. He had many disguises and as a magician he once invited some Toltecs to a party where he danced and played the drum, in this way exciting his guests who then danced, led by Tezcatlipoca, to a ravine into which they fell and were turned into stones. The evil magician then destroyed the bridge so those who followed also fell into the abyss and became petrified. All this was done to amuse Tezcatlipoca (Sahagún, II:23).

But this god was not all bad. Among his positive aspects was his personification as Telpochtli, the young god who was so fleet of foot that he was the first to arrive at the feasts of the gods. Telpochtli also was the patron of the *telpochcalli,* "house of youth," the school where the macehualtin (commoners) and also the *pipiltin* (nobles) studied, and boys were trained for warlike activities. So, Tezcatlipoca was a patron of youth (Durán 1971:112).

The many facets of the Smoking Mirror can be seen in the different names by which he was addressed in Book 6 of Sahagún's Florentine Codex (1969). I have counted 360 of these; some are repetitions but are used in different context and some are considered gods in their own right; for example, Omacatl. I shall list a few of these personalities of Tezcatlipoca:[1]

Icnoacatzintle: The Merciful One
Ilhuicahua Tlalticapaque: Possessor of the Sky, Possessor of the Earth
Ipalnemoani: He for Whom We Live
Monantzin Motatzin: Your Mother, Your Father
Monenequi: He Who Is Arbitrary, He Who Pretends
Moyocoani, or Moyocoyotzin: He Who Creates Himself
Necoc Yaotl: The Enemy on Both Sides
Ome Acatl, or Omactl: Two Reed

Calendar name of the god: Omacatl (see Figure 11.1) is considered a separate god, the Lord of Reeds, the patron of banquets. He carries not an obsidian mirror but a mosaic or tlachialoni, which, however, is basically the same, as it is an object used for observation (Simeón 1988:567).

Pilhoacatzintli: Revered Father, Possessor of the Children

Teiocoyani: The Creator (of people)

Telpochtli: The Youth

Tepeyolotl: Heart of the Hills

In this title, the god is related to the jaguar and the night sky, to caves and darkness; it is not included in Book 6 of the Florentine Codex but is an aspect of Tezcatlipoca.

Titlacauan: He Whose Slaves We Are

Tlacatle Totecuyo: O Lord, Our Master

Tlazopilli: The Precious Son, the Precious Noble

Tloque Nahuaque: The Possessor of Nearness, the Possessor of That Which Surrounds Us (He Who Totally Envelops Us)

Yaotl, or Yaotzin: The Enemy

Youalli EhÉcatl: Night, Wind

By extension, this implies the invisible, the impalpable, the intangible

Nicholson (1971:412–13) has described Tezcatlipoca as

> the virile, ever-youthful, omnipotent, omnipresent deity, before whom all creatures were completely helpless. It was the ascription to Tezcatlipoca of total power which, above all, characterized this remarkable deity. He bore almost as many names and appellations as Ometeotl [creator duality]; some of these were identical with those applied to the latter, pointing up his partial merger with this figure. . . . Some other deities apparently considered to have been aspects of Tezcatlipoca were: Itztli (a "calendar deity"), Ixquimilli-Itzlacoliuhqui (a rather obscure conception, probably connected with punitive justice), Tepeyollotl (probably originally an independent eastern Mexican jaguar-earth god), Tecciztecatl-Metztli (the male lunar deity), and Chalchiuh-totollin (his commonest theophanic form and another "calendar deity"). . . . Befitting Tezcatlipoca's omnipotence was his role as archsorcerer, associated with darkness, the night, and the jaguar, the were-animal *par excellence* of the Mesoamerican sorcerer-transformer. Tezcatlipoca's ultimate origins might go back to the obsidian mirror, an instrument used for divinatory scrying. No deity better expressed the pessimistic, fatalistic

Figure 11.1. Omacatl, an Aspect of Tezcatlipoca and the God of Banquets. His instrument for observation is the itlachiaya (his visual power). From the Florentine Codex, Book 1. All drawings for Chapter 11 are by Aarón Flores.

> *weltanshauung* that prevailed in late pre-Hispanic central Mexico. The basic attitude of dread and submission before Tezcatlipoca's capricious omnipotence is particularly well expressed in a famous series of Sahaguntine prayers. . . . This god, true to his name, provides a mirror in which the whole character of a culture is clearly reflected.

Perhaps some of the awe inspired by Tezcatlipoca was due to the fact that he was the firstborn of the creator pair, Ometecuhtli and Omecihuatl, together known as Ometeotl (two god), also called Tonacatecuhtli and Tonacacihuatl (lord and lady of our flesh or sustenance) and as Nicholson states — shares some characteristics with this dual creative force.

Tezcatlipoca, when born, appeared in four forms, associated with the world quarters: the black or true Tezcatlipoca (north); the red Tezcatlipoca or Xipe Totec (east); the blue Tezcatlipoca or Huitzilopochtli (south); the white Tezcatlipoca or Quetzalcoatl (west) (Caso 1962:19–21; Historia de los Mexicanos por sus Pinturas 1973:23–24. Tezcatlipoca also ruled over the first of the Four Suns or Worlds, called Four Jaguar, when giants lived on the earth.

Tezcatlipoca's statue in Tenochtitlan was made of "shining black stone, black as jet, the same stone of which sharp blades and knives are fashioned" (Durán 1971:98). The stone undoubtedly was obsidian, which is volcanic glass.[2] In other cities the god's image was made of wood, painted black "from the temples down," the color with which Tezcatlipoca's priests covered themselves. The black "paint," called teotlacualli (divine food, or food of the gods), was made of soot from "smoke from torches . . . which torches and smoke were highly revered and were special offerings to the gods" (Durán 1971:115), mixed with spiders, scorpions, centipedes, vipers, and other poisonous creatures, all ground together with tobacco and *ololiuhgui* (*Rivea corymbosa*). When applied to the body, this pitch protected the wearer from harm, especially at night when he went to the hills and into caves where figures of the gods were kept, and where the priests communicated with the gods. The pitch also had medicinal properties. I suggest that the black color of priests, color of divine pitch, was an imitation of Tezcatlipoca's body, which was made of obsidian, the black volcanic glass.[3] Since Tezcatlipoca was omnipresent, this black unguent, made of unpleasant things but bringing positive results — just like Tezcatlipoca's character — would always remind men who performed rituals of the intangible but ever-present god (see Heyden 1988:222).

Pictorial representations of the god Tezcatlipoca or of his impersonator show him carrying the diagnostic obsidian mirror in his hand (see Figure 11.2), with the mirror as part of his head ornaments (see Figure 11.3), or as a substitute for his foot (see Figure 11.4), to name a few. Often, smoke comes out of the mirror, making this a name-glyph, since Tezcatlipoca means "smoke from the mirror." However, the smoke also resembles a speech scroll, which would mean that Tezcatlipoca is both a speaker and an observer, because the mirror, called itlachiaya (his visual power, or place from which he watches, according to Durán [1971:99]), indicated "that Tezcatlipoca could see all that took place in the world."

Figure 11.2. Tezcatlipoca as Seen by the Informants of Sahagún. He carries the mirror in his hand. From the Florentine Codex, Book 1.

But the mirror has other implications. The *Histoyre du Mechique* (Historia de México 1973:114–115) tells us that there was a mirror in the temple of Quetzalcoatl in Tula that controlled the rain: If rain was lacking, all the people had to do was ask the mirror for it. But one day Tezcatlipoca went to the temple where he found the guards sleeping, so he stole the

Figure 11.3. Tezcatlipoca in the Codex Magliabechiano. The circular breast pendant is characteristic of this god.

mirror. Thus, it became his mirror and because of this Tezcatlipoca caused a drought. Eventually, he tired of the game and told an old woman he met on the road where to find the rain-making mirror, which he had hidden underneath the palace. So, the rains could come again.

Mirrors have, in all cultures, been used for divination. On Tezcatlipoca's foot, head, or in his hand, his mirror could have functioned in part as an instrument for predicting when the dry season would begin or end.

Mendieta (1945, vol. 1:95) equates Ipalnemohuani or Moyucuyatzin with the sun, which is the source of heat and, when rain does not come,

Figure 11.4. Tezcatlipoca. As seen by Fray Diego Durán, the god is a well-formed young man whose smoking mirror forms part of his headdress.

causes drought. I have suggested elsewhere (Heyden 1984:608) that the smoke emerging from the mirror may have been associated with the smoke coming out of the fields that were burned in May, time of Toxcatl, in order to prepare the earth for planting. Smoke in many cultures is a means of communication between humans and the gods, in a similar manner, perhaps, to the offering to the sun, among the Aztecs, of vapor from a recently extracted heart.

In Book 6 of the Florentine Codex, we are told that the Aztec ruler was the mirror of Tezcatlipoca, since the god was the supreme judge of man's actions. Tezcatlipoca and his mirror played an important part in ascension rites, and at times the god was joined to Xiuhtecuhtli in image and insignia, since Xiuhtecuhtli was the patron of rulers (see Noguez 1971) and Tezcatlipoca guided the ruler's actions. One meaning of the mirror, then, was that it was a metaphor for rulership, for power.

Toxcatl

Toxcatl, the fifth month and fiesta of the year, has, like Tezcatlipoca, many meanings. As I have mentioned, Durán interprets the word as "something dry." According to Simeón's Nahuatl-language dictionary (1988:723), to Clavigero, Orozco y Berra, and Dibble and Anderson (FC, II:66), the term Toxcatl is derived from the garlands of toasted maize, symbolizing the dryness of the season, worn by participants in the fiesta: Durán (1971:102–107, 426–27) explains that Toxcatl was not only the name of the festival but also of the maize garlands worn at that time, "which indicated the barrenness of the season." He adds that Toxcatl symbolized drought and that the aim of the rites was to petition rain, "much like our own pleas and litanies which usually fall in the month of May" (Durán 1971:102).[4] "A native informant [continues Durán] told me that around this time of the year rain was (so) scarce (that) the people begged it of the god whose feast they were keeping. . . . The Indians also had a proverb, titotoxcahuia, which means 'to dry up with thirst', and so it is that Toxcatl means . . . Lack of Rain" (Durán 1971:427).

The end of the dry season was symbolized by the sacrifice of Tezcatlipoca's ixiptla, or impersonator, at the beginning of the Toxcatl fiesta.[5] Like Tezcatlipoca, this image of the god had to be a youth without physical defects, a model of young perfection (see Figure 11.5). He was chosen from among captives of war and during a year was trained in singing, the playing of musical instruments, and in speaking well. He lived in luxury and was treated like the god himself.

Sahagún (FC, 1981:66–69) describes this ixiptla, who lived as the god for a year before his sacrifice, who was the "human form" given Tezcatlipoca. The image was chosen from among about ten selected war captives, each one fair of body, "fair of countenance, of good understanding, quick, of clean body, slender, reed-like, long and thin, like a stout cane, like a stone column all over, not of overfed body, not corpulent, not very small, nor exceedingly tall." If he were very tall, women would taunt him by calling him "tree-shaker, star-gatherer." He was the image of perfect youth — fair of face, perfect of body, without flaw or blemish. The emphasis was on youth and virility.

During the year he represented the god, this model of perfection was first trained in the home of a steward: "The greatest care was taken that he be taught to blow the flute, that he be able to play his whistle; and at the same time he held all his flowers and his smoking tube" (FC, 1981:68;

Figure 11.5. Tezcatlipoca's Ixiptla. *Above:* The deity's human image is being prepared for his role as representative of the god during one year. *Below:* Tezcatlipoca's representative is taught to play the flute correctly. The flute was a diagnostic element of the god. From the Florentine Codex, Book 2.

Figure 11.6. Tezcatlipoca's Ixiptla Dressed for the Toxcatl Fiesta. He carries the tlachieloni, mirror, and a tube of smoking tobacco. From the Florentine Codex, Book 2.

see Figure 11.6). He went about day and night, playing his flute, smoking tobacco, and smelling flowers.[6] When he passed by, the people bowed before him and performed the earth-eating ceremony in his honor. They treated him like a god. His face was painted black, characteristic of the deity he represented. Eagle down was pasted to his face; these fine feathers were symbolic of sacrifice. His attire was splendid and included turquoise, gold, shell, and feather adornments. He wore a crown of popcorn flowers and a cape of the same — that is, even though his legs were covered with gold bells, the *oyoalli,* and his feet wore sandals of obsidian and jaguar skin, the popcorn flowers and toasted maize garlands were an ever-present reminder of the dryness of the season, of the importance of the fecundity of the earth, dependent upon rain, over nonvegetative wealth.[7]

Aside from the popcorn garlands and sumptuous vestments worn by the impersonator, the huey tlatoani adorned him on numerous occasions and showered him with gifts, "for verily he took him to be his beloved god" (FC, 1981:69).[8]

Twenty days before the sacrifice of the ixiptla — when it was still the fourth month, Huey Tozoztli — his physical appearance was transformed into that of a warrior. He had been a warrior who was captured, and he ended his life as a warrior. During the interim, his year as impersonator of Tezcatlipoca, he represented the more peaceful, positive aspects of the god but at the end reverted to the bellicose aspect. Perhaps this reflects Tezcatlipoca's aspect as the patron of the telpochcalli, the school where youths were trained to be warriors. López Austin (personal communication) translates *yaotequiua*, one of the appellations referring to Telpochtli, as "he whose occupation is the military."

The impersonator's long hair was cut and then was bound in a kind of "pony tail," to which were attached quetzal and heron feathers. He was given four young women as wives. They, too, had lived for a year in their own quarters, carefully guarded, and were named for goddesses. So they were also *teixiptlauan*. Five days before the Toxcatl fiesta, Tezcatlipoca's image and his wives sang and danced in specific places: the first day at Tecanman; the second at the home of the man who had guarded the image of the god; the third a Tepetzinco in the middle of the lagoon; the fourth at Tepepulco; the fifth at Acaquilpan or Caualtepec, a place reached by boat. Here he was left by the four women.

The servitors accompanied the young man, who then ascended the steps of a temple called Tlacochcalco (house of darts, a shrine dedicated to war) in Tlapitzauayan. At each step he shattered a flute or a whistle.[9] When the impersonator reached the summit, he was seized by the priests, thrown on his back on the sacrificial stone, and his heart was cut out. The heart was then raised to the sun in an act of offering that took place after every human sacrifice. The body was carefully lowered and his head, severed, was placed on the tzompantli, or skull rack.

The four young women given to Tezcatlipoca's impersonator during the last twenty days of his year's portrayal of the god represented four goddesses of agricultural fertility and water: Xochiquetzal, goddess of plant life and vegetation in general; Xilonen, young maize goddess; Atlatonan, patroness of lepers but also a goddess of maize; and Uixtociuatl, goddess of salt and sister of the Tlaloque, rain deities. I interpret this "marriage" of Tezcatlipoca's impersonator with these images of earth's fertility as a symbolic substitution of sterility by abundance. While they lived with the ixiptla, the women were impregnated with his seed, so when he (the dry season) disappeared, the seed flourished within the images of sustenance, of water, of fruits of the earth. That is, the sacrifice of Tezcatlipoca signifies the end of the dry season. Tezcatlipoca's smoke is replaced with water from the sky, the dry gives way to the wet (Heyden 1984, 1986). And the four symbols of agricultural abundance are free to bear fruit.[10]

HUITZILOPOCHTLI

Huitzilopochtli's (Sahagún FC, 1981:71–77) festivities followed the sacrifice of Tezcatlipoca's ixiptla; Sahagún states that Ixteucale (also named Tlacauepan and Teicauhtzin), who had lived together with Titlacauan (Tezcatlipoca), was sacrificed and his head placed on the skull rack next to that of Tezcatlipoca's impersonator. The important thing here is that honors to Huitzilopochtli, who was an avatar of Tezcatlipoca according to Nicholson, were held at the *end* of Toxcatl, when Etzalcualiztli, time of rain and abundance, was about to begin. Furthermore, Huitzilopochtli's statue was made entirely of seeds, mainly amaranth. Thus, in the Toxcatl fiesta, Huitzilopochtli was portrayed as a symbol of sustenance. This is a different picture from the one we usually have of Huitzilopochtli as the war god and tutelary deity of the Aztec-Mexica. It is one example of the complex character of the Aztec deities who, like Tezcatlipoca, were omnipresent and had many faces and many attributes.

NOTES

1. I am indebted to Karen Dakin for her assistance in translating from the Nahuatl these names of the deity.
2. Obsidian was called "the steel of the New World" by Cobean et al. (1971).
3. Obsidian is, although certainly black, touched with green, gray, gold, or red lights.
4. These traditions are still alive in Mexico. May 3 is the Day of the Holy Cross and is celebrated in many ways: For example, in the cities it is "el día de los albañiles" (construction workers), when crosses covered with flowers adorn buildings being erected; in the country, rites to the earth and petitions for rain are held. In Ostotempa, Guerrero, offerings are made to four giants who supposedly live in four caves at the bottom of a great *pozo* or hole, part of a geological fault. In these caves all kinds of grains grow, especially maize of four colors. Crosses (in pre-Hispanic times representing life-giving plants) are set up on the sacred hill and around the pozo and caves. Three pilgrimages a year are made to the site, in April, May, and October, to petition for rain and to give thanks for the harvest. These pilgrimages coincide with the pre-Hispanic months Toxcatl, Etzalcualiztli, and Tepeilhuitl (Sepúlveda 1973:11–12).
5. According to Sahagún, Tezcatlipoca's ixiptla was sacrificed on the first day of the fiesta. As soon as he was sacrificed, a new impersonator was chosen to represent the god for another year. Transgressions were pardoned during Toxcatl also, but this took place every four years, says Durán (1971:99).

6. These were some of the elements by which Tezcatlipoca was recognized. Even after the conquest, in certain processions whose date corresponded to that which would have been Tezcatlipoca's fiesta, the participants carried flowers instead of the usual candles. Durán (1971:103), recognizing this syncretism, simply shrugged and said, "I see these things but I am silent . . . so I pick up my staff of flowers like the rest and walk along, thinking of our gross ignorance, for great evils may be concealed under these customs."
7. This is reminiscent of Huemac's downfall in Tula, according to one myth. Huemac played ball with the Tlaloque, rain gods, and, when victorious, insisted upon receiving jade beads and quetzal feathers instead of maize, after which drought and famine besieged Tula (Davies 1977:394).
8. In the Florentine Codex's representation of the Toxcatl fiesta and the ixiptla's actions, this impersonator of Tezcatlipoca wears a flayed skin. The accompanying text does not mention flaying and I have yet to find a satisfactory explanation for the drawing. The Texcatlipoca impersonator resembles the *xipeme,* men who wear flayed skins in the Tlacaxipehualiztli fiesta. Perhaps the same artist illustrated all the fiestas for the Florentine Codex and simply contributed his own interpretation.
9. Remains of flutes in archaeological excavations are generally taken to indicate the presence of Tezcatlipoca's impersonator, or rites in honor of the god. Such remains are abundant at the Templo Mayor. Music from flutes, drums, or whistles constituted a sacred message, as did smoke. Nevertheless, flutes were played in rites at different times of the day, a custom perhaps similar to the ringing of church bells today.
10. It has been suggested that it would be impossible for the four wives to give birth to Tezcatlipoca's offspring because they were sacrificed in the succeeding months. However, the chronicles state that impersonators of the goddesses usually were maidens from prominent families (see, e.g., Durán 1971:242), in which a girl's virginity was carefully protected; therefore, they would not possibly have been the same girls who had spent twenty days as Tezcatlipoca's concubines. Some goddess images were slaves, about twelve or thirteen years old (Durán 1971:223), and two maidens sacrificed in Xochiquetzal's fiesta, Pachtontli, had their legs crossed after death, "to signify they had died as virgins" (Durán 1971:244). More than one young woman could have been given the name of a goddess for ritual purposes. Each year, for example, there was a different ixiptla of Xochiquetzal, of Xilonen-Chicomecoatl, of Uixtociuatl, and of Atlantonan, each one bearing the name of "her" goddess. We are ignorant of the fate of the children born to the "four wives of Tezcatlipoca," but it would have been to the interest of the Aztec-Mexica to incorporate them into society as a fusion of the sacred and the secular.

References

Aguilera, Carmen

1982 Xolpan y Tonalco. *Estudios de Cultura Náhuatl* 15:185–207.

Broda, Johanna

1970 Tlacaxipehualiztli: A reconstruction of an Aztec calendar festival from sixteenth-century sources. *Revista Española de Antropología Americana* 5:197–274.

1971 Las fiestas aztecas de los dioses de la lluvia, *Revista Española de Antropología Americana*:245–327.

Carrasco, Pedro

1976 La sociedad mexicana antes de la Conquista. In *Historia general de México,* vol. 1:165–286. Mexico City: El Colegio de México.

Caso, Alfonso

1962 *El pueblo del sol.* 2d ed. Mexico City: Fondo de Cultura Económica.

Codex Borgia

1976 *Códice Borgia,* with commentary by Karl Anton Nowotny. Graz: Akademische Druck- und Verlagsanstalt.

Davies, Nigel

1977 *The Toltecs: Until the fall of Tula.* Norman: University of Oklahoma Press.

Durán, Fray Diego

1971 *Book of the gods and rites and the ancient calendar.* Translated and edited by Fernando Horcasitas and Doris Heyden. Norman: University of Oklahoma Press.

Heyden, Doris

1984 El espejo de Tezcatlipoca. *Investigaciones Recientes en el Area Maya* 3:603–10.

1986 Diosas del agua y la vegetación. *Anales de Antropología* 20:129–45.

1988 Black magic: Obsidian in symbolism and metaphor. *In Smoke and mist: Mesoamerican studies in memory of Thelma D. Sullivan,* edited by J. Kathryn Josserand and Karen Dakin. BAR International Series, no. 402. Vol. 1. Oxford.

Historia de los mexicanos por sus pinturas

1973 Historia de los mexicanos . . . In *Teogonía e historia de los mexicanos: Tres opúsculos del* siglo *XVI,* edited by Angel María Garibay K. Mexico City: Porrúa.

Historia de México

1973 Historia de México (Histoyre du Mechique). In *Teogonía e historia de los mexicanos: Tres opúsculos del siglo XVI,* edited by Angel María Garibay K. Mexico City: Porrúa.

Mendieta, Fray Gerónimo de

1945 *Historia eclesiástica indiana.* 4 vols. Mexico City: Salvado, Chávez Hayhoe.

Navas, Fray Francisco de las

n.d. *Calendario de Fray Francisco de las Navas, de don Antonio de Guevara y Anónimo Tlaxcalteca.* Colección Ramírez Opúsculos Históricos, vol. 21; Colección Antigua, vol. 210. Archivo Histórico del Museo Nacional de Antropología, Mexico City.

Nicholson, Henry B.

1971 Religion in pre-Hispanic Mexico. In *Handbook of Middle American Indians: Archaeology of Northern Mesoamerica,* edited by Gordon F. Ekholm and Ignacio Bernal. Austin: University of Texas Press.

Noguez Ramírez, Francisco Javier

1971 El Hueitlatoani y su relación con el complejò del dios del fuego Xiuhtecuhtli. History thesis, Universidad Nacional Autónoma de México, Mexico City.

Sahagún, Fray Bernardino de

1950–1982 *Florentine Codex: General history of the things of New Spain.* Translated and edited by Arthur J. O. Anderson and Charles E. Dibble. 13 books. Book 1: *The Gods,* 1970. Book 2: *The Ceremonies,* 1981. School of American Research and the University of Utah. Monographs of the School of American Research.

Sepúlveda, María Teresa

1973 Peticíon de lluvias en Ostotempa. *Boletín INAH* 2, no. 4:9–20.

Simeón, Remi

1988 *Diccionario de la lengua Náhuatl o Mexicana.* Translated from the French by Josefina Oliva de Coll. 6th ed. in Spanish. Mexico City: Siglo Veintiuno.

Part III

Changing Voices

12

Reflections on the Miraculous Waters of Tenochtitlan

Lawrence E. Sullivan

Yesterday we ascended Tepeyac and were asked to look and to see. Like so many great seers throughout history, we have been taken up onto a high mountaintop by Johanna Broda (see Chapter 7, above). One thinks of the scene that was witnessed by fellow visionary pilgrims: Elijah, Moses, Zarathushtra, the Buddha, Jesus, Mohammed. Like them we were shown the glories of the world below. And David Carrasco, with a presiding sweep, said, "Behold." And Johanna Broda exhorted, "Look over there." And Tony Aveni pointed south-southwest and asked, "What's your take on that angle?" And Nick Nicholson responded, "It's surely Ixtacalco, Nextipan, Atlazolpa, and Ixtapalapan." In response to which several others wondered out loud, "Isn't one of those names also a species of plant, Bob [Bye]?" and "Isn't there a day-name connected with that?" or hypothesized that "the Maya equivalent for that name may be 'suq,' which means either a 'necklace of mandibles' or a 'small dog.' "

All this high-level talk was in service of better sight. And we hit the heights at Tepeyac — if not of Cuautepec — on what Johanna Broda has described in her paper as "one of those rare occasions when, due to propitious winds, the smog suddenly clears up and reveals a magnificent view." She pointed out that it was a view that also deeply impressed Cortés and Bernal del Castillo in 1519. And, like a good seer herself, she described for us "lakes, distant mountain ranges, the high volcanoes to the southeast, and the towns . . . with their imposing ceremonial architecture." I suggest that for the Aztecs it was not only a spectacular view, as it is for us, but

Professor Sullivan's response to Johanna Broda's paper was given the day after our field trip to Tepeyac.

also a *specular* view, in a way that we must try to imagine.

For the Aztecs, but not for us, the city of Tenochtitlan and its surrounding mountains, especially the stunning mountainous natural features marked by the special shrines for pilgrimage and sacrifice — these lofty signs, could be seen reflected in the water below as in a dark mirror. From the mountaintops, the mirror of Lake Texcoco and Lake Xochimilco would re/double and re/flect reality, giving the sky, the city, and each mountain, each sight line, and each heliacal rising, a curiously double aspect, a speculative existence. In the mirror of the waters, all realities appear together in one material substance, join on one plane or moving, flowing place. And this terrible symmetry of water—the water of this especular world of sky, mountains, and land—converges toward the world center of Tenochtitlan, the theatrical state in which all reality is mirrored in rite and drama. This is the world wherein Tezcatlipoca, the "dark mirror," is everywhere.

The ritual sequences of pilgrimages to a rotation of shrines is mapped out by Johanna Broda in Chapter 7. The ritual rotation assured that this speculative view was appreciated from many angles, in the festivals of Atl Caualo, Huey Tozoztli, Etzalcualiztli, and Tecuilhuitontli, which took place, regulated by the rhythm of the rains, on the various mountains surrounding the lake. But nowhere was it more spectacular and specular than from the Cerro de la Estrella, which takes its peculiarly strategic place "at the divisory line among Lake Texcoco, Lake of Mexico, and the southern lakes of Chalco and Xochimilco." It dominates all sections of the lake, the sweet and the salty. It is not surprising that Broda describes it for us as "one of the most important sacred places" in the Valley.

And from Zacatepetl, the four-thousand-meter "sacred hill to the south" and the highest peak of the western range, one speculates on reflections of the Yoaltecatl-Tepeyac–Sierra de Cuautepec, which, even as they strain toward the highest heights of the sky, point downward, in watery reflection, to the central shrines of Tenochtitlan.

Zacatepetl is the sacred mountain par excellence. Ironically — and curiously — the sacred place is associated with barbarous "others," the Chichimec hunters whose emblem is the zacapan, the spread-out grass of the mountains. From this peripheral place of the other, the outsider, one "sees" with that seering glance that speculates on the center and with that specular, troubling vision, that reflective revision, that constitutes a cosmos. These mountains were not only reflected on waters, and not only climbed as sacred places when each, in its calendrical turn, offered a different angle from which to reflect upon the specular world of Tezcatlipoca. These sacred mountains were even more deeply implicated in this economy of reflexive relations. They were the sources of their own medium of reflection (a phrase applicable also to gods and humans, whose reflexivity is, each in its own fashion, related to the mountain and water). After all, the sacred mountains were the storehouses of the chaotic, consuming waters whose flow from on high to the inhabited lake and plains brought life to all below — the material life of grain and the especular life of reflexive human beings, arranged in a hierarchy of views displayed in the ritual theater and demarcated by the precincts of the holy city. The mountains were the boundaries whose sides physically enclosed the waters. Their positions in the space of the Valley of Mexico — or perhaps the better term is the *Basin* of Mexico — marked the reflective periphery of the specular state they defined with their vistas, with their self-contained view, and with the mirrory waters they contained within and among them. The entrapment of resources within the catchment area of the mountains allows that view to double back on itself, through the refractive lens of imperial power and fertilizing lake water. Thus bound and doubled, vision is "re/viewed" and transformed into re/ligious cosmovision. The mountains with the waters they contain, within each one singly and among them all collectively, formed the cosmovision that was the Basin of Mexico.

Water comes in different forms; its containers are essential structures of the cosmos. Waters inhabit the sky and fill its clouds; waters dwell in named mountains, spill out of mountain springs and caves, cascade down irrigation canals, nestle in lakes, spurt as salty blood from Huixtocihuatl, recycle through whirlpools that perhaps lead to the consuming sea. Or, in transforms of salt, *atole,* pulque, or maize, the waters insinuate themselves into human containers, driven by the consuming appetite for life. Each of these water forms requires response. The acts of agriculturalists were responses. The acts of labor and the gestures of ritual, from seedtime to harvest, were the proper responses to well-timed rain, mirrored vision, and the consumptive fire that nourishes reflective life in the cosmos and organizes social life. These gifts of power from sacred water mountains create debts. Life in abundance instigates a network of relations and reciprocities wherein debts are repaid with the first offerings of chosen fruits.

Among the offerings were children sacrificed from Tepeilhuitl (October) to Huey Tozoztli, the sowing ritual and petition for rain that marks with hope the end of the dry season in late April, just before the onset of the rains. At Etzalcualiztli (the beginning of June), adults were given in sacrifice to Tlaloc and Chalchiuhtlicue, the swelling god of sweet-water rain and the patroness of the renewed specular lake. The gods themselves are dispatched in the sacrifice at the lakeshore by canoeing priests, even as the gods carry out their role as resource for the cosmos and its vision of itself, a vision appropriated in speculation and symbolic act.

The gods, as fully present powers, are dispatched into absence, into a dimension speculated upon only in the religious imagination, in order that they may be present in their life-giving signs of rain, mountain water, and the sweet water of the lake. Their hearts are thrown into the whirlpool. If I understand Broda's analyses correctly, it is remarkable that these rainy season rites are not celebrated on high, on the heights of the rain-storing mountains that reflect on the waters below. Rather, they are celebrated right on the rising shoreline or on the waters themselves.

The two seasons mirror one another: The ritual activities are mirror re/versals of one another, just as the fertile signs of divine power at work in the ritualized cosmos reflect the fullness of divine beings who once dwelled in a now-dispatched mythic condition. Across the entire dry season stretch the child sacrifices, from October to April, the "going of the young tassled corn." Through an explicit economy of powers, these first fruits are directly related to the rainy season and its fruits, but in the manner of transmuted mirror images. For as the corn was taken and the rains received, now the children are offered as debt payments for that rainy season and its fruits.

There are more mirrored images in which dry season rites are cast as reflections of those in the rainy season. The dry season rites described by Johanna Broda, Anthony Aveni, Philip Arnold, and Ed Calnek are performed on *high,* and on the perimeters of the horizon. But the sacrifices of the rainy season are of mature adults, who are apparently the gods themselves. And they are not sacrificed "up and out," on the reflective edge of the valley, but in the center, down low, on the water's edge. Furthermore, their hearts, the inner germ of their bodies, are thrown into the central waters below, whereas the entire seed body, the husk or outer envelope, of "the paper streamers" ("the baby corn") is deposited into the dry, craggy ridge high on the periphery.

Over the course of the year, the inside is made to reflect what is outside, what is up reflects what is down, the dry reflects the wet — but always through alienated forms and debt-incurring exchanges, just as debts reflect gifts earlier received, signs reflect powers whose full presence was previously dispatched from the scene, and dark, mirroring waters reflect the reality of mountain and sky. The dry season reveals the rain-driven cosmos, mountains, vitality, richness, and center in its reflections, its debts, its night side, its dark-cast images and deaths. The lofty heights of celestial light and mountainous matter are seen as dark shadows, *tonalli,* speculations on water. We must take care not to reduce these reflections to meteorology, to a primitive agriculturalist's science of the weather. The seasons, wet and dry, and their appropriate acts become images and vehicles for reflecting on all those forces that *must* oppose one another in order to reproduce abundant life.

In July, in the height of the rains, when the clouds and rainwaters obscure the spectacular views of and from the mountains and during that time when the Night Sun journeys through the underworld, another set of rites was enacted that composed the Huey Tecuilhuitl. It is noteworthy that these rainy season rites, too, were not performed on the reflective heights but on the sandy shores of the lake. At this time, the young maize germinates in the presence of Xilonen, Cinteotl, Xochipilli, Piltzintecuhtli, and Cihuacoatl. The air and earth are thick with gods and waters and growing maize. This is, then, the fitting time to celebrate the "Small and Big Festival of the Lords," the Tecuilhuitontli and Huey Tecuilhuitl, with its forty days of ritual banquets.

The inhabitants of the whole Basin of Mexico poured into the lake, into the city, like the rains streaming in from the peripheral mountains. And, like the lords of the rains and the mountains, each individual visitor was fed by the tlatoani a generous ration of twenty tamales a day, while the nobles feasted on limitless fare behind closed doors. All this royal bounty was sprung from the storehouses of the sacred king, just as the rains and waters poured from the storehouses of the sacred mountains, for, it is good to bear in mind, the maize for that year's crop had not yet ripened to full fruition and the time for harvest had not yet come. This capacity of king and gods to accumulate abundance over time may appear to work for the common good, but it does so through an economic asymmetry and a hierarchy of unequal reciprocities. There is a shocking arbitrariness attached to the dispensing of the rains, foods, and ceremonies; and a shocking arbitrariness to the dispensing of young children, the "young dwarf maize plants with fresh tassels" — in the spring of their life. Their lifeblood pays the debts incurred through rainwater and pollinates the dry season of the enigmatic, dark-mirror world.

The nextlaoalli pays for the bounty to come from fine lands made fertile with rain. The decapitated body was thrown into lonely mountain crags and crevasses on the heights of speculation, far above the reflective waters that will have flown from its blood. The waters allow cosmovisionists to review every arbitrary move.

In this world, transactions and exchanges cannot be exacted with equal power on all sides. For instance, only the periphery has the power to bind. The periphery is defined in the alterity of the mountains and sky, in the "others" who lie in more hills or beyond them, in the waters that scribe the city's limits, in the ordinary others (the macehualtin) who fill the human reservoirs of the holy city's profane classes and the precincts that surround the priestly sites, and in the extraordinary others who are the supernatural over and against whom the human world stands as an economy of reproductive relations.

But somehow, strangely, arbitrarily, *terribly,* that power to define or bind the city limits, to bind the years, to bind space into sacred and profane parcels, to bind the ethnic others as captives, to bind children for death, and to bind Tezcatlipoca's omnipresence and omniscient vision with ritual vestments and movements mapped on ritual landscape — that power to bind falls firmly into the hands of those who govern speculation. By holding up the mirror of ritual, these speculators control the human mode of seeing the world. They dramatize social and economic relations. They refract sacred powers through their own symbolic gestures, adornments, and speech. They ritually preside over the population's vision of the valley by providing a god's-eye view into the smoking mirror, looking down from the sacred mountains, through the ritual dramas, into the miraculous waters below.

Perhaps in the most arbitrary and ironic act of all, the power to speculate on the Basin of Mexico, its inhabitants and meanings, has fallen into the hands of investigators who often turn a blind eye to the ancient citizens' capacity to create a specular, reflective culture. In frustration, we recognize that this is frequently the case with early Spanish witnesses to the conquest, but it may apply as well to us as intellectuals who bind Aztec history between the covers of books whose premises reflect our own speculations and whose revisions of history overdetermine the views that the Aztecs may have had of themselves.

We find it difficult to look on waters as *truly miraculous.* We have difficulty in discovering what this might mean for us. Miraculous waters make us *mirar* — look at or see or admire — what we could not otherwise see. On the miraculous waters that flowed from Tepeyac and other sacred mountains, we see reflected below a reality that is strangely doubled in water, in myth, in art, in ritual, in the reproductive acts of couples that yield new generations and seeds that yield abundant harvests.

Let us be clear about one thing: No one has ever made precise observations of nature, of water, say, or mountains, or stars, if one thinks by that phrase that someone has confronted and grasped nature *in se* directly. Even our word *nature* has an exposable history that makes it a very suspicious word to use in order to represent anything real, anything that really matters. The movements of sun, star, water, and mountains-on-the-waters always come to human beings through the travail of their understanding, their materially and culturally defined place in the world. As Anthony Aveni has said, his exactions are always a function of his point of view and his instruments. These instruments, in turn, are material interpretations of a cosmology that comes replete with commitments — often mythic commitments — about the nature of what is real and how that reality is constituted.

In this book and in other provocative works, Johanna Broda shows us that the cosmovision of the Basin of Mexico is not a vision of things *as they are,* a phrase that might tempt us to evaluate it as a foreshadowing of "modern empirical science," but a vision of reality as it is *reflected* in the Mexican religious imagination, in the specular landscape that mirrors sacred mountains and a divinely populated sky and waters controlled by gods. Exact Aztec sciences flourished in an imaginal world — a world of matter and material elements, to be sure, but a material world reflected against, and reflected upon, by matter of vastly different kinds.

These different reflections on matter and these reflections on the material differences among sky, earth, water, blood, and image yield a cosmovision that is creative, abundant, and terrifying. In the obscurity of our tutored imaginations, can we see — do we want to see — the darkened reflections of history, no longer precisely visible, but cast on the Basin floor, where once, but no longer, the miraculous waters cast reflections back toward Tenochtitlan?

13

Vamos a Rezar a San Marcos: A Tlapanec Pilgrimage

Peter L. van der Loo

This brief chapter will describe a short Mesoamerican pilgrimage. In the framework of the conference of 1989 we discussed some of Victor Turner's illuminating concepts of pilgrimages in Mexico in his *Dramas, Fields and Metaphors.* It is not my intent to discuss all possible theoretical implications, but several of the general characteristics of pilgrimage, furnished by Turner in Chapter 5 of his book, will be easily discernible in the Tlapanec example: the concept of liminality related to, and intensifying with, the crossing of space, and the idea of nonutilitarian normative communitas; both are appropriate here. Also present are the development of the act of pilgrimage from voluntary to obligatory, and the communitas resulting from the sharing of meals, which for the Tlapanecs begins before the actual pilgrimage.

After describing the Tlapanec pilgrimage I will indicate a few areas where I think that Turner's model may be expanded for the Mesoamerican case.

The Tlapanecs are a Mesoamerican people living in the northeast of Guerrero state on the border of Oaxaca in the heart of the Sierra Madre del Sur. They speak Tlapanec and share the main features of the Mesoamerican peoples in their culture.

One of their religious observances is a ritual that must be performed to petition the rain deity for a good rainy season. This ritual is performed roughly one month before the start of the rainy season, on the twenty-fourth of April. It is common in the whole Tlapanec region and also in the neighboring Nahuatl and Mixtec areas. It is usually referred to as "going to pray to Saint Mark" or simply "to beg for the rain."

The official day is April 25, the ritual taking place during the eve and night before. April 25 is in the Roman Catholic calendar the day of Saint Mark, who is also the rain god of the Tlapanecs. This deity also has a name in Tlapanec. We may safely assume that during autonomous times the offering also took place on the eve of what is now called the twenty-fifth day of April. The name of the appropriate Catholic saint was simply added in early colonial times to prevent conflict with the Roman Catholic clergy. This process may have been facilitated by the fact that in rural European Roman Catholic communities Saint Mark's day is a day to petition for a good harvest.

The appropriate place for the ritual is a cave or a mountaintop, both traditional abodes of the rain deity in Mesoamerica. On that prescribed day "all the mountains smoke," as I have been assured by many Tlapanecs.

I was granted an opportunity to witness this ritual as performed by the people of one Tlapanec village, Malinaltepec. In the Tlapanec dialect of Malinaltepec the rain god's name is Wi'Ku. This name is used interchangeably with the Spanish San Marcos.

The place to which this village brings its offering is the highest mountaintop in the vicinity: La Lucerna. It is an arduous five-hour walk uphill from Malinaltepec to that mountaintop. The participants leave around noon on April 24, stay overnight, and return the next day.

In 1984 the people of Malinaltepec, represented by the *mayordomía* of Saint Mark, graciously allowed me to share and document the experience of this short pilgrimage.

After having been away from Malinaltepec for visa matters in Mexico City, I returned on April 21st, the day before Easter. I went to see the *mayordomo* of Saint Mark to ask for permission to be included in the group that would ascend La Lucerna on the twenty-fourth. I was asked to explain my motivations. I clarified that I wished to document the ritual that takes place for the rain god, because I believe similar rituals are depicted in preconquest codices. I referred to some of my writing on that topic that was available in the city hall of Malinaltepec. The mayordomo listened carefully and told me to come back the next day when he would have come to a decision.

The next day, I was granted permission and several rules were explained to me. I was to embark on a trip of crucial importance to the village and would have to follow all instructions from the performer (Ndikaa Wi'Ku) of the ritual. I had to understand clearly that any malevolent act or intent on my part could seriously jeopardize the well-being of the village and would be dealt with accordingly. I would have to do my share in the carrying of materials necessary for the ritual, and I must promise never to use the acquired knowledge in any harmful way.

My ready acceptance of these conditions was greeted with a cheer from the other members of the mayordomía. At this time I was introduced to the other people who would undertake the trip, an occasion that was marked by shoulder clapping and broad smiles. I then was offered a bowl of atole with chile. The mayordomo, who was not to go himself, explained that sharing this meal with my fellow walkers cemented my commitment to make the trip and only the most extreme of circumstances might excuse me.

It is interesting to note that on this occasion several persons independently assured me that I had nothing to fear; only turkeys, chickens, and, possibly, goats would be sacrificed.

The mayordomo took me aside and warned me to be aware of the fact that I would leave the protective surroundings of the village and that I might be subject to attack by malevolent forces, dangerous to the village and therefore dangerous to all people on a journey for the benefit of the village. The middle part of the trip would be the most perilous as I would be far from the protection of both the village and the Place of Saint Mark. Nearing the site, I would be relatively safe, but even in the placa itself I had to be careful because that place, especially on that date, was an extraordinary place and time where one might meet with either great good or bad, for oneself or for the whole community.

The staff of the mayordomía prepared for the event by going to church to pray three times a day, on April 21, 22, and 23. Green twigs and candles were left before the altar as offerings.

On April 24, at 11:30 in the morning, my group left, rather unceremoniously, burdened down by all the materials necessary for the ritual. In addition, many villagers had entrusted to the group their gifts of candles, eggs, liquor, and a turkey to be offered to Saint Mark. Another party had left earlier to cut the reed for the counted bundles that would be an important part of the ritual (see van der Loo 1982). The total number of persons going up to the Place of Saint Mark was eight.

La Lucerna towers approximately twenty-three hundred meters above the village. The lower part of the walk over the mountain paths was very hot. Regular stops were made to drink pulque in the traditional ritual circle (see van der Loo 1987, chs. 11 and 22). On this occasion the women also participated in the ritual; normally, only men drink in the ritual circle.

After approximately one hour of walking the Ndikaa Wi'Ku told me to walk beside or, if that was impossible, immediately behind him. He was apparently keeping a special eye on me. People spoke very little and only for necessary instructions or to decide on the best path. After two and a half hours we met up with the other part of the group carrying the offertory reed. This was seized as a good opportunity to eat and rest.

Then the really steep ascent of the Lucerna proper began. Nevertheless, the mood was cheerful now, opposed to the apprehensive quietness of the first part of the trip. The Ndikaa Wi'Ku did not care anymore if I was directly beside or behind him. People engaged in animated conversations about any topic.

After four hours we started to encounter piles of rocks, laid down in horseshoe shapes. In the whole Tlapanec region this is a traditional form for a mountain altar, called *tecorale,* where one prays or performs a ritual, mainly to petition for health, safety, and prosperity. The four tecorales that we passed on our way to the top were deliberately placed along the route. The Ndikaa Wi'Ku stopped at each of them, made a small offering of pulque and said a prayer. The rest of the company waited at a short distance, looking on but not showing any specific sign of devotion.

We arrived at the top of La Lucerna at 6:00 P.M. The Place of Saint Mark is actually a large tecorale (c. four meters in diameter) with a smaller one (c. one meter in diameter) right behind it. In this smaller one stands a cross. Immediately upon arrival the preparations for the ritual began. The ritual itself was to last from c. 7:30 P.M. to 3:15 A.M. Elsewhere I have described this ritual in more detail (van der Loo 1987:162–63).

An interesting incident illustrates the sacrality of the Place of Saint Mark. The ritual requires drinking by the Ndikaa Wi'Ku, who has to drink with Saint Mark and becomes quite inebriated or, in terms of that religious event, reaches a sacred state. The other participants in the pilgrimage also drink but have no ritual reason to inebriate themselves. As is wont to happen at a feast, some did get drunk anyway. The next morning a girl of about fifteen was quite sick. I assumed that probably she had never in her life drunk so much alcohol and was having a normal physical reaction. For the others this was not sufficient explanation. A special divination ritual with maize kernels was performed to determine the meaning and reason of the girl's sickness in the Place of Saint Mark on that date. This shows poignantly how much the sacred place is felt to be outside of the normal world of cause and effect.

The walk back on the morning of April 25 was done without any of the apprehension of the way up. The Ndikaa Wi'Ku did stop to pray in the tecorales along the road.

Upon our return to the village, the mayordomo came to greet us and inquired diligently about all the details of the trip and the ritual. He came over to me to ask if I had received any special dreams while sleeping at the Place of Saint Mark. This same question was asked by many in the following days.

It rained on May 15, which is considered a good omen for the whole rainy season. Accordingly, the trip was then judged as having been successful. This caused a rise in status for the performing Ndikaa Wi'Ku and also for the other participants, even for me, the participating stranger.

Now we return to the characteristics defined by Turner that I mentioned before. In this account the liminal state is shown by how the trip is conceived: as having dangers and being especially dangerous where the people are far from their village but not yet close to the Place of Saint Mark. The mere existence of the mayordomía of Saint Mark indicates the normative communitas. The development of the trip from voluntary to obligatory is clear in the way I was first granted permission, then, after sharing the symbolic meal, obligated to go. The sharing of the meal also established the special communitas of the group. Thus, this simple example of a short pilgrimage shows many of the distinctive features Turner observed for far longer ones.

It appears that some expansion of Turner's model should be made for the particular case of Mesoamerica. Turner does recognize the difference between the mestizo and indigenous participation in the long pilgrimages, but this difference needs more illumination than the classification as "culturally distinctive" (Turner 1974:210–11).

For many Mesoamerican indigenous peoples, the pilgrimage places are indeed the continuation of a tradition that was established long before the site and its sacredness were put into a Christian context. In the times that have passed since the beginning of colonization, some Christian concepts have been embedded firmly in the indigenous religion. In this fusion a totality has been formed that fulfils the religious needs of the indigenous people who observe it. However, in the eyes of the Roman Catholic church and even for many scholars this represents a "syncretistic" religion; the word *syncretistic* often involves a value judgment to be understood as: contaminated; polluted; of lesser value. This aspect is not clearly identified by Turner (1974:228) when he writes: "Such a superimposition may involve a conscious rejection at the same time as an unconscious acceptance of the old religion." Rather than seeing this in terms of rejection or acceptance, I would recommend exploring the element of both conscious and unconscious resistance against a superimposed value system, a resistance manifested in acknowledging and venerating the continued sacredness of a certain place on indigenous terms and time schedules, independently of the interpretation the established powers may dictate. This leads to a second point that may be of importance for the understanding of indigenous pilgrimage in Mesoamerica: the relation between time and space. Time and space or direction are thought of as inseparable in Mesoamerican religion. Turner (1974:212) describes how different villages organize pilgrimages to the same place according to a pattern divided over the year. It would be interesting to investigate if this pattern of Roman Catholic pilgrimage rests on an indigenous system that assigns villages in certain directions to certain times.

Finally, if we want to do justice to the trading and market element that is present in Mesoamerican pilgrimage, it must be noted that the role of the walking merchants or pochteca (Nahuatl) may have influenced the present-day Mesoamerican pilgrimage patterns. This topic also requires further research. The fact that the activity of the pochteca had its religious implications is demonstrated, for instance, by their presence in the Codex Fejérváry-Mayer. We see them walking, associated with certain periods of the ritual calendar, on pages 31–32 and 36–37, while the top of page 43 seems to indicate a merchant ritual, with divisions of time periods over space.

Following the guidelines of Turner, more research on these topics is needed to increase our understanding of the history and present, time and place of Mesoamerican culture.

References

Loo, Peter L. van der

1982 Rituales con manojos contados en el grupo Borgia y entre los Tlapanecos de hoy día. In *Los indígenas de México en la época prehispánica y en la actualidad*, edited by M.E.R.G.N. Jansen and Th. J. J. Leyenaar. Leiden: Rijksmuseum voor Volkenkunde.

1987 *Códices costumbres continuidad: Un estudio de la religión mesoamericana.* Leiden: Archeologisch Centrum Rijksuniversiteit Leiden.

Turner, Victor W.

1974 *Dramas, fields and metaphors: Symbolic action in human society.* Ithaca and London: Cornell University Press.

14

Eating Landscape: Human Sacrifice and Sustenance in Aztec Mexico

Philip P. Arnold

The Aztec deity Tlaloc, god of rain, earth, and vegetation, literally embodied the Mexican landscape. Material attributes of the Aztec environment were necessities that occasioned ritual interaction between human and divine worlds. Material reality, particularly the material components that constituted the human body, was taken as evidence of a "hidden" reality that undergirded human existence.

To explore this dimension of Aztec thought, I have recently translated the ceremony Atl Caualo from Nahuatl as recorded by Sahagún. Language used to describe the ceremony gives us some indication of an Aztec understanding of their relationship to their environment. "Eating landscape" translates an Aztec understanding of their life situation in the Valley of Mexico based on an active interchange between Tlaloc and the people of the valley. Child sacrifice at specific points in the Valley was a food exchange that was substantive, material, and meaningful, and the agent of Tlaloc-Aztec communication. The text indicates several "correspondences" between ritual and landscape elements. Elements of earth, water, wood, and food are explicitly used in Atl Caualo and must be accessed in their material and ritual situations. An examination of these elements contributes to an understanding of Aztec correspondences between physical and hidden reality.

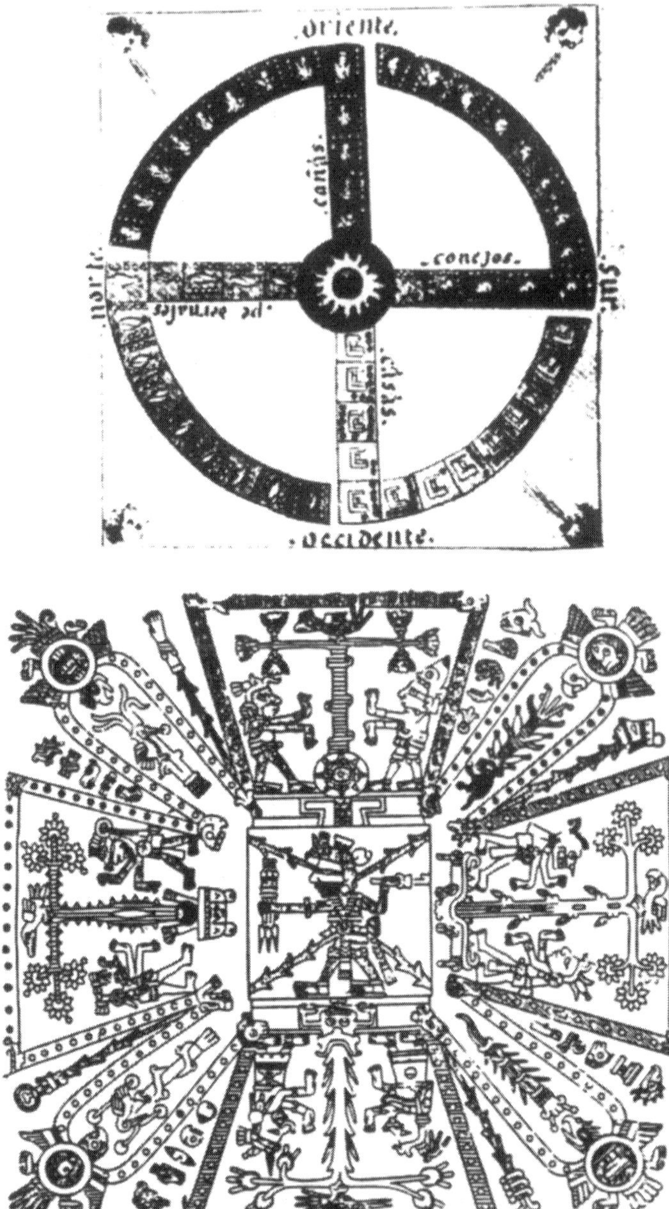

Figure 14.1. The Aztec Cosmos. *Above:* In Durán's depiction of the fifty-two-year calendar, the east appears at the top and the years are counted in counter-clockwise fashion. Reprinted from Aveni, *Skywatchers of Ancient Mexico* (Austin, 1980), by permission of the publisher. *Below:* In the Fejérváry-Mayer depiction of the cosmos, the east is again at the top. Reprinted from van der Loo, *Códices Costumbres Continuidad* (Leiden, 1987), by permission of the publisher.

ATL CAUALO (WATER LEFT)

1. Thus, Chapter 20,
   For its part it tells of it the festival day and the payment of debt:
   When they used to make it during one whole festival month;
   When they named it, they called it Atl caoalo (water left),
   or Quauitl eoa (to raise up the staff)
2. Quauitl eoa, this day they would leave:
   and when this one, there they would celebrate the festival of tlalocs:
3. The debts would be paid by someone, everywhere on mountaintops,
   and they would be made into paper streamers.
   There the debts would be paid by them at Tepetzinco (honorable hill),
   also there from well into the middle (belly) of the water,
   its namesake place Pantitla (banner row);
4. There they used to leave it the paper streamers,
   and there they would raise up a pole,
   it is named cuenmantli (cultivated land), very long, only attached to it goes being three, its freshness, its sprouts, its shoots.
5. And there they would leave them the little (noble) children,
   which they used to be called human paper streamers:
   the (ones with) two cowlicks, whose day signs were good:
   everywhere they were being sought, they were costly:
   it was being said "indeed they are precious blood sacrifices (debt payments),
   they (the tlalocs) happily receive them, they want them,
   thus they are very content, thus they are well pleased,"
   so that thus indeed rain was asked for, rain was requested.
6. And when everywhere on the house, everybody's homes:
   and on (each) young man's house on the calpulli,
   everywhere they would raise it, long thin poles, pole top,
   on them they would arrange paper streamers,
   with rubber, rubber-spattered things, the rubber-splashed thing.
7. And in many places they would be abandoned.
8. Quauhtepec (tree hill place): and with those who were dying there,
   the same place went being, Quauhtepetl: his paper vestments darkened.
9. Thus in two places they were dying, on top of the hill Yoaltecatl (night dweller):
   at the same place (time) its name goes being, the human paper streamers,
   Yoaltecatl: his paper vestments (were) black, (and) red-striped.

10. Thus (the) third place, Tepetzinco there they went dying a girl,
her name Quetzalxoch (feather flower), on top of it they would seize her, the sacred hill,
they would name her Quetzalxoch, her vestments were blue.
11. Thus the fourth place, Poyauhtlan (color-darkened place),
only its base, only in front of the hill, Tepetzinco:
its name goes being with them (who) were dying Poyauhtecatl (dark dweller),
thus all were made to go, rubber-covered, a rubber-whipped thing.
12. Thus the fifth place, there in water in it its namesake place Pantitlan,
there at that place he would die, his name goes being, Epcoatl (shell snake):
the vestments in which they would dress him (were) set with shells (or pearls).
13. Thus the sixth place: there they would carry him on top of Cocotl (sore, pimple),
his name would go being Cocotl: his adornment was divided,
one side painted red, one side painted black.
14. Thus the seventh place, on top of Yiauhqueme (his sacrificial offerings):
also its name went along Yiauhqueme, the human paper streamers:
the vestment went along, a gift, black-stained.
15. Thus they would die their payment, human paper streamers:
16. And their hairbands went along, crammed with queztal feathers, corn tassel feathers:
their precious green stone necklace went along, and would go along bracelet-bedecked,
they would go along bedecking them with bracelets (of) precious green stone:
they were made rubber-faced, they made them become rubber-faced,
they made themselves amaranth-faced, and their rubber sandals,
their rubber sandals went along, all of them went in honor,
everything they arranged, everything they made adorned, all (with) precious things,
which on them went along,
they went with fine things they put paper leaves (wings) on them, paper,
each paper-wing wearer: to be carried by litter, they would be carried,
they would go quetzal feather-housed,

when there they were going being spread out (in procession),
they would go blowing (flutes) at them.

17. Very much it would let them show compassion,
it would make people cry, it made one break down crying,
it caused them great pain, which indeed resulted in much sighing.
18. And when they are brought (to) vigil place, in mist house, there one-night vigil is kept,
they would keep them (the children) vigil the tlamacazque (serving priests):
and the quaquacuilti (sacrificial priests), who were old tlamacazque.
As for the tlamacazque, if any one of them there give up their places to someone,
they were called abandoned ones: no longer do they go to meet someone singing,
nowhere are they wanted, nowhere are they respected.
19. And the little noble children, if they go along crying, if their tears keep flowing,
if their tears keep falling, it was said, indeed it will rain: their tears signify it, the rain,
thus they are contented, thus their hearts are contented: as they say,
indeed already it will arise the rain, indeed already we will be rained on.
20. And if somewhere someone is, dropsical they would say, not to us abundant rain.
21. And already it will emerge the rain, and already it will end on its top:
Then already thus it speaks the curve-billed thrasher, his sign, it comes,
thus it will raise itself the steady rain: After that they come this way,
Franklin gulls also and they come this way sparrowhawks, little falcons,
they go screeching, their sign is soon it comes the ice, soon it will freeze.

It is important when discussing the ritual of Atl Caualo, that one discuss it with regard to its physical elements. Elements of earth, water, plant life, and human children conjoin in a powerful way within the activity of the ritual. Death of human children was the dramatic condensation of elements into physical correspondence. *Yetiuh* (lit. "they go being," "went along," or "goes to be") is a linguistic device used throughout the text to denote correspondence. I have arranged my analysis of Atl

Caualo with reference to correspondences of elements,[1] between the attributes of the ceremony and their landscape referents.

EARTH

The text mentions seven sites where children were sacrificed: (1) Quauhtepec (tree hill place); (2) Yoaltecatl (night dweller); (3) Tepetzinco (honored hill); (4) Poyauhtlan (color-darkened place); (5) Pantitlan (banner row); (6) Cocotl (sore or pimple); and (7) Yiauhqueme (sacrificial offerings).

Quauhtepec is located north of Mexico City in the Guadalupe range. Quauhtepec is a sierra region (2,750 m and above) that was chiefly exploited for its wood and quartzite (used as building material), papermaking materials, and maguey(Arnold 1986:15–19; Sanders, Parsons & Santley 1979:81–85, Maps 1, 24).[2] Yoaltecatl is located just north of the Guadalupe shrine.[3] It is the middle piedmont (2,350–2,500 m) where rainfall agriculture was practiced in addition to some mining. Tepetzinco was a small island in the middle of Lake Texcoco (saline), known for its hot springs. Poyauhtlan is said to be a peak in Tlaxcala (east of the Valley) but was enshrined in an altar on Tepetzinco's flank. Pantitlan is alternatively referred to as either where the lake drained or where it spouted out of the earth. This is topographically the lowest point in the Valley and one of its richest resource areas. The salt lakes of the Valley were a yearly migratory stop for a large variety of geese and ducks, which were caught in large nets. Many different kinds of fish, frogs, polliwogs, mollusks, turtles, and aquatic insects and their larvae were gathered seasonally. Wild rice and blue-green alga were saltwater vegetable resources. Reeds and water grasses were gathered for mat and basket weaving. Salt was manufactured along the lakeshore and was a lucrative trade item throughout Mesoamerica.

Cocotl is a small hill rising abruptly out of the deep soil alluvium. It divides the fertile Amecameca subvalley and the sweet-water lakes in the southern Valley region. The Amecameca Valley is one of the most fertile unirrigated areas of the Valley. Situated in the drainage basin from the volcanoes Popocatepetl and Iztaccihuatl, it receives a constant nutrient flow from eroding volcanic material. On the other side of Cocotl, to the west, in the shallow sweet-water regions of Lakes Xochimilco and Chalco were the famous *chinampas* or raised fields. Chinampas produced astounding yields of maize, squash, beans, flowers, medicinal herbs, tomatoes, chiles, and other crops (Armillas 1971; Coe 1964).[4]

Yiauhqueme cannot be readily identified today but its approximate location lies somewhere between the lower- and middle-piedmont regions (2,255–2,350 m and 2,350–2,500 m respectively) on the western slope of the Valley. In this area wooded hills are cut by seasonally running waters. It was used for its wood resources and for hunting wild game.

These sites cut across the major ecological resource areas vertically from sierra to the lakes and horizontally from the hilly piedmont to the alluvial plain.

To Sullivan (1972:216), Tlaloc is "he who is the embodiment of the earth." As earth, Tlaloc, who is iconographically identified by goggle eyes and a fanged mouth, is expressed as Tlaltecuhtli or the earth monster "whose joints were entirely made up of eyes and predacious mouths." In another account of creation, the gods Quetzalcoatl and Tezcatlipoca transform themselves into great serpents;

> one of whom took [Tlaltecuhtli's] right hand and left foot and the other, her left hand and right foot and they twisted her with such force that they split her in two. From one half they created earth and from the other, the heavens. To compensate her for the damage she had suffered, all the gods ordained that the sustenances of life issue from her. From her hair they made trees and the flowers and plants: from her skin and its tiny hairs, the small plants and flowers; from her numerous eyes, the springs and fountains and caves; from her mouths, the rivers and great caverns; from her nose, the valleys and mountains [Sullivan 1972:103, citing Garibay; the description of events is contained in the *Histoyre du Mexique*].

This passage imparts an important attribute of landscape as a coherent bodily structure. Elements of the material world were seen as evidence of cosmogonic violence; therefore, at points in the landscape body, direct communication with Tlaloc's body could be achieved by sacrificial violence. Killing was the regenerative act within an eating landscape formed from an original violence. The several sites of Atl Caualo were openings or mouths of the landscape body that sustained its inhabitants. Broda has discussed the Templo Mayor as the principal earth opening. Examining the iconography of the earth deity complex and the enormous number of fertility offerings, she concludes "that on a mythological level Templo

Mayor, the sacred mountain, was the earth itself, the earth as a voracious monster devouring human victims and blood. At the same time, the earth contained regenerative forces that linked it to agricultural growth and fertility in general" (Broda et al. 1987:105).

In Atl Caualo the sacrificial blood and souls of children were "happily received." The bodies of children served as food for the tlalocs who reciprocated by releasing elements from the openings of the earth. Human flesh and bone corresponded to the earth. Tlaloc's flesh and a child's body constituted a correspondence whose relationship was physically circumscribed by the sacrificial event. This correspondence concretely expressed the reciprocal relationship of human body and earth. The earth (Tlaloc) physically sustained the human body both through its wild resources and fruits of agriculture — fruits of the human body (children) sustained the earth.

Water

Atl Caualo literally means "water left" or "drought" and was performed before the rainy season to secure enough moisture to ensure successful harvest. This need is accounted for in the ritual in at least two ways: First, the arrangement of sites corresponded to important hydrological features of the Valley; second, water cosmology corresponded to the incidence of bodily fluids, particularly blood, which was given special status in the ritual.

Everything was encapsulated by water. In a description of the sea, Sahagún records what the Aztec called *ilhuicatl* (sky or celestial water). The Aztec "thought and took as truth that the heavens were just like a house; it stood resting in every direction, and it extended reaching to the water. It was as if the water walls were joined to it. And hence they called it 'water which reaches the heavens,' because it stretched extending to the heavens" (Sahagún 1950–1982, XI:247). The earth was called Cemanahuac (the place surrounded by water). According to Broda, the earth "was conceived as a disk or huge alligator (cipactli) floating on the waters. These waters proceeded from Tlalocan as springs to form rivers, lakes, and the sea" (Broda et al. 1987:101). Oceans entered the land and spread underneath it filling all the cavities within the earth, thus becoming potable waters on their journey. Tlaltecuhtli was depicted as either a crocodile or as a gigantic, crouching toad with snapping mouths at the knee and elbow joints. Tlaltecuhtli devoured the blood and hearts of sacrificial victims and the souls of the dead and floated in *teoatl* (the divine water), which was conceived of as the foundation of the earth plain.

Total envelopment of a phenomenal world by water appears in the ritual in the form of the children being carried on litters that were housed in an arrangement of quetzal feathers. These feathers were an insignia of status and wealth. The plumes were deep blue and green colors associated with water, fertility, and Tlaloc. Housing the children, whose lives and bodies directly corresponded to earth and its fruits, within quetzal feathers was a model of a cosmological understanding. Earth and phenomenal existence were encapsulated by divine/celestial water, and this relationship was meaningfully reconstructed in ritual accoutrements that surrounded the children.

In Atl Caualo the sites of sacrifice themselves have correspondences to particular expressions of Valley hydrology. Most types of waters are accounted for in the ritual circumambulation: Quauhtepec is a sierra site with a connection to celestial water and rain (mountains were containers of celestial waters and were duplicated in architecture such as the Templo Mayor);[5] at the base of Yoaltecatl there still gushes an enormous spring; Tepetzinco, the island site, has hot springs and is surrounded by the salt lake; Pantitlan is the lowest point of the Valley, the place where salt water either drained or spouted; Cocotl is located at the pre-Columbian shore of the sweet-water lakes and the Amecamecan subvalley drainage; Yiauhqueme may be in a similar situation because of its location along the western drainage. These sites hydrologically express several correspondences between rain and lake water, vertical and horizontal water, interior and exterior water, hot and cold water, still and running water, sweet and salt water, and death-dealing and life-sustaining water.

At these sites child sacrifice physically constituted the central theme of correspondence between human life and the landscape: blood and water. The former is a bodily water and the basis of human life, the latter is an earthly or heavenly blood and logically the basis of Tlalocan or the landscape's life. The reciprocal nature of life and death was a central element in most of Aztec religious life. The ritual acquisition of water required paying a high price in children's blood, which offset the costs of the sacrifice given by Tlaloc.[6] The exchange was a liquid one.

Just as blood and body interacted to create life (children and mobility), so it was with the landscape. The blood of Tlaloc-Tlaltecuhtli (water) interacted with the body (earth) to create life (animal and vegetal sustenance). This system of correspondences was widened to include other bodily fluids. Mentioned explicitly in the text are the tears of both the children and participants, which correspond to rain. Ritual weeping and sorrow over the deaths of these children were the emotional impetus that resulted in rainfall. Far from portraying Aztecs as cold toward human life, they seemed keenly aware of the high cost of sacrificing children, fruits of their bodies, for a larger world concern. Wrenching life from the body in the forms both of sacrificing children and emotional catharsis was seen as part of a larger ecological picture of life.

Wood

The use of paper, rubber, and wooden poles is one of this ritual's most central characteristics (Quauitl Eua = to raise up the staff). Everywhere in the Valley, people would raise poles with paper banners spattered with rubber. On all the young men's houses these poles were raised.

Paper was highly regarded among the Aztecs. Traditional papermaking was a labor-intensive activity that utilized all the elements we have discussed.[7] The bark of the amatl tree was placed in a pool of running water; the soaked wood was then boiled, and the remaining pulp was felted together with a beater typically made from a grooved stone. The sheets of paper were then dried. Catholic priests identified paper and papermaking so closely with indigenous religious practices that they virtually eradicated its production.

Seven children were adorned in different-colored papers. They went to the tlalocs adorned with the destroyed plant life for which their lives were given. The use of paper physically collapsed the significance of the sacrificial act. Earth, water, and plant life coalesced through human intervention, created a sign. "Human paper streamers" was a fitting name for children who died in this cause. Moreover the use of color on paper was sometimes a general metaphor for blood and bloodletting.[8]

Banners were raised at each of these sites. The poles were freshly cut from trees in bud, as children corresponded to sprouting (to a tree's "greenness" or budding). This correspondence represents new growth and potential both in terms of the human body and plant life.

Rubber also played an important part in this ceremony. The children wore it on their feet, faces, and costumes; it was also splattered on the paper banners. Rubber, a latex sap from trees, was another element of the blood-water correspondence. Its counterpart was plant life, which completed the cycle of sustenances. Landscape, plant life, and human beings were locked in an eating relationship. The sacrifice physically promoted this relationship. Atl Caualo was performed to ensure adequate plant growth and harvest. Wearing rubber collapsed the sacrificial theme of correspondences between life-sustaining fluids.

Food

Two criteria are given for choosing children to be sacrificed. First, they must have two cowlicks at the crown of their heads. The idiom for cowlick in Nahuatl was *cuezcome,* a large ceramic pot used to store grain, and refers to mountains. The second criteria was that they be born under a good (i.e., "comestible") day sign. Correspondence between a human child's attributes and sustenance was established and maintained throughout the ritual imagery.

Children, as fruits of the body, were the gift to Tlaloc at the beginning of the germinating season. In exchange for the children, the Tlalocan landscape reciprocated by releasing those elements of earth, water, and plant life, in the proper order and proportion for human use.

The Aztec symmetry of human sacrifice and maize has long been understood. In the second half of the month Atl Caualo, Aztec warriors began presentation ceremonies of their captives who were to die in the famous gladiatorial sacrifice. After the victim was vanquished, his skin was donned by his captor. This flaying, a tribute to Xipe Totec, was said to correspond to the growth of new maize (Seler 1960, vol. 2:849–53). Child sacrifice, however, corresponded to the maize flower, or to the preproducing stage of agricultural growth. Sahagún tells us that their headbands were crammed full of feathery tassels of maize. The children's hair and head corresponded to the delicate, flowering stage of the agricultural cycle.

Living in the consumptive landscape of the Aztec world assumed a level of material interaction within that environment. The necessity of food exchange with Tlaloc was also an occasion for meaningful exchange. Although predicated on the idea of securing a successful harvest, rituals such as Atl Caualo are also occasions for meaningful orientation. Eating was not a discrete activity among the Aztec; rather, it assumed a host of interactions within an intrinsically meaningful life system. Eating landscape satisfied a number of criteria for conjoining material and religious concerns. The brutal conditions of life and death to sustain a life system were isolated in ritual action. Atl Caualo forced life to a meaningful outcome by the surrendering of the precious lives of children.

With stunningly succinct clarity a contemporary Nahua group puts it this way:

> We live HERE on the earth (stamping on the mud floor)
> we are all fruits of the earth
> the earth sustains us
> we grow here, on the earth and lower
> and when we die we wither in the earth
> we are ALL FRUITS of the earth (stamping on the mud floor).
>
> We eat of the earth; the earth eats us.[9]

Broda, in her careful reconstruction of rituals to deities of rain, has concluded that child sacrifices were not devotional activity but understood by common people in the Valley as fulfilling their part of a contractual agreement with Tlaloc. The ritual arbitrated between mythic and material realties, and "the media for its representations were the word, song, dance, accoutrements, liturgical objects, offerings, and above all, human sacrifices" (Broda 1971:319). Ritual activities directly overcame communicative difficulties between realities. On the one hand these were imaginative strategies developed by Mesoamerican cultures to orient themselves within a meaningful cosmos. On the other hand these imaginal structures formed the substantive basis of continued material existence and enabled Aztec people to act appropriately within a physical landscape.

NOTES

Field work during January 1988 and 1989 was made possible by grants from Sigma Xi. I want to thank Jane Rosenthal, my Nahuatl teacher, for her guidance in retranslating Atl Caualo. I presented this paper at the American Academy of Religions, section on Human Sacrifice in November 1988 and want to thank panelists Kay Read, Frank Neumann, and Peter van der Loo for their comments. Many thanks to Anthony Aveni, Johanna Broda, Doris Heyden, and Norman McQuown for reading earlier drafts. Thanks also to my teachers David Carrasco and Lawrence Sullivan for giving me the opportunity and occasion to voice my ideas. Special thanks to my wife Sandy Bigtree who has helped in every aspect of this chapter's creation. Atl Caualo is recorded in Nahuatl by Sahagún in Book 2, Ch. 20 of the Florentine Codex (See Sahagún 1950–1982 , 2:42–46).

1. López Austin (1988:347) talks of many correspondences existing between the human body and the universe. Citing many examples of contemporary groups from Knab's work, he says "the central world of Tlalocan and water [were connected] to yollotl (heart)." My use of *correspondences*

is similar to, and substantiated by, Carrasco's (personal communication) use of the term *intimacies.* While *intimacies* expresses a tight locative sense, *correspondences* seems to fit into the translation better, giving the impression that certain elements really are the same as other elements.

2. Broda, and her students and associates, led Aveni and me to this site in January 1989. Calnek had positively identified this site in the previous year from a seventeenth-century document. On the summit and in the saddle between east and west peaks there was a large amount of cut stone probably used to construct ceremonial buildings. This stone was quarried at the base of Quauhtepetl and carried to the summit. From the top one can see the whole of the northern part of the Valley including Teotihuacan, Texcoco, and perhaps the Tula valley; to the south Mexico City and the volcanoes were completely visible. Quite striking is the growth of pine trees on the north side of the peak and maguey on the south. Quauhtepetl, like most sierra sites, hosts contrary ecological niches at different times and places. The gods of maguey were also intimately associated with the mountain deities (Broda 1971:263).

3. Aveni, Broda, Calnek, and I visited this site in January 1988. There was a lot of stone used for penning animals and dividing fields. We postulated that this may be evidence of a large ceremonial precinct. We found a scatter of Late Aztec sherds around a small mound. This site was not shown on the Basin survey.

4. For the political implications of chinampas, see Parsons (1985a, 1985b). Chinampa agriculture has seen a recent resurgence in Mexico; see Gómez-Pompa et al. (1982) on the construction of raised fields.

5. The Templo Mayor was regarded as a sacred mountain, expressing a relationship between ritual architecture and Valley topography (see Aveni, Calnek & Hartung 1988, 1989).

6. The ritual is literally expressed in economic terms of "making a payment." For example, children are referred to as being either "precious" or "costly."

7. Sandstrom and Sandstrom (1986:11–31) reconstruct pre-Columbian papermaking techniques and how paper was used by combining primary texts with practices of contemporary groups.

8. *Tlapalli* — something dyed or colored — metaphorically referred to blood and bloodletting. (Karttunen 1983:289).

9. This quotation is published in Broda et al. (1987:107) from Knab's work among the Nahuas of San Miguel.

REFERENCES

Armillas, P.

1976 Gardens on swamps. *Science* 174:653–61.

Arnold, P. P.

1986 The Aztec ceremonial landscape in the Valley of Mexico: Implications of examining religion and environment. M.A. diss. submitted, University of London.

Aveni, A., E. E. Calnek, and H. Hartung

1988 Myth, environment and the orientation of the Templo Mayor of Tenochtitlan. *American Antiquity* 53, no. 2:287–309.

1989 The role of astronomical orientation in the delineation of world view: A center and periphery model. *Imagination of matter: Religion and ecology in Mesoamerican tradition.* BAR International Series, no. 515. Oxford.

Broda, J.

1971 Las fiestas aztecas de los dioses de la lluvia: Una reconstrucción según las fuentes del siglo XVI. *Revista Española de Antropología Americana.* 6:245–327.

Broda, J., D. Carrasco, and E. Matos Moctezuma
1987 *The Great Temple of Tenochtitlan: Center and periphery in the Aztec world.* Berkeley: University of California Press.

Clendinnen, I.
1985 The cost of courage in Aztec society. *Past and Present* 107:44–89.

Coe, M. D.
1964 The chinampas of Mexico. *Scientific American* 211, no. 1:90–98.

Gómez-Pompa, A., et al.
1982 Experiences in traditional hydraulic agriculture. In *Maya subsistence: Studies in memory of Dennis E. Puleston,* edited by K.V. Flannery. New York: Academic Press.

Karttunen, F.
1983 *An analytical dictionary of Nahuatl.* Austin: University of Texas Press.

López Austin, A.
1988 *The human body and ideology: Concepts of the ancient Nahuas.* Translated by Thelma and Bernard Ortiz de Montellano. 2 vols. Salt Lake City: University of Utah Press.

Parsons, J. R. et al.
1985a Chinampa agriculture and Aztec urbanization in the Valley of Mexico. In *Prehistoric intensive agriculture in the tropics,* edited by I. S. Farrington. BAR International Series, no. 232. Oxford.

1985b Political implications of pre-Hispanic chinampa agriculture in the Valley of Mexico. Paper presented at the symposium Land and Politics in the Valley of Mexico, Forty-fifth International Congress of Americanists, Bogotá, July 1–6, 1985.

Sahagún, Fray Bernardino de
1950–1982 *Florentine Codex: General history of the things of New Spain.* Translated and edited by A.J.O. Anderson and C. Dibble. 13 bks. Santa Fe: School of American Research and the University of Utah.

Sanders, W. T., J. R. Parsons, and R. S. Santley
1979 *The Basin of Mexico: Biological processes in the evolution of a civilization.* New York: Academic Press.

Sandstrom, A. S., and P. E. Sandstrom
1986 *Traditional papermaking and paper cult figures of Mexico.* Norman: University of Oklahoma Press.

Seler, E.
1960 *Gesammelte Abhandlungen.* 5 vols. Graz: Akademische Druck- und Verlagsanstalt.

Sullivan, T.
1972 Tlaloc: A new etymological interpretation of the god's name and what it reveals of his essence and nature. *Proceedings of the 40th International Congress of Americanists,* vol. 2. Genoa: Tilgher-Genova.

15

Religious Rationalization and the Conversions of the Nahuas: Social Organization and Colonial Epistemology

J. Jorge Klor de Alva

In 1987 I began to analyze the links between three related processes: the confessional practices used in sixteenth-century Central Mexico; the colonization of Nahua minds and bodies (as opposed to institutions); and the birth of modern anthropology as a by-product of the first two endeavors. The brief discussion here is necessarily sketched in very broad strokes. In the spirit of a work in progress, I seek to evoke rather than convince or document, knowing very well that these latter ends must await further research and reflection.

In particular, I want to outline a series of issues relevant to the periodization of widespread postcontact ceremonial activity and the conflict precipitated in New Spain by the clash of contrasting rationalizing principles. From all indications, distinct systematizing assumptions among Nahuas and Spaniards, who did not share a common ethos and worldview, helped to sustain sociocultural discontinuities and, explicit forms of antagonism throughout the colonial period. (see, e.g., Lockhart 1985; Klor de Alva, in press). The widespread application of these frequently contrasting visions of order — used to make sense of and solve the chaos of everyday life activities — were a frequent occasion of ethnic conflict and helped to shape the diverse images of alterity that delimited social possibilities, ideological verities, economic tactics, and political strategies. In effect, power flowed in both directions across the fields energized by polar epistemologies. And no matter how effective either force may have been, a will to dominate on either side necessarily met a will to resist on the other.

Rationalizing the Self as a Colonial Practice

Elsewhere I have studied the differences between the ideas of the self that Nahuas held and those common among Spaniards (see Klor de Alva 1988), and I have pointed to the need recognized by the missionaries to deploy new self-forming techniques that would bring Nahua concepts of the self in line with the modes of Christian self-idealization and self-presentation. My argument can be summarized as follows.

Sacramental confession meant that native would-be penitents had to be convinced to inform to Europeans on themselves and others; but, equally important for the individual, they had to be taught the European techniques of self-examination and autobiographical representation that, when successfully accomplished, transformed them into Christian actors on the social stage. A "good" confession required the mastery of a number of difficult, self-forming, and, figuratively, self-destructive practices. First, the unstable Nahua self, composed of a collection of forces that constituted the cosmic and cyclical continuum of which it was a part, needed to be destroyed and replaced by an autonomous, bipolar self, whose two aspects were antagonistic. One of the poles required that the physical body as a polysemic microcosm of the universe (see López Austin 1980) be replaced by a semantically restricted desiring body, center of libidinal and deviant inclinations. Thus, the transformation of the Nahua body into a morally and physically corruptible entity called for the transfer of many of its former qualities to its new antithesis: the Christian soul. With this bimodal self, the Nahua narrative of self-representation (familiar to ethnohistorians and ethnographers), with all its (to us) digressions and discontinuities, its symbolic chronology of contemporaneous successions of events, and its divisions between mythical and "real" times, its tropological exuberance, and its focus on seemingly insignificant details of everyday life, was exchanged for a two-part discourse on the self: the story of the desiring body, which Christianity characterized as the life of sin; and the story of the soul, the tale of salvation (see Freccero 1986).

A close examination of the canons of confessional narrative, found in the extant Nahuatl sermons and the many manuals for confessors of Indians, the doctrinal works, and devotional texts that circulated widely in New Spain, reveals that the discourse that was expected was supposed to be linear, chronologically ordered, punctuated by conflict between the desires and the moral will, and internally coherent, that is, rationalized in the Western sense of linearity. Yet, as the historical (e.g., Durán 1967; Ruiz de Alarcón 1982) and ethnographic (e.g., Madsen 1960; Montoya Briones 1964; Taggart 1983) record discloses, for the Nahua ethical subject, whose key preoccupation was to equilibrate the desires and thereby to promote harmony between the opposing influences of external and internal forces, the bifurcated Christian autobiography, focused on the scrutiny of intentions and the elimination of desires, was no way to tell the story of the true self (see Foucault 1985).

In contrast, Nahua self-portraiture was of necessity chronologically discontinuous and nonlinear in structure or content (since the Christian logic of conversion/separation was not always there to sustain the sequentialized narrative). It was also more concerned with harmony (balance) than conflict (given that the conceptual self lacked an autonomous moral will) and more semantically charged with tropes and symbols than was expected to result from self-examination exercises modeled on sacramental confession.

Nevertheless, when successful, the deployment of the penitential system, with its imposition of self-forming tactics of introspection, its diffusion of a consciousness of new modes of deviant behavior, and its insistence on autobiographical discourse aimed at divulging the most private thoughts and acts of the individual, contributed to the transformation of the Nahuas into the "other" not only of the Europeans, but of themselves. The new techniques of self-constitution introduced by the confessional practices created new subjects who recognized a now-alienated part of themselves (their body, their desires) as the object of their will. This new truth about the native self, made up of novel self-conceptualizations drawn in the image of the Christian sinner, reformulated native self-identities and generated a new knowledge of themselves as actors in a significantly restricted cosmos. Christianized Nahuas could no longer be sure of the importance of their role as an essential force of balance in a precarious universe when sacramental confession, supported by penitential discipline, shrank their world to tragicomic clashes between good and evil played out on the tiny stages of their desiring bodies and their repentant souls. Bodies, which were once the microcosm of the cosmic dramas that made and destroyed universes (León-Portilla 1966; López

Austin 1980:58–98), became the other of those Christian natives pursuing personal purity and individual salvation.

However, in the diminutive theater of the Christian ethical subject a universal drama was indeed reenacted, as Nahuas who were taught to sin in the same process that required them to be sorrowful, repentant, and loquacious about their sins, were trained to understand their phenomenological lives as reflections of a coherent story of sin, redemption, and salvation. Consequently, confessional autobiography's insistence on conversion as its theme gave rise to a humbling new truth about the self and its representation. New Nahua identities as sinners in search of forgiveness tended conceptually to delimit the possible options open to them to resist, accommodate, or redefine the truth of the Europeans. The ideology of the confessional thus promoted the subjection of the *self*, through self-discipline, and the subjection of the *body*, through the assent to the claims of those who asserted an expertise in the ways of bodies and souls.

To tell one's life to another is always a dangerous thing, and in sixteenth-century Mexico the risk was particularly high even if not always apparent. Confessional autobiography, when successfully implanted, led to the reconstruction and the diminution of the Nahua self, and this transformation contributed in subtle and not so subtle ways to the tightening of the European world's hold on native bodies, selves, and fortunes. The ultimate result for those caught in this grip was the disappearance from public life and individual consciousness of their native selves and their reappearance as poor peasants.

For the Nahuas, then, rationalization along Christian lines meant adapting themselves to an epistemology that defined a new sense of self, inaugurated a novel cognitive framework, and introduced an alternative spirituality. I now turn from the diminution of self implied by this new epistemology to the changing geography of Nahua beliefs and ceremonial space that resulted from the colonial contests of ordering principles.

The Ironic Reversal of "Conversion"

My thesis is simple: For the Nahuas of Central Mexico, the conquest of Tenochtitlan and the resulting demographic alterations and sociopolitical effects spelled the circumscription of ceremonial space and the localization of religious knowledge. The transformations can be periodized as in Table 15.1.

Table 15.1 Periodization of Sociocultural Transformations

Phase	Dominant Form of Labor Organization	Characteristic Linguistic Shifts	Prominent Religious Response
1. 1521–1550/60	Encomienda	No borrowing	Extensive participation in public, "Christian" ceremonies
2. 1560–1640	Repartimiento	Borrowing of great numbers of nouns	"Fluorescence" of traditional rites and beliefs
3. 1640–	"Free" labor	Borrowing of nouns, verbs, conjunctions, prepositions, and whole idioms	Disarticulation: traditionalist forms and popular Christian practices

Note: The research on the linguistic shifts has been done primarily by Frances Karttunen and James Lockhart (e.g., Karttunen and Lockhart 1976; Karttunen 1985); the timing of the shifts in relation to the dominant forms of labor has been studied by Lockhart (n.d. [a, b]). For the history establishing the periodization of the phases see, e.g., Gibson (1964).

I believe the first phase represents a continuation of precontact state-level forms of ceremonialism and use of ritual space as well as precontact forms of state rationalization: widely disseminated abstract ideological ideals; well-articulated systems of deities, rituals, and cosmological beliefs; and an abundance of generally phrased moral dicta. Because this is a time when interethnic, interaltepetl (the altepetl being the basic provincial sociopolitical unit) integration was still present, this period was characterized by the same large-scale, public ritual activities, covering great distances and making ceremonial use of extensive spaces, that were common in the precontact world. Consequently, given that the native nobility was still in place, that a limited local penetration of Christianity was the rule, and that the Nahua state religious organization was in shambles, the missionaries were able to make use of the surviving precontact state structure to stage ostensibly Christian rituals of great magnitude. As a result, at this point the popular religion of the Nahuas, in which magically motivated behavior and local beliefs predominated, was less evident than it would be in the future.

Phase two marked the end of the precontact state-level arrangements as interaltepetl links were progressively weakened. To this disarticulation must be added the effects attendant on the fact that by the 1560s there were very few Nahuas left who had been socialized by way of the institutionalized mechanisms of precontact state discipline. In the meantime, the contraction in number and size of the *encomiendas* by the 1550s, following on the direct and indirect effects of the restrictive New Laws of 1542 (Gibson 1964:62), forced large numbers of Nahuas, for the first time, to come in intimate and sustained contact with Spaniards. At the same time, the declining plague-ridden native populations were being concentrated — through the *congregación* policies — into denser settlements, each of which, in asserting its rights to land and resources, increased the centrifugal pressures then fragmenting the *altepemeh* (pl. of altepetl). This growing independence (decentralization) of the altepemeh coupled with the internal *cabecera-sujeto* conflicts — that is, the conflicts between the core and peripheral settlements of the provinces — contributed to the localization of religious knowledge and ritual activity.

With all these factors in play, and with the weakening of the thrust of the mendicant friars precipitated by both the secular priests and the maturing viceroyalty, the popular religiosity of the Nahuas was left more exposed than ever. Not surprisingly, the friars Bernardino de Sahagún and Diego Durán, along with many others, began to pine for the golden days of missionary triumphs or began to assert (correctly) that these had in fact never been (Klor de Alva 1988b). Indeed, at every turn the sources speak about resurgences of "idolatry, sacrifices, and offerings," and Nahua religious life began to be described as a constant and widespread practice of precontact rituals taking place in isolated villages, ravines, mountains, rivers, and lakes; everything pointing, of course, to far more restricted ceremonial spaces than ever before.

At the level of cognition and epistemology, the gradual disappearance of widely connected state forms of rationalization, based on a millennium of Mesoamerican reflection, and their replacement by highly articulated though obviously new Christian ways of making sense (e.g., doctrinal orthodoxy logically framed, laconic catechismal understandings, mechanical confessional verbalizations of intimate practices and inchoate beliefs) promoted a paradoxical situation. On the one hand, although framed by the cosmological and ethical logic of the Catholic doctrine, which sought to generate order out of the "false beliefs" (see Sahagún 1980), what took place was a derationalization of overarching (Nahua) cosmologies, coupled with an inevitable ideological fragmentation. This resulted in what I claim was the proliferation of concretely defined and loosely ordered deities and rituals, which by their very nature were less vulnerable to the Christians' attacks. On the other hand, the systematized forms of Christian religious expression and conceptualization that were deployed gave rise to new categories of religious understanding, but these by their very nature promoted a widespread, more or less uniformly disarticulated content.

In other words, Christian rationalization, in an ironic twist, led to the growth of widely distributed types of similarly derationalized beliefs. Although I have not yet sorted the data adequately, it appears that some Christian practices, such as learning by rote the tenets of the faith, facilitated the integration of the Catholic doctrines into the systems of religious understanding common among the Nahuas. Thus, rather than locating the Nahua beliefs in the Christian religious categories, the opposite seems frequently to have taken place. Therefore, the Nahuas could come to know (perhaps even believe) the doctrines found in the catechisms without being committed to the ethos they implied or the worldview they asserted.

Lastly, I believe that the attendant lack of geographic uniformity with regard to the understanding of Christian cosmological principles, doctrinal assumptions, identities and functions of supernaturals, and symbolic codes was inevitable given that the Christian order had to be imposed on a derationalized native religious ideology that could not be otherwise after the disarticulation into provincial units of the formerly linked state polities. I propose, then, that the first "triumphant" decades registered by Fray Toribio (de Benavente) Motolinía (1971, 1973), Fray Pedro de Gante, and others represented the continuation of precontact patterns of state-level religious rationalization, organization, and extensive use of public ceremonial space. Moreover, the subsequent assumed "loss" of religious fervor was the result of a transformation in the altepemeh from a state structure of integration to a loosely linked network of relatively independent political and social units. Thus, the old state-level religious responses were replaced by a perceived "fluorescence" of the — always existing, but generally backgrounded — popular responses, which were local in nature, magical in orientation, and narrowly circumscribed geographically.

Given the very limited research done for the third phase, I will limit myself to some necessarily broad generalizations. Beginning in the late sixteenth century, especially following the Third Provincial Council of 1585, which had the effect of bringing home the counterreforms of the Council of Trent, the functions of the church at the local parish level became highly institutionalized and, consequently, more routinized than ever (Schwaller, 1987; Poole 1987). By the 1650s this standardizing process was clearly reflected in native religious practices, which continued the movement to Catholic-like transformations that had characterized the previous 130 years. However, widespread disarticulation of traditional patterns was accelerated by the explosive growth of a liminal mestizo population and by the rising numbers of Spaniards pressing against native lands and lives. Thus, this period seems to have been dominated by an increase in the variety of popular Christian rites and beliefs and by the routinization of often separate, sometimes comingled, forms of religiosity. Given the generational and cultural distance between the practitioners and the precontact past, the native ways that harked back to non-Christian assumptions and rituals were necessarily understood by the faithful as Christian-indigenous constructs (see Klor de Alva, in press). This multiplicity of faiths, with Nahua beliefs spread across a spectrum from strongly indigenous to clearly Catholic, but more commonly located along the center of the continuum, would last until the present, wherever secular modernizing forces have remained marginal and native cultural contours are still recognizable as such.

THE CONTEST OF ORDERING PRINCIPLES

The accelerated study of Nahuatl documents that has been taking place in the last fifteen years, coupled with careful iconographic and informed empirical research, and supplemented by more-critical hermeneutical and interpretive frameworks than those used in the past, have all combined to make more-credible — if not yet fully convincing — assertions about Nahua epistemology, cognition, and axiology. In particular, the work of James Lockhart (1985, n.d. [a, b]), Alfredo López Austin (see, e.g., 1980 [Eng. ed. 1988]), Serge Gruzinski (1988, 1989), along with that of others (see, e.g., Klor de Alva 1988b, 1988c, 1989), is seeking to deromanticize our understanding of Nahua ideology and to speculate on its content in the light of its own logical and ethnographic limits.

A useful example of some of the more salient competing rationalizing frameworks, whose seeming polarization is meant to invoke contrasts rather than to essentialize differences, is outlined in the continua listed below. For a close discussion of a number of the characteristics noted here, the work of Lockhart must be consulted, since it was he who, in several very insightful published and unpublished essays, first explicitly proposed and/or documented some of the following points:

NAHUA RATIONALISM ⟵⟶	SPANISH RATIONALISM
Symmetry	Hierarchy
Horizontality	Verticality
Autonomy/ Independence	Centralization/ Dependence
Interchangeability	Fixity
Rotational/Cyclical	Linear/Discrete
Continuity	Discontinuity

Without going into details, I would like to summarize some possible, relevant implications.

1. I think it reasonable to affirm, as has been done by others, that the precontact Nahua pantheon tended toward a symmetrical order, wherein relatively independent deities (abstracted under certain conditions as *tonalli*-like forces) interchanged positions of predominance in a regular, cyclical order.

2. Increased penetration of Christian beliefs, the result of greater Spanish missionary–Nahua contacts in the second phase, put this ordering principle in crisis. Although I cannot develop it here, in future work I shall attempt to show that, in part, the crisis arises when individual Nahuas were coaxed or convinced by the missionaries to do two things closely associated with the confessional practices I noted earlier: (1) to verbalize their spiritual beliefs and (2) to explain their religious practices.

3. As is evident from the informants of Sahagún and Olmos (see Baudot 1983), Nahua state religion was highly systematized, particularly as to the ordered cycles of ritual activity and the details of ceremonial protocol, but it was not very rationalized, if at all, in what Europeans would call doctrinal dogma and casuistry. Thus, more important than the beliefs

and rituals of Christianity, what the missionaries sought to introduce through the confessional practices and to propagate through the *doctrinas* was, first of all, an epistemology of catechismal order, a fixity of doctrinal beliefs, and an accompanying casuistical framework (one based on purely abstract principles) for the analysis of ethical issues and the resolution of moral dilemmas.

The cognitive acceptance of the new social and moral order the Europeans attempted to impose required what I call a "colonial epistemology." This epistemology is one that was introduced in order to set novel limits to knowledge that make certain traditionally held concepts, and their related practices, appear impossible to conceive or deviant if performed. Therefore, the successful inculcation in the minds of the Nahuas of a Christian colonial epistemology implied the acceptance by them of new rules of understanding and criteria of proof, new truth values, and a new calculus of moral assessment.

Although the ultimate goal of the missionaries was to make Nahuas believe the truths of Christianity and accept the authority of the Spanish regime, the will to linear, fixed hierarchical order, inherent to colonial Christianity, was at the core of the colonial epistemology they introduced. By using their religious and sociopolitical technologies to superimpose a new grid of organization on the personal and public landscape of the Nahua world, the missionaries attempted to make their will to order satisfy their "will to know" (see the discussion on the "will to know" in Foucault 1980). As an exercise of power, this will to order had a dual object: (1) to promote the hierarchical, centralized, and linear rationalization of the Nahua worldview, so that the disciplinary techniques of Christianity could be effectively deployed; and (2) as stated above, to elicit discourses that could generate new and useful knowledge about native customs, desires, and intentions. In effect, my future research will focus on how, to what extent, and with what effects Nahua religion was Eurorationalized in the sixteenth century as a result of the attempt to make Nahuas verbalize their spiritual beliefs and explain their religious practices.

I am arguing that this colonizing effort took place primarily through the systematization of religious rituals, dogmas, and ethics through the imposition of a casuistical, rationalistic calculus of sin and ideological deviation (see Burkhart 1989). This calculus was regularly taught in the course of formal and informal religious instruction and was continually reinforced by a network of confessional practices (see Klor de Alva 1988a).

These premises suggest the utility of analyzing the significance of conversion by privileging the epistemological sense of Weber's concept of rationalization ("a making sense of," "an ordering and systematizing of"), as opposed to focusing, as is commonly done, on conversion as a form of social assimilation through the religious acculturation that follows the adoption of new dogmas and rituals. Put another way, I am studying how the inculcation of new cognitive styles, rather than new beliefs, affected the way the Christian missionary project served the colonizing ends of the Europeans. In effect, Christianity through the doctrinas provided an uneasy solution: requiring responses by rote over belief, and knowledge of over "commitment to." Therefore, although Christianity replaced the state religious apparatus of rationalization, it left much of the popular religiosity intact not only as a guide for the first generations of natives, but as an object for anthropologists to witness today.

REFERENCES

Baudot, Georges

1983 *Utopía e historia en México: Los primeros cronistas de la civilización mexicana (1520–1569).* Translated by Vincente González Loscertales. Madrid: Espasa-Calpe.

Burkhart, Louise M.

1989 *The slippery earth: Nahua-Christian moral dialogue in sixteenth-century Mexico.* Tucson: University of Arizona Press.

Durán, Fray Diego

1967 *Historia de las indias de Nueva España e islas de la tierra firme,* edited by Angel María Garibay K. 2 vols. Mexico City: Porrúa.

Foucault, Michel

1980 *The history of sexuality.* Vol. 1, *An introduction.* Translated by Robert Hurley. New York: Vintage.

1985 *The history of sexuality.* Vol. 2, *The use of pleasure.* Translated by Robert Hurley. New York: Pantheon.

Freccero, John

1986 Autobiography and narrative. In *Reconstructing individualism,* edited by Thomas C. Heller et al. Stanford, CA: Stanford University Press.

Gibson, Charles

1964 *The Aztecs under Spanish rule.* Stanford, CA: Stanford University Press.

Gruzinski, Serge

1988 *La colonisation de l'imaginaire: Sociétés indigènes et occidentalisation dans le mexique espagnol XVIe–XVIIIe siècle.* Paris: Gallimard.

1989 *Man-gods in the Mexican highlands: Indian power and colonial society, 1520–1800.* Translated by Eileen Corrigan. Stanford, CA: Stanford University Press.

Karttunen, Frances

1985 *Nahuatl and Maya in contact with Spanish.* Texas Linguistic Forum, no. 26. Austin: University of Texas Department of Linguistics and Center for Cognitive Science.

Karttunen, Frances, and James Lockhart

1976 *Nahuatl in the middle years: Language contact phenomena in texts of the colonial period.* Publications in Linguistics, no. 85. Berkeley: University of California.

Klor de Alva, J. Jorge

1988a Contar vidas: La autobiografía confesional y la reconstrucción del ser nahua. *Arbor* 515–16:49–78.

1988b Sahagún's misguided introduction to ethnography and the failure of the "Colloquios" project. In *The work of Bernardino de Sahagún: Pioneer ethnographer of sixteenth-century Aztec Mexico,* edited by J. J. Klor de Alva, H. B. Nicholson, and E. Quiñones Keber. State University of New York at Albany Institute for Mesoamerican Studies and University of Texas, Austin.

1988c Sahagún and the birth of modern ethnography: Representing, confessing, and inscribing the native other. In *The work of Bernardino de Sahagún: Pioneer ethnographer of sixteenth-century Aztec Mexico,* edited by J. J. Klor de Alva, H. B. Nicholson, and E. Quiñones Keber. State University of New York at Albany Institute of Mesoamerican Studies and University of Texas, Austin.

1989 Language, politics, and translation: Colonial discourse and classical Nahuatl in New Spain. In *The art of translation: Voices from the field,* edited by Rosanna Warren. Boston: Northeastern University Press.

In press Nahua colonial discourse and the appropriation of the (European) other. In *Imagenes interétnicas en el nuevo mundo. Interpretaciones contemporáneas.*, edited by Manuel Gutiérrez Estévez et al. Madrid: Siglo XXI.

León-Portilla, Miguel

1966 *La filosofía náhuatl estudiada en sus fuentes,* 3d ed. Prologue by Angel María Garibay K. Mexico City: Universidad Nacional Autónoma de México.

Lockhart, James

1985 Some Nahua concepts in postconquest guise. *History of European Ideas* 6:465–82.

n.d.(a) The Nahuas after the conquest. Unpublished manuscript.

n.d.(b) Postconquest Nahua society and culture seen through Nahuatl writings. Unpublished manuscript.

López Austin, Alfredo

1980 *Cuerpo humano e ideología: Las concepciones de los antiguos nahuas.* 3 vols. Mexico City: Universidad Nacional Autónoma de México.

1988 *The human body and ideology: Concepts of the ancient Nahuas.* Translated by Thelma Ortiz de Montellano and Bernard Ortiz de Montellano. 2 vols. Salt Lake City: University of Utah Press.

Madsen, William

1960 *The Virgin's children: Life in an Aztec village today.* Austin: University of Texas.

Montoya Briones, José de Jesús

1964 *Atla: Etnografía de un pueblo náhuatl.* Mexico City: Instituto Nacional de Antropología e Historia.

Motolinía, Toribio de Benavente

1971 *Memoriales o libro de las cosas de la Nueva España y de los naturales de ella.* Mexico City: Universidad Nacional Autónoma de México.

1973 *Historia de los indios de la Nueva España,* edited by Edmundo O'Gorman. Mexico City: Porrúa.

Poole, Stafford

1987 *Pedro Moya de Contreras: Catholic reform and royal power in New Spain, 1571–1591.* Berkeley: University of California Press.

Ruiz de Alarcón, Hernando
1982 *Aztec sorcerers in seventeenth-century Mexico: The treatise on superstitions.* Translated and edited by Michael D. Coe and Gordon Whittaker. Albany: State University of New York at Albany Institute for Mesoamerican Studies.

Sahagún, Fray Bernardino de
1980 Coloquios y doctrina christiana. Translated and edited by J. Jorge Klor de Alva from 1564 Nahuatl original. In The Aztec-Spanish Dialogues of 1524. *Alcheringa: Ethnopoetics* 4:52–193.

Schwaller, Frederick
1987 *The church and clergy in sixteenth-century Mexico.* Albuquerque: University of New Mexico Press.

Taggart, James M.
1983 *Nahua myth and social structure.* Austin: University of Texas Press.

16

Remnants of the Shaman

Jane Stevenson Day

Tezcatlipoca as revealed in the rituals of the month of Toxcatl is interpreted by Heyden and other scholars as the symbol of the end of the dry season, the time of the coming of the rains, the change from sterility to fertility. Indeed, the activities of the festival indicate that this was the meaning of the elaborate drama played out ritually each year by the ixiptla of the deity. Yet a number of questions come to mind when we consider Tezcatlipoca in this particular role.

As Heyden mentions, this god had many personalities and aspects, but above all he was the god of kings, the reflection of the Aztec state, the only deity with total power. However, at the core he still appears as the eternal shaman — capricious, clever, ever changing shape and form. Neither of these aspects of the god fits the pattern of the Toxcatl drama. What has this imperial god or shaman to do with the deities of nature and the natural phenomena of the changing seasons? Yet we see him sacrificed in what appears to be a petition for rain.

The antiquity of Tezcatlipoca is unquestionable. He was the first created, the god of the First Sun, and as shaman the living image of humankind's earliest religion. Perhaps we see him first depicted in jaguar form among the Olmecs, shifting as the shaman does from one shape to another. In his aspect as Tepeyollotl (jaguar, heart of the mountain), he lingers on into late Postclassic times still in his original role as master of the animals. His accoutrements in the Toxcatl ceremony continue to suggest this ancient tradition as we see him with his magical mirror, smoking tubes, and flute. Mirrors in Mesoamerica are evidenced archaeologically as early as the Olmecs and are recognized in many areas of both the Old and New Worlds as devices for reflecting the unknown and predicting the future. The smoking tubes used ritually for inhaling or smoking various hallucinogens suggest the deity's ancient shamanistic role as healer, the hallucinogens providing the doorway to the spirit world where the shaman battles for the soul of his patient.

The breaking of the flutes in the Toxcatl sacrificial ceremony is particularly interesting in relationship to Tezcatlipoca as shaman. Even today in Central Asia the breaking of the shaman's musical instrument (in this case a drum) indicates his death, the silencing of his voice and power. Finally, the traditional sexual power and energy of the shaman are symbolized in the Tezcatlipoca ritual by the impersonator's final period of sexual activity with the female ixiptlatin of four goddesses.

Even our first historical view of Tezcatlipoca is as shaman, when at Tula he vies with Quetzalcoatl for command. Here, he still uses the power of the shaman to vanquish his opponent and astounds the Toltec people with his sorcerer's tricks. Perhaps it was at Tula, following the disposition of Topiltzin-Quetzalcoatl, that he first made the formal transition to identification with the ruling lineage. If so, this association with Toltec nobility would surely have strengthened his role among the Aztecs as they strove to prove themselves the true descendants of Tula.

We cannot escape Tezcatlipoca's connection with the shaman, yet among the Aztecs he was this and so much more. We see him as the young warrior, the eternally virile youth, the embodiment of kingship, the god of whom perphaps the king himself is only the ixiptla. His change over time from the great shaman to the personification of the Aztec world must have been gradual. By the time that Sahagún recorded the Toxcatl rituals, Tezcatlipoca was obviously far more than the prototype of a tribal shaman. He incorporated aspects of many gods and beliefs and had titles so numerous one can scarcely list them. However, we cannot ignore the significance of his shamanistic powers, graphically symbolized in the objects he carries. It is almost as if at the very pinnacle of empire the Aztecs were unable or chose not to separate themselves from their distant tribal origins and gods. Perhaps, as in other areas of the pre-Columbian world, beneath the veneer of elite, urbanized religious rituals, common people continued to cling to older folk beliefs and the ancient traditions of shamanism.

Index